RIVER PUBLISHERS SERIES IN COMMUNICATIONS AND NETWORKING

The "River Publishers Series in Communications and Networking" is a series of comprehensive academic and professional books which focus on communication and network systems. Topics range from the theory and use of systems involving all terminals, computers, and information processors to wired and wireless networks and network layouts, protocols, architectures, and implementations. Also covered are developments stemming from new market demands in systems, products, and technologies such as personal communications services, multimedia systems, enterprise networks, and optical communications.

The series includes research monographs, edited volumes, handbooks and textbooks, providing professionals, researchers, educators, and advanced students in the field with an invaluable insight into the latest research and developments.

Topics included in this series include:

- Communication theory
- Multimedia systems
- Network architecture
- Optical communications
- Personal communication services
- Telecoms networks
- Wifi network protocols

For a list of other books in this series, visit www.riverpublishers.com

The Autonomous Edge – Intelligence Embedded in Industrial Applications

The Autonomous Edge – Intelligence Embedded in Industrial Applications

Editor

Ovidiu Vermesan

SINTEF, Norway

Fetze Pijlman

Signify, Netherlands

River Publishers

Routledge
Taylor & Francis Group
NEW YORK AND LONDON

Published 2026 by River Publishers
River Publishers
Broagervej 10, 9260 Gistrup, Denmark
www.riverpublishers.com

Distributed exclusively by Routledge
605 Third Avenue, New York, NY 10017, USA
4 Park Square, Milton Park, Abingdon, Oxon OX14 4RN

The Autonomous Edge – Intelligence Embedded in Industrial Applications / by Ovidiu Vermesan, Fetze Pijlman.

Routledge is an imprint of the Taylor & Francis Group, an informa business

ISBN 978-87-4381-525-9 (hardback)
ISBN 978-87-4381-528-0 (online)
ISBN 978-87-4381-527-3 (master ebook)
ISBN 978-87-4381-530-3 (ePub)

DOI: 10.1201/9788743815273

Printed on acid-free paper.

Dedication

"Discovery consists of looking at the same thing as everyone else and thinking something different."

– Albert Einstein

"The key question isn't 'What can AI do?' but 'What should AI do?"

– John C. Havens

"Creativity is a natural extension of our enthusiasm."

– Earl Nightingale

Acknowledgement

The editors would like to thank all the contributors for their support in the planning and preparation of this book. The recommendations and opinions expressed in the book are those of the editors, authors, and contributors and do not necessarily represent those of any organizations, employers, or companies.

Ovidiu Vermesan
Fetze Pijlman

Contents

Preface

The Edge of Creation, Generative and Autonomous Systems

This book explores the profound technological transformation occurring at the intersection of artificial intelligence, edge computing, and autonomous industrial systems. As intelligence increasingly migrates from centralised cloud infrastructures directly into vehicles, robots, smart cities, and embedded devices, new engineering paradigms are required.

To address this need, the chapters outlined below examine how next-generation edge AI systems are designed to navigate operational constraints, including real-time latency, energy efficiency, privacy, and safety. Highlighting innovations ranging from lightweight neural networks and vision transformers to digital twins and distributed AI pipelines, the following summaries detail how these advancements are being optimised for edge hardware to power the decentralised intelligent systems of the future.

Chapter 1 – The AI-Defined Vehicle: Navigating the Convergence of AI and Autonomous Systems

This opening chapter explores the transformation of the automotive industry from traditional, hardware-centric vehicles to software- and AI-defined vehicles. It explains how advances in artificial intelligence, generative AI, vehicle-to-everything communication, and embedded sensing technologies are reshaping transportation systems into adaptive and autonomous ecosystems.

The authors introduce AI-defined vehicles as self-evolving platforms capable of autonomous reasoning, scenario synthesis, and continuous learning, while also discussing the societal, ethical, and regulatory implications of this increasingly intelligent transportation.

Chapter 2 – From Complexity to Efficiency: Pruning Vision Transformers in Practice

This chapter investigates the optimisation of Vision Transformers for embedded and real-time edge AI applications. Although Vision Transformers achieve high performance on computer vision tasks, their computational demands make deployment on constrained hardware challenging.

The authors analyse pruning strategies that reduce computational complexity by removing redundant tokens or patches. Practical deployment experiments on NVIDIA Jetson hardware reveal that lower computational workloads do not always directly translate into lower latency due to GPU scheduling and framework overhead. The chapter provides valuable insights into the gap between theoretical AI optimisation and real-world edge deployment.

Chapter 3 – GStreamer Plugin for RDMA Offload on BlueField-3 for Edge Applications

This chapter presents an edge computing architecture that leverages Remote Direct Memory Access (RDMA) and BlueField Data Processing Units (DPUs) to accelerate multimedia AI applications. By moving processing tasks closer to the data source, edge systems reduce latency and improve responsiveness.

The work introduces a GStreamer RDMA plugin that efficiently streams video data directly to DPUs for AI processing. Through a virtual try-on demonstration, the chapter illustrates how edge infrastructures can optimise resource utilisation while reducing CPU dependency in distributed AI systems.

Chapter 4 – On-Device Continual Learning for Unsupervised Visual Anomaly Detection in Dynamic Manufacturing

This chapter tackles the challenge of deploying adaptive visual anomaly detection systems in modern manufacturing environments characterised by frequent product variations and limited training data.

The proposed approach extends the PatchCore architecture with lightweight continual learning capabilities that allow models to adapt directly on industrial edge devices without cloud retraining. The solution enhances detection performance while reducing memory usage and training time, demonstrating the feasibility of adaptive AI inspection systems for flexible smart manufacturing.

Chapter 5 – In-GPU GNN-based Intrusion Detection System

This chapter focuses on cybersecurity for edge and communication systems powered by Graph Neural Networks (GNNs). Traditional intrusion detection systems often suffer from delays caused by graph construction overhead.

The proposed framework accelerates both graph generation and inference entirely inside GPU memory. By optimising graph processing and node-feature computation, the system achieves faster, real-time intrusion detection while maintaining accuracy. The work demonstrates how hardware-aware AI optimisation can strengthen cybersecurity in latency-sensitive environments such as 5G infrastructures.

Chapter 6 – Vision-language Embeddings in Large-scale LiDAR SLAM for Terrain Segmentation

This chapter presents a semantic mapping framework that combines LiDAR data, vision-language embeddings, and Simultaneous Localisation and Mapping (SLAM) technologies for autonomous robotics. The proposed system constructs vector-based semantic maps that facilitate terrain understanding and open-set perception.

The framework enables robots to retrieve semantic information via vector-similarity searches with text or image queries. Experimental results demonstrate strong terrain segmentation performance for outdoor navigation, illustrating how multimodal AI can enrich environmental understanding in autonomous robotic systems.

Chapter 7 – Investigating Target Class Influence on Neural Network Compressibility for Energy-Autonomous Avian Monitoring

This chapter examines how lightweight AI models can support biodiversity monitoring through edge-based birdsong recognition systems deployed directly in the field.

The research explores the relationship between the number of target species and neural network compressibility on microcontrollers. Findings indicate that significant model compression can be achieved with minimal performance loss, enabling energy-efficient, autonomous wildlife monitoring systems to operate on low-power hardware.

Chapter 8 – When a Model is not Enough: A Complementary AI Pipeline for Ultra-Safe PCBA Defect Detection

This chapter introduces a multi-stage AI inspection pipeline designed for safety-critical manufacturing domains, such as automotive and avionics, where defect-detection reliability requirements are extremely strict.

The proposed cascaded architecture progressively improves detection precision while maintaining high recall. Through mathematical analysis and simulations, the chapter demonstrates that multi-stage pipelines significantly outperform single-model approaches in reducing defect escapes. The work highlights the importance of combining AI robustness, redundancy, and statistical validation in industrial inspection systems.

Chapter 9 – Towards Automated Liability Determination for Autonomous Vehicles in Road Accidents

This chapter investigates how edge intelligence and graph-based AI can facilitate automated liability assessment for autonomous vehicle accidents.

The framework processes vehicle, infrastructure, and environmental data locally using lightweight AI models and constructs event identity graphs to analyse causal relationships. The system incorporates traffic regulations, insurance rules, and ethical considerations to enhance transparency and explainability. The chapter illustrates how AI can support objective and scalable decision-making in future intelligent transportation ecosystems.

Chapter 10 – Edge-Optimised Modular Architecture for Real-Time Vehicle Re-Identification

This chapter presents an edge AI architecture for vehicle re-identification across multiple cameras in intelligent transportation systems.

The proposed modular pipeline combines lightweight object detection and re-identification models optimised via quantisation, pruning, and TensorRT acceleration. The work demonstrates how real-time analytics can be achieved on edge hardware while preserving privacy and maintaining operational reliability in smart city deployments.

Chapter 11 – Edge Deployment of Multi-Task Vision Models for Smart City Infrastructures

This chapter explores the efficient deployment of multi-task vision models capable of simultaneously performing object detection, segmentation, and depth estimation on edge devices.

The proposed optimisation workflow balances model accuracy and computational efficiency for distributed smart city infrastructure. By processing data locally, the system reduces bandwidth consumption, enhances privacy, and enables robust urban analytics. The chapter lays a strong foundation for scalable edge-native smart city applications.

Chapter 12 – Experiences in Deploying a Weapon Detector in a Smart City

This chapter details the real-world deployment of a handgun detection system operating on constrained edge hardware within a smart city environment.

The authors analyse different AI pipeline configurations and evaluate trade-offs between accuracy and inference speed. The final solution integrates lightweight YOLO models with MQTT and IoT communication platforms for real-time alerting. The chapter highlights practical engineering challenges in deployment, optimisation, and operational robustness for public safety applications.

Chapter 13 – A 3D Simulation Framework for Behaviour Cloning on Edge AI-Enabled E-Scooters in Smart Cities
This chapter presents a simulation framework for training autonomous navigation systems tailored to edge-enabled e-scooters.

The framework combines physics-based simulation with lightweight behaviour cloning models that operate efficiently under constrained computational resources. Experimental results demonstrate near-real-time performance on CPU-only systems, illustrating the practicality of AI-driven micro-mobility solutions for future smart cities.

Chapter 14 – Edge AI Ready Lightweight Digital Twin for Anomaly Prediction: A Case Study on Hydrogen Refuelling Station Data
This chapter proposes a lightweight digital twin framework for anomaly prediction in hydrogen refuelling stations leveraging edge AI technologies.

The methodology combines unsupervised learning, supervised refinement, and model optimisation techniques such as quantisation and pruning to create deployable edge-ready AI systems. By simulating real-time streaming environments, the work demonstrates how digital twins can bolster operational safety, reliability, and maintenance efficiency in critical industrial infrastructures.

List of Figures

List of Tables

List of Contributors

Albandea Merino, Hugo, *VISILAB, University of Castilla-La Mancha, Spain*

Anicic, Darko, *Siemens AG, Germany*

Arents, Janis, *Institute of Electronics and Computer Science (EDI), Latvia*

Barnhill, Alexander, *Friedrich-Alexander-Universität Erlangen-Nürnberg (FAU), Germany*

Bati, Emrecan, *HOP, Türkiye*

Bercy, Victor, *Université Paris-Saclay, CEA, List, France*

Bohara, Rohit *asvin GmbH, Germany*

Cancelliere, Francesco, *Deepsensing s.r.l., Italy*

Cugini, Filippo, *CNIT, Italy*

Deniz, Oscar, *VISILAB, University of Castilla-La Mancha, Spain*

Dimitrakopoulos, George, *Harokopio University of Athens, Greece*

Dorofeev, Kirill, *Siemens AG, Germany*

Faro, Alberto, *Deepsensing s.r.l., Italy*

Faro, Robin, *Deepsensing s.r.l., Italy*

Fomi Wamba, Francis, *Framatome GmbH, Germany*

Frascolla, Valerio, *Intel Deutschland GmbH, Germany*

Fu, Yuqian, *INSAIT, Sofia University "St. Kliment Ohridski", Bulgaria*

Geis, Simon, *Fraunhofer Institute for Integrated Circuits IIS, Germany*

Georgiadis, Dimitrios, *Harokopio University of Athens, Greece*

Girolamo, Salvatore Di, *NVIDIA, Switzerland*

Gool, Luc Van, *INSAIT, Sofia University "St. Kliment Ohridski", Bulgaria*

Greitans, Modris, *Institute of Electronics and Computer Science (EDI), Latvia*

Hashemi, Vahid, *AUDI AG, Germany*

Ibrahim, Ahmed Salah Tawfik, *CNIT, Italy*

Joglekar, Omkar, *asvin GmbH, Germany*

Judvaitis, Janis, *Institute of Electronics and Computer Science (EDI), Latvia*

Köhle, Kay, *Technical University of Munich, Germany; Siemens AG, Germany*

Kanelos, Tassos, *G.N.T. Information Systems S.A., Greece*

Karathanasopoulou, Konstantina, *Harokopio University of Athens, Greece*

Kasper, Maximilian, *Fraunhofer Institute for Integrated Circuits IIS, Germany*

Kranenburg, Rob van, *Martel Innovate, Switzerland*

Mahdi, Mohammad, *INSAIT, Sofia University "St. Kliment Ohridski", Bulgaria*

Mineo, Raffaele, *Deepsensing s.r.l., Italy*

Muñoz, Juan Daniel, *VISILAB, University of Castilla-La Mancha, Spain*

Muzzini, Filippo, *HiPeRT, University of Modena and Reggio Emilia, Italy*

Nina Brolich, *Fraunhofer Institute for Integrated Circuits IIS, Germany; Fachhochschule Erfurt, Germany; Universität Erfurt, Germany*

Öztürk, Esin, *Framatome GmbH, Germany*

Pani Paudel, Danda, *INSAIT, Sofia University "St. Kliment Ohridski", Bulgaria*

Paolini, Emilio, *Scuola Superiore Sant'Anna, Italy*

Paolucci, Francesco, *CNIT, Italy*

Plinge, Axel, *Fraunhofer Institute for Integrated Circuits IIS, Germany*

Politi, Elena, *Harokopio University of Athens, Greece*

Poreba, Martyna, *Université Paris-Saclay, CEA, LIST, France*

Pouillard, Romain, *Université Clermont Auvergne, France / Scuola Superiore Sant'Anna, Italy*

Prisadnikov, Nedyalko, *INSAIT, Sofia University "St. Kliment Ohridski", Bulgaria*

Pype, Patrick, *NXP Semiconductors, Belgium*

Račinskis, Pēteris, *Institute of Electronics and Computer Science (EDI), Latvia*

Raphael Frantz, *NVIDIA, Italy; Eindhoven University of Technology, The Netherlands*

Ren, Haoyu, *Technical University of Munich, Germany; Siemens AG, Germany*

Ross, Mirko, *asvin GmbH, Germany*

Ruiz-Santaquiteria, Jesus, *VISILAB, University of Castilla-La Mancha, Spain*

Sanudo Olmedo, Ignacio, *HiPeRT, University of Modena and Reggio Emilia, Italy*

Scribano, Carmelo, *HiPeRT, University of Modena and Reggio Emilia, Italy; Institute of Informatics and Telematics, National Research Council, Italy*

Seuß, Dominik, *Fraunhofer Institute for Integrated Circuits IIS, Germany; Center for Artificial Intelligence and Robotics (CAIRO), Technische Hochschule Würzburg-Schweinfurt, Germany*

Soulmani, Ahmed, *Université Paris-Saclay, CEA, List, France*

Stefanidou, Artemis, *Harokopio University of Athens, Greece*

Szczepanski, Michal, *Université Paris-Saclay, CEA, List, France*

Tüfekçi, Burak, *TÜBİTAK B İLGEM, Türkiye*

Tafur Monroy, Idelfonso, *Eindhoven University of Technology, The Netherlands*

Tsaousi, Eleni, *Harokopio University of Athens, Greece*

Vegas Olmos, Juan Jose, *NVIDIA, Denmark*

Vermesan, Ovidiu, *SINTEF AS, Norway*

Verucchi, Micaela, *HiPeRT, University of Modena and Reggio Emilia, Italy*

Yalabuk, Ihsan Can, *TÜBİTAK B İLGEM, Türkiye*

Zutis, Tomass, *Institute of Electronics and Computer Science (EDI), Latvia*

List of Abbreviations

AI	Artificial Intelligence
AE	Autoencoder
CBM	Condition-Based Maintenance
CNN-AE	Convolutional Neural Network–based Autoencoder
CS	Compressor System
DT	Digital Twin
DS	Dispenser System
EDGE-AI	Artificial Intelligence deployed on resource-constrained edge devices
ES	Entrance System
FA/h	False Alarms per Hour
FCV	Fuel Cell Vehicle
HP	High-Pressure System
HRS	Hydrogen Refueling Station
KD	Knowledge Distillation
LP	Low-Pressure System
MLP	Multilayer Perceptron
NIS	Nitrogen Inserting System
PdM	Predictive Maintenance
QAT	Quantization-Aware Training
RAM	Random Access Memory
RSS	Resident Set Size (process-level memory usage)
SL	Supervised Learning
UL	Unsupervised Learning

ONNX	Open Neural Network Exchange (model format)
IQR	Interquartile Range
τ^*	Optimal reconstruction-error threshold
EW_HORIZON_SEC	Early-warning horizon in seconds (900 s = 15 min)

1

The AI-Defined Vehicle: Navigating the Convergence of AI and Autonomous Systems

Ovidiu Vermesan[1], Valerio Frascolla[2], Patrick Pype[3], and Vahid Hashemi[4]

[1]SINTEF AS, Norway
[2]Intel Deutschland GmbH, Germany
[3]NXP Semiconductors, Belgium
[4]AUDI AG, Germany

Abstract

The automotive landscape is experiencing a paradigm shift, driven by the pervasive integration of artificial intelligence (AI) across all functional layers, the availability of previously unattainable data-processing capabilities, and an increasingly tight convergence of sensors, actuators, and advanced communication technologies. This perspective article explores the evolution from connected vehicles to Software (SW)-defined vehicles (SDVs), focusing on the emerging frontier of AI-defined vehicles (AIDVs) as a self-evolving architecture that integrates generative AI (GenAI) for scenario synthesis and agentic AI for autonomous decision-making. This article discusses the technology evolution and the role of AI and vehicle-to-everything (V2X) communication in enabling this transformation. The architecture of SDVs and the conceptual framework of AIDVs are examined, highlighting the transition from Hardware (HW)-centric to SW- and AI-centric designs. Recent advances and future directions are also discussed, presenting a multifaceted view of the opportunities and challenges by synthesising insights from research and industry trends and offering a forward-looking perspective

DOI: 10.1201/9788743815273-1

on the technological, societal, and ethical factors shaping the evolution of automated intelligent transportation systems (ITSs).

Keywords: AI-defined vehicle, software-defined vehicle, autonomous vehicles, vehicle communication AI, V2X, edge computing, edge AI.

1.1 Introduction

The concept of the automobile is being fundamentally redefined, with recent vehicles evolving into cyber-physical, interconnected, and intelligent platforms. This transformation is underpinned by three key technological pillars: widespread embedding of sensing and actuation, advanced communication largely through V2X technologies, and pervasive integration of AI. In addition, as modern vehicles are increasingly SW-defined, the control and compute infrastructure using AI becomes a strategic asset, with central domain and zonal controllers replacing fragmented Electronic Control Units (ECU) architectures [1]. This shift increases reliance on high-performance microprocessors, AI, machine learning (ML), deep learning (DL), GenAI, agentic AI (AI systems with the capacity to perceive, reason, make decisions, act autonomously, and take multi-step actions to achieve specific goals with minimal human oversight), accelerators, and real-time controllers. The journey began with the connected vehicle, a concept that has steadily evolved into today's advanced automated vehicle systems [2, 3].

Advanced autonomous vehicles leverage novel ML/AI-based computational methods combined with new architectures and platforms [4]. The evolution of these vehicles enables ITS, which is seen as the future of transportation systems integrating sensors, information, and computing and communication technologies. AI applications, which are steadily enhancing the human-like intelligence into ITS, and advanced autonomous vehicles share common challenges, such as demanding real-time requirements, cybersecurity threats, and network bandwidth constraints [5]. As vehicle architectures advance, key issues including trustworthiness, intellectual property (IP), and insurance liability underscore the need for robust regulation to support the integration of autonomous vehicles in transportation systems and the smart cities of the future [6].

Technology developments in ITS are firmly evolving in the era of the SDV, where vehicle functions are increasingly decoupled from HW and updatable over-the-air (OTA), and real-time sensor notification and warning systems enhance overall safety [7], a shift that analysts see as the future of

Table 1.1 The evolution of the of vehicle architecture.

Traditional Architecture	**Software-Defined Vehicle (SDV) Architecture**	**AI-Defined Vehicle (AIDV) Architecture**
HW-Defined: Functionality tied to specific ECUs.	**SW-Defined:** Decoupling of SW from HW via HW Abstraction Layer (HAL). Centralized computation and processing.	**AI-Defined:** AI embedded in vehicle operation and user experience.
Inflexible: Difficult and costly to update or add new features.	**Flexible and Scalable:** OTA updates for new features, performance improvements and upgrades.	**Adaptive and Learning:** Continuous learning and personalization based on real-time data.
Siloed Systems: Limited communication and data sharing between ECUs.	**Service-Oriented Architecture (SOA):** Enables integration and communication between SW components.	**Data-Driven and Predictive:** Proactive maintenance, personalized experiences, and anticipatory actions.
Focus on Mechanics: Core value in the vehicle physical engineering.	**Focus on SW and Services:** Value shifts to the user experience and connected services including new business models.	**Focus on Intelligence and Autonomy:** Core value in the vehicle ability to perceive, infer, and act intelligently.

the automotive industry [8]. Looking ahead, the horizon is dominated by the concept of the AIDV, a system in which AI, at the core of operations and user experience, is the main driver of the evolution of the vehicle, as sketched in Table 1.1.

V2X communication serves as the nervous system of this intelligent transportation ecosystem and can be considered as a general concept that encompasses vehicle-to-vehicle (V2V), vehicle-to-infrastructure (V2I), vehicle-to-pedestrian (V2P), vehicle-to-network (V2N), vehicle-to-grid (V2G), vehicle-to-home (V2H), vehicle-to-maintenance (V2M), vehicle-to-owner (V2O), vehicle-to-users (V2U), and other interactions [9, 10]. It provides the real-time data streams necessary for advanced driver-assistance systems (ADAS), cooperative autonomous driving, and efficient traffic management. Concurrently, AI provides vehicles with the equivalent of a brain, enabling vehicles to perceive the environment, make complex decisions, and learn from experience, building on a long history of development in autonomous systems.

The development of SDVs and AIDVs requires architecture and technology solutions that integrate cooperation and real-time communication into their design specifications. The collaboration and exchange of data and information depend on trust among humans, vehicles, and infrastructure. In advanced autonomous systems, trust is earned through the dependability of vehicle systems and subsystems, as reflected in the trustworthiness concept [11]. Complex AI systems integrated into SDVs and AIDVs deepen the existing challenge of safety assurance of autonomous driving. A solution to mitigate this challenge is to utilize a set of techniques like spatio-temporal prediction [1, 12], explainable AI (XAI) [13] and interpretable AI (IAI) [14] methods for safe and trustworthy autonomous driving, focusing on key aspects such as data, model, and agency in the defined operational design domain (ODD) of the vehicle.

The autonomous functions required by SDVs and AIDVs are executed by the vehicle modules integrated into the vehicle architecture to perform perception, planning, and control and communicate with other vehicles, road users or the road infrastructure.

Communication technologies play an essential role in SDV Network (SDVN) architectures, added to the SDV architectures by integrating novel electrical and electronic (E/E) architectures, operating systems (OS), open-source HW, SW tools, processing at the edge, OTA updates/upgrades techniques, features-on-demand, and the deployment of Digital Twins (DT) and immersive triplets technologies for modelling, simulation, and operations. SDV refers to transforming vehicles from primarily HW-driven to embedded and SW-centric platforms. This shift implies that SW drives much of the functionality of a vehicle functionality, customization, and performance enhancements rather than mechanical or HW changes. This approach allows for continuous updates, upgrades and improvements of the features and functions of vehicles and more in general of mobile autonomous systems.

Vehicle architectures have evolved to achieve full autonomous functions, as illustrated in Figure 1.1.

The evolution includes domain-based, body-zonal, cross-domain zonal, and consolidated computing architectures, where zonalization and consolidation of the computing tasks drive the developments of the vehicle architecture. The domain-based functions in the vehicles are grouped progressively into zonal controllers. While several applications still require isolation for performance, safety, or security requirements, in the future, complete consolidation of the electronic functions into a central vehicle computer is expected. In the consolidated compute vehicle architecture, sensors and actuators data are collected in I/O aggregator units placed in their proximity. While reducing the system complexity, zonalization and consolidation introduce new safety and

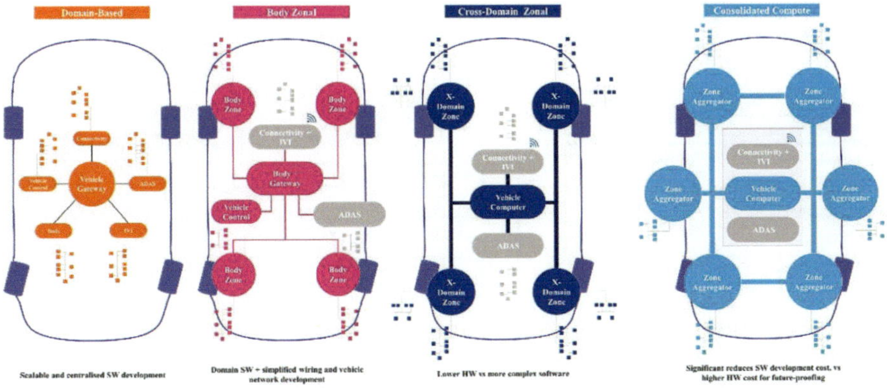

Figure 1.1 Evolving vehicle architectures.

security concerns. Mixed-critical applications share HW resources, such as communication links or vehicle processors, potentially interfering with each other. The system must separate the execution of safety-critical, real-time applications from the execution of non-critical ones. Isolation, safety, and security mechanisms must be taken into consideration in the very early phases of the architectural design of new vehicles, as they will be key elements for commercializing future mobile autonomous and robotic systems.

The transition from conventional vehicles to SDVs illustrates a fundamental shift in automotive perspective, architecture, and capability. Traditional vehicles are primarily HW-defined, with their functions and performance inherently linked to the physical and electromechanical components installed in the vehicle during manufacturing. Upgrades or new features generally require physical modifications or component replacements, which are often performed at a dealership. A distributed network of multiple ECUs characterizes the vehicle architecture, each with a specific, usually isolated function, connected by intricate wiring harnesses that add weight and limit integration possibilities. Innovation cycles are tied to model years and HW changes, resulting in slower evolution.

The integration of sensors, actuators, connectivity, and AI into the vehicle-edge-cloud continuum requires managing data effectively, reliably, securely, and privately via various data-, model-, and code-centric architectures, combining proprietary and open-source building blocks. The evolution of the E/E architecture for SDV to AIDVs is envisioned in Figure 1.2.

One of the core elements of autonomous SDVs and AIDVs lies in the decision-making and planning systems that interpret sensor data,

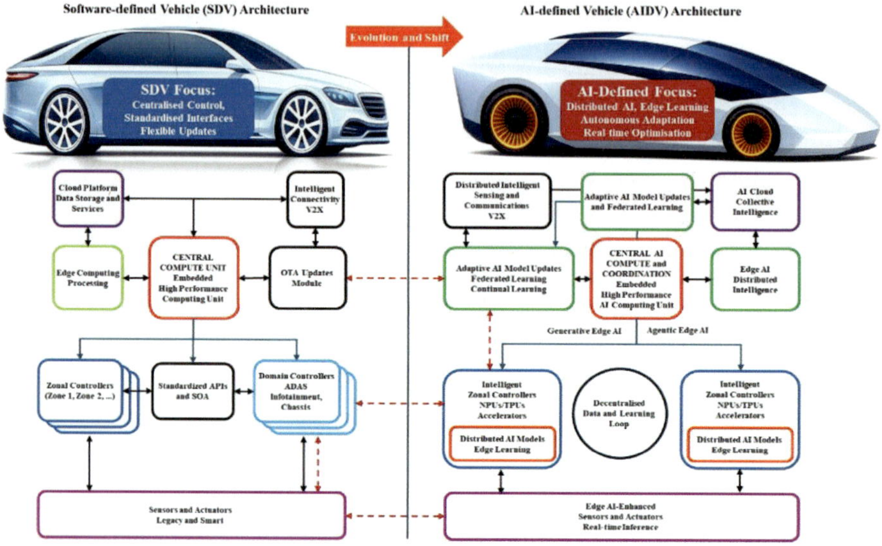

Figure 1.2 E/E Architecture types: SDVs vs. AIDVs.

predict traffic behaviour, and determine optimal driving actions. Traditional rule-based systems, while offering transparency, often lack the flexibility needed for unpredictable real-world scenarios. End-to-end AI models that integrate perception, prediction, and planning have shown promise in this domain. Research emphasizes the use of reinforcement learning (RL), imitation learning, and advanced neural network architectures that combine these elements for real-time decision-making [15].

Emerging techniques that leverage deep RL have the potential to scale decision-making by dynamically adapting to new driving environments. Incorporating multi-modal data, such as real-time weather updates, V2X information, and historical traffic patterns, can significantly enhance prediction accuracy and planning reliability. Improving these models requires rigorous simulation and field testing, along with advanced synthetic data generation methods, to replicate rare yet critical driving scenarios and provide explainable solutions for autonomous vehicles [16].

In this context, challenges remain in effectively combining multimodal, multisource, internal, and external vehicular data to support real-time decision-making, as well as in addressing synchronisation, formatting, and management issues. Integrating vehicular system intelligence with human knowledge requires robust frameworks that ensure secure, private, yet efficient data management pipelines, focusing on adaptive techniques that integrate newly emerging data modalities and sources.

The deployment of ML, DL, and GenAI solutions requires optimised energy and resource use for processing and communication. As the models can run in vehicles using specialised HW accelerators, task prioritisation, management, and optimisation are necessary for effective decision-making. Decision-making in real-time using large-scale sensor data analytics and GenAI relies on novel algorithmic innovations, including federated learning (FL), neural networks, and agentic AI. As a result of specific tasks performed by SDVs and AIDVs, the models must be personalised in the vehicular environment based on human responses.

Personalisation can be critical for the driving experience, where environments and road events vary constantly. Creating models for every vehicle, again and again, is inefficient, as (re)training is resource-intensive and vehicles are constrained environments that require lightweight frameworks capable of handling large-scale datasets as part of the data processing pipeline [17].

This article presents a perspective on the synergistic evolution of AI by the pervasive integration across all functional layers in shaping the future of autonomous systems and ITSs, by exploring architectural shifts from traditional vehicles to SDVs and AIDVs, discussing the current state of the art and future research directions, and offering a view of the extensive potential and significant challenges that lie ahead.

1.2 Architectural Evolution: From HW to AI-Defined

The transition from HW-centric to AI-defined architectures is a multi-stage evolution, with each phase building upon the capabilities of the previous one.

The autonomous vehicle architecture began with a modular pipeline approach [18, 19] used in the design of the driving systems, separating each part of the system into distinct SW and HW components, split which created significant challenges in optimising and synchronising the system. The modular pipeline approach breaks down the task of the autonomous driving system into perception, prediction, planning, and control. In this approach, each module is developed separately and is responsible for a specific functionality in the whole system. To address the development of autonomous vehicles, an end-to-end pipeline approach [19, 20, 21] was introduced to integrate separate components into a unified system and optimise the entire system in a differentiable manner. The end-to-end pipeline manages autonomous driving as a single learning task using imitation and RL, taking raw sensor data as input and directly outputting the control signal, optimising final planning performance as its primary objective, thereby providing greater safety and reliability than a modular pipeline approach. These approaches are part of the evolution towards new architectural concepts for SDVs and AIDVs.

1.2.1 The Rise of the SW-Defined Vehicle

Traditionally, vehicle functionalities have been tightly coupled with dedicated ECUs. The ECU-based architecture, while reliable, is limited in its ability to update and introduce new features, leading to a complex, costly upgrade process. An SDV architecture marks a significant departure from this model by centralising computing resources and abstracting SW from the underlying HW, a concept that has been thoroughly surveyed in the context of SDVNs [22] and AI-defined wireless networking [23, 24].

SDVs represent a shift from HW-centric design to a model where SW governs functionality, performance, and user experience. As vehicles integrate increasing numbers of sensors, ECUs, and connectivity features, they generate large volumes of data related to performance, driver behaviour, and system health. SDVs leverage this data to continuously improve vehicle capabilities, enabling manufacturers to refine features, diagnose issues, and deploy enhancements throughout the vehicle lifecycle.

A key technical enabler of SDVs is the use of DTs and immersive triplets, which act as virtual representations of real-world vehicles [25]. By transmitting operational data to the cloud, vehicles can provide detailed insights into battery health, performance of ADAS, and feature usage under real driving conditions. This continuous feedback loop allows original equipment manufacturers (OEMs) to accelerate development cycles, identify recurring faults, and implement corrective actions before issues become widespread, particularly in complex domains such as autonomous driving.

V2X communication further extends the value of SDVs by enabling secure data exchange between vehicles, infrastructure, and other road users. Information such as vehicle speed, position, and lane departure warnings can be shared in real time to enhance situational awareness and improve traffic safety. This interconnected environment relies on robust data handling and secure communication protocols, both of which are central to SDV platforms.

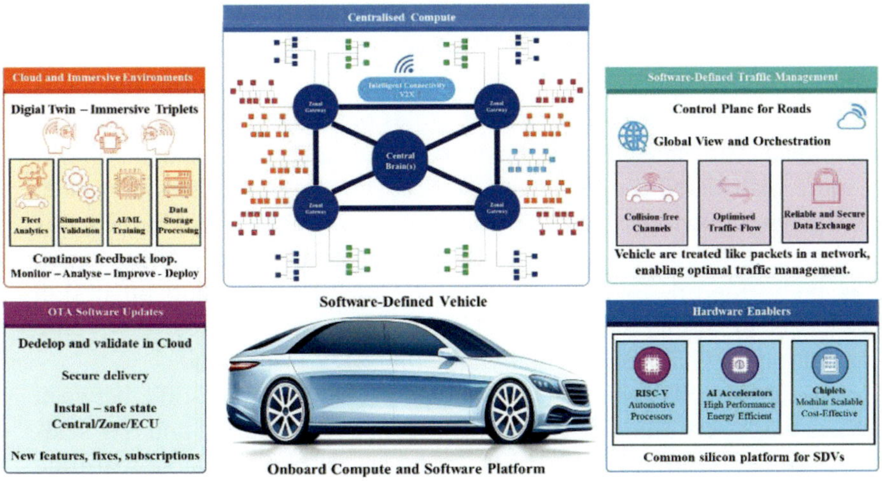

Figure 1.3 SDV architecture.

A defining feature of SDVs is the ability to update and expand functionality through OTA SW updates, which are developed and validated in cloud environments before being securely delivered to vehicles. Once downloaded, updates can be installed across central computing systems, zone controllers, or edge ECUs, typically requiring a system restart in a safe vehicle state.

OTA capabilities allow OEMs to introduce new features, fix SW defects, and offer subscription-based services without requiring physical access to the vehicle.

The transition to SDVs is closely tied to the evolution of electrical and electronic E/E architectures. Traditional distributed and domain-based architectures are being replaced by zone-based networks that reduce wiring complexity and support centralised SW control. In a zone architecture, the vehicle is divided into physical regions, each managed by a zone control module that aggregates inputs from sensors and actuators within its area.

Within these architectures, OEMs adopt different SW deployment strategies. In a fully centralised approach, a single high-performance computer controls most vehicle functions, simplifying SW management and enabling consistent updates. However, this model introduces challenges related to real-time control latency and functional safety, particularly if communication links between the central unit and peripheral components are disrupted.

A hybrid approach distributes SW responsibilities between a central computer and zone controllers. High-performance applications such as ADAS and infotainment are typically centralised, while time-sensitive control functions may remain closer to the HW in zone modules or edge ECUs. This balances computational efficiency with responsiveness and safety requirements.

A more distributed model retains several domain controllers alongside zone modules, allowing a gradual transition from legacy systems. In this configuration, different zones may handle varying combinations of functions, such as body control, lighting, or chassis systems, depending on design choices. This flexibility enables OEMs to tailor architectures to specific vehicle platforms while incrementally adopting SDV principles.

The design of SDV architectures requires careful trade-offs between latency, network performance, functional safety, cybersecurity, and SW scalability. OEMs must align HW and SW strategies to ensure reliable real-time control while enabling the flexibility and continuous innovation that define SDVs.

From a road perspective, a collection of individual vehicle decisions is inevitably sub-optimal, and it is essential that roads directly intervene (control/assist) in vehicle operation to enable optimal traffic management. Solutions such as SW-defined traffic management (SDTM), which incorporate SW-Defined Network (SDN) concepts, are being used in the transportation environment. In SDTM, each vehicle is handled like a packet in an SDN, and its movement can be assisted/controlled using a global view of the road. In this concept, the SDTM enables reliable interaction between vehicles and infrastructure by allocating collision-free channels to vehicles, reducing their messaging interval by fully utilising available channel resources, and redistributing sensitive information from the infrastructure [26].

The maturity of open-source SW (e.g., Linux-based solutions) has demonstrated how shared platforms can reduce duplication, lower entry barriers, foster innovation, and enhance interoperability. This success needs to be replicated in the domain of silicon by enabling the co-development of a common European platform of RISC-V-based automotive processors and AI-accelerators. Chiplets are small, specialised integrated circuits (ICs) designed to perform specific functions within a larger system. This is considered a strategic approach to mitigate the substantial design costs associated with newer, smaller process geometries and to address the challenges posed by large, monolithic die sizes of 300 mm and above, which often result in poor yields. Additionally, providing diverse processing elements for both low- and high-power loads is a game changer in the continuously evolving market for commercial processing elements (CPUs, GPUs, AI accelerators, etc.).

1.2.2 The Dawn of the AI-Defined Vehicle

AIDVs represent a decisive shift in automotive system design, moving beyond the SDV paradigm toward architectures where AI is the primary driver of functionality, behaviour, and evolution. While SDVs introduce abstraction, modularity, and updatable SW layers, AIDVs embed intelligence as a foundational property of the vehicle. In this model, AI does not merely support isolated features but defines how the vehicle perceives, decides, adapts, and interacts across all domains of operation.

At the architectural level, AIDVs build on centralised and zonal computing frameworks that consolidate previously distributed ECUs into high-performance computing platforms as illustrated in Figure 1.4, where AI is the primary driver for functionality, behaviour and evolution.

These platforms integrate CPUs, GPUs, NPUs, and dedicated AI accelerators, enabling the execution of complex ML models with strict real-time constraints. The shift toward centralised compute reduces latency, improves data coherence, and supports advanced sensor fusion. Robust sensor fusion involves integrating data from cameras, LiDAR, radar, and other

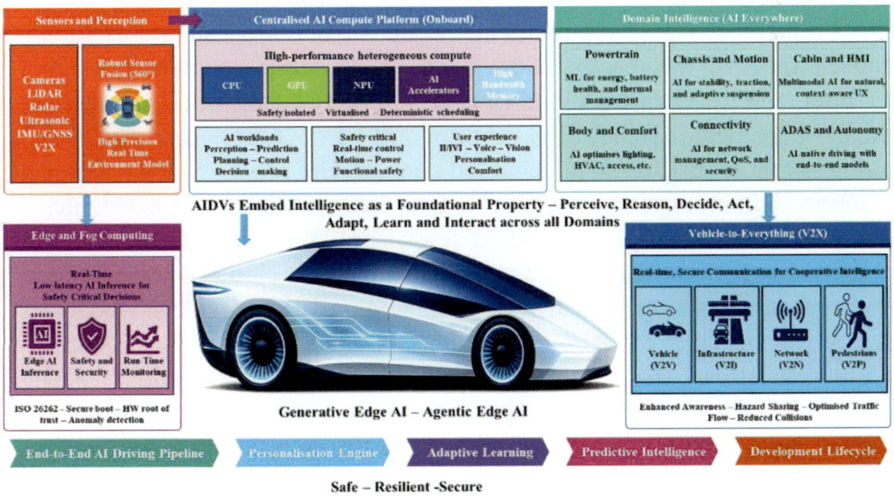

Figure 1.4 AIDV architecture.

sensing devices to create a detailed and reliable picture of the environment and enhancing DL methods for object detection and localisation to handle complex, dynamic environments. Enhancing these technologies is critical to optimising traffic flow and reducing casualties during unforeseen events [27, 63].

AI workloads are deployed across a heterogeneous computing fabric, where safety-critical tasks coexist with high-level perception, planning, and user-experience functions, under strict isolation and scheduling policies.

A defining characteristic of AIDVs is pervasive AI integration. Instead of limiting intelligence to ADAS, AI is embedded across the entire vehicle stack. In the powertrain domain, ML models optimise energy efficiency, battery health, and thermal management in real time. In chassis and motion control, AI enhances stability, traction, and adaptive suspension behaviour by continuously learning from driving conditions and driver intent. Within the cabin, multimodal AI systems fuse voice, vision, and contextual data to deliver adaptive human–machine interfaces that respond naturally to occupants. This pervasive intelligence is enabled by tightly coupled sensor networks and high-bandwidth in-vehicle communication systems, often based on automotive Ethernet.

Fog and edge computing are critical enablers of AIDVs, providing low-latency processing for safety-critical decisions [28]. AI models deployed at the edge process raw sensor data from cameras, radar, LiDAR, ultrasonic sensors, and inertial units in real time. These systems must meet stringent functional safety requirements, often aligned with standards such as ISO 26262 [29], while also addressing cybersecurity concerns through secure boot, HW roots of trust, and runtime anomaly detection. The vehicle effectively becomes a secure, high-performance computing node capable of operating autonomously even in degraded connectivity scenarios.

Continuous learning is another core pillar of the AIDV concept. Vehicles continuously collect data from onboard sensors, V2X communications, and user interactions. This data is selectively transmitted to cloud infrastructure, where large-scale training and validation pipelines refine AI models. Updated models are then deployed back to the fleet via OTA updates. This closed-loop lifecycle allows the vehicle to improve over time, adapting to new environments, edge cases, and usage patterns. Importantly, mechanisms for data governance, privacy preservation, and dataset curation are integral to ensuring both regulatory compliance and model robustness.

Personalisation in AIDVs extends beyond static user profiles to dynamic, context-aware adaptation. AI systems learn driver and passenger preferences across multiple dimensions, including driving style, seating position, climate control, infotainment choices, and navigation habits. These preferences are continuously refined using behavioural data and contextual cues such as time of day, location, and occupancy. The result is an in-cabin experience that evolves with the user, delivering a level of customisation that approaches individualised mobility services. This personalisation is often supported by multimodal user identification and cloud-synchronised profiles that persist across vehicles.

Predictive and prescriptive capabilities distinguish AIDVs from reactive systems. By integrating real-time sensor data with historical and fleet-level insights, AI models can anticipate hazards, optimise routes, and predict component degradation. Predictive maintenance algorithms analyse vibration patterns, thermal signatures, and usage data to forecast failures before they occur, reducing downtime and maintenance costs. Similarly, predictive energy management systems optimise battery usage, charging strategies, and regenerative braking to maximise efficiency and range. These capabilities rely on both onboard inference and cloud-based analytics, forming a hybrid intelligence model.

A major technological trend underpinning AIDVs is the shift toward continuous end-to-end AI pipelines, particularly in autonomous driving. Traditional autonomy stacks rely on modular pipelines that separate perception, localisation, prediction, planning, and control. In contrast, end-to-end models use deep neural networks to map raw sensor inputs directly to control outputs such as steering, acceleration, and braking. These models are trained on large-scale datasets collected from vehicle fleets and augmented with synthetic data generated through high-fidelity simulation. While end-to-end approaches can reduce system complexity and improve adaptability, they also introduce challenges in interpretability, validation, and safety assurance.

The development lifecycle of AIDVs is tightly coupled with continuous integration and continuous deployment practices. AI models are iteratively trained, validated, and deployed across a computing continuum that spans cloud and edge environments. Cloud platforms provide the computational resources for large-scale training and scenario simulation, while edge platforms execute optimised models in real time. Emerging techniques in GenAI and agentic systems are being integrated into these pipelines, enabling automated scenario generation, data augmentation, and even autonomous system tuning. This accelerates development cycles while improving coverage of rare and safety-critical scenarios.

AIDVs represent a convergence of advanced AI, high-performance computing, and connected vehicle ecosystems. By embedding intelligence into every aspect of the vehicle and enabling continuous evolution through data-driven pipelines, AIDVs redefine the vehicle as an adaptive, learning system. This transformation has implications not only for vehicle performance and safety but also for the broader mobility landscape, where vehicles become intelligent agents operating within a dynamic, interconnected environment.

1.2.3 The Transition to Self-Evolving Vehicular Architectures

While SDVs decouple SW from HW, AIDVs introduce a paradigm shift toward "Self-Evolving Architectures" integrating GenAI and agentic AI technologies. The core challenge lies in moving from static OTA updates to dynamic, self-supervised learning loops. The defining characteristic of the future AIDV architecture is its "self-evolving" capability, a departure from static, rule-based systems toward a dynamic, continuous evolving ecosystem. This evolution is driven by the cyclical interaction between the AI paradigms, such as GenAI and agentic AI [30].

The synergy allows the system to move beyond supervised learning on pre-labelled datasets into a continuous, self-supervised learning cycle, where GenAI functions serve as a knowledge generator, and foundation models synthesise high-fidelity virtual environments by ingesting vast streams of real-world driving data, including telemetry, sensor fusion logs, and V2X communication packets.

The trajectory toward AIDVs is accelerating as advances in connectivity, compute, foundation models, GenAI, and agentic AI begin to converge into an AI-centric vehicle stack. Beyond incremental improvements, the field is shifting toward architectures in which perception, planning, communication, and user interaction are co-optimised through shared AI models and continuous learning loops spanning fleet, edge, and cloud.

AI-powered V2X communication is evolving from static protocol optimisation to fully adaptive, learning-driven network orchestration. Recent trends integrate RL and graph neural networks to model highly dynamic vehicular topologies, enabling predictive scheduling, interference mitigation, and semantic-aware communication while transmitting only task-relevant information. This reduces bandwidth pressure while improving latency bounds for safety-critical services. The transition toward 5G-Advanced and early 6G concepts further introduces integrated sensing and communication (ISAC), allowing the communication infrastructure itself to act as a distributed sensor [31]. In this context, AI-native air interfaces and cross-layer optimisation are expected to support sub-10 ms end-to-end latency and ultra-reliable low-latency communication (URLLC) at scale, which is essential for cooperative autonomy [32].

Cooperative perception and manoeuvring are moving beyond simple data sharing toward collective intelligence. Instead of exchanging raw sensor feeds, vehicles increasingly share compressed feature maps or object-level abstractions generated by deep neural networks, reducing communication overhead while preserving semantic richness. Emerging approaches use multi-agent RL and distributed consensus algorithms to coordinate manoeuvres such as platooning, merging, and intersection negotiation. This enables intent-aware driving, in which vehicles not only perceive the environment but also anticipate others' actions [33]. Progress in uncertainty quantification and trust-aware fusion is critical here, ensuring robustness against noisy, delayed, or malicious inputs in open environments.

Edge and cloud computing are being redefined by the rise of heterogeneous AI accelerators and AI-defined compute fabrics. Modern AIDV platforms integrate GPUs, TPUs, NPUs, neuromorphic, and domain-specific accelerators optimised for transformer-based workloads, enabling real-time execution of increasingly large foundation models and agentic AI workflows. A key trend is the emergence of split computing paradigms, in which inference pipelines are partitioned across the vehicle, roadside edge, and cloud based on latency, privacy, and energy constraints. FL and continual learning frameworks enable fleets to collaboratively improve models without centralising raw data, addressing both scalability and regulatory concerns. At the same time, AI-defined infrastructure enables dynamic deployment of AI services OTA, effectively turning vehicles into nodes of a distributed learning system.

GenAI in the cabin is advancing from conversational assistants to context-aware, multimodal copilots. These systems integrate speech, vision, and vehicle telemetry to provide proactive assistance, such as anticipating driver needs, explaining vehicle decisions, or adapting interfaces in real time. The underlying models are increasingly domain-specialised small language models (SLMs) and vision-language models (VLMs) fine-tuned for automotive safety and reliability [34]. On-device inference is becoming feasible through model compression and distillation, reducing reliance on cloud connectivity. A key research direction is aligning generative models with safety constraints

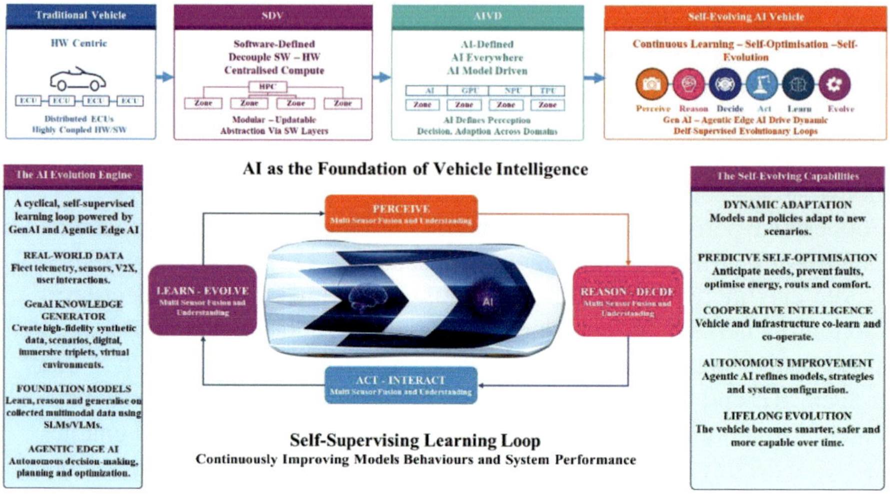

Figure 1.5 The vision of self-evolving vehicular architecture.

and human factors, ensuring that natural interaction does not compromise driver attention or trust.

DTs are evolving into high-fidelity, continuously synchronised replicas that allow for not only validation but also real-time decision support and lifecycle optimisation. Advances in simulation realism, driven by neural rendering and physics-informed AI, allow DTs to capture complex environmental and behavioural dynamics. The concept of immersive triplets extends this by integrating spatial computing and mixed reality interfaces, enabling engineers and even vehicles themselves to interact with virtualised environments. Emerging frameworks incorporate secure attestation mechanisms that validate AI models and OTA updates against their DT counterparts before deployment, enhancing safety and cybersecurity [35, 36]. Looking ahead, closed-loop integration between fleet data, simulation, and model retraining is enabling a "simulation-driven development at scale" paradigm, significantly shortening innovation cycles.

These trends indicate a shift from isolated intelligent functions to fully integrated, learning-driven vehicular ecosystems. The defining characteristic of next-generation AIDVs will not be any single capability, but the ability to continuously adapt, collaborate, and improve through tightly coupled AI, communication, and compute infrastructures.

Looking ahead, the integration of 6G communication technologies is expected to be a significant catalyst for AIDVs. The ultra-low latency, high bandwidth, massive connectivity, integrated sensing, precise localisation, and embedded AI of 6G will enable even more evolved V2X applications.

Recent developments have significantly expanded the scope of V2X research by integrating generative models and advanced game theory into trajectory planning, particularly at the intersection of aerial and ground vehicular networks. In path planning, Generative Adversarial Networks (GANs) have emerged as a tool for navigating complex, high-dimensional spaces. Visual data is utilised to autonomously generate energy-efficient flight paths, highlighting the potential for generative models to solve optimisation problems in dynamic, three-dimensional traffic environments where traditional heuristic methods struggle [37].

Complementing these generative approaches are advancements in modelling the interactive decision-making processes between vehicles during critical manoeuvres, such as on-ramp merging. Moving beyond static rule-based logic, an integrated motion planning framework based on Stackelberg Game modelling can be used [38].

Advancements in neuromorphic and cognitive computing, which mimic the structure and function of the human brain, could lead to more efficient and powerful AI HW for the various electronic components integrated into diverse vehicle domains.

Security solutions in ITS standards, based solely on Key Performance Indicators (KPI), leave several areas for reconsideration, and new approaches and solutions are required for SDVs and AIDVs to ensure vehicular communication is indeed secure so that the overall objective to make the roads safer and reduce road accidents can be achieved, rather than providing a new target for cyberattacks. The development of SDVs and AIDVs towards autonomous cyber-physical systems, utilising vehicular communication as a key domain for exchange between vehicles, infrastructure, and traffic participants, is crucial to ensure that the connectivity system is not suboptimal, thereby avoiding physical damage. To prevent such losses, new relevant security and privacy aspects of vehicular communication for SDVs and AIDVs must be addressed [39].

1.3 Opportunities and Challenges

The shift toward AIDV represents a fundamental overhaul of automotive architecture, moving from distributed ECUs to centralised, high-performance computing platforms. This AI-centric approach allows for continuous OTA updates and predictive maintenance, turning vehicles into evolving intelligent agents rather than static HW. However, this reliance on complex AI models requires immense processing power and data management, challenging manufacturers to build robust, scalable systems that support real-time decision-making without latency.

As vehicles become hyper-connected, trustworthiness and security emerge as a paramount challenge; a single vulnerability in the SW and AI stack could compromise fleet safety or user privacy. To mitigate these risks, the industry must navigate a complex landscape of evolving regulation and standardisation. Establishing universal protocols is essential not only for preventing malicious cyberattacks but also for ensuring interoperability between different manufacturers and smart infrastructure, preventing a fragmented ecosystem of incompatible safety standards.

The widespread adoption of autonomous capabilities will trigger a profound transformation of jobs, disrupting traditional roles in logistics, transportation, and ride-hailing services. While the demand for human drivers may decline, a new spectrum of opportunities can emerge in SW engineering, teleoperations, and fleet oversight. The challenge lies in managing this workforce transition equitably, requiring significant investment in upskilling to ensure that the creation of high-value technical roles balances the displacement of manual labour.

The deployment of these vehicles introduces complex ethical dilemmas regarding algorithmic accountability and decision-making during unavoidable accidents. Programming a machine to make life-or-death value judgments raises difficult questions about moral priority and legal liability. Furthermore, ensuring that these AI systems are free from data bias, such as detecting pedestrians of all demographics with equal accuracy, is critical to gaining public trust and preventing the convenience of automation from coming at the cost of equitable safety.

The key opportunities and challenges of AIDV vehicles are presented in Table 1.2, further described in the subparagraphs below and illustrated in Figure 1.6.

1.3.1 AI

AI is likely to disrupt the way vehicles are developed and built, the solutions used, the intrinsic characteristics of automotive components and systems, and how consumers interact with them. The first stages of AI development, from ML and DL to generative and agentic [40], are already evident in new vehicle

Table 1.2 Key opportunities and challenges of AI-defined vehicles.

Opportunities	Challenges
Enhanced Safety: Drastic reduction in accidents caused by human error [39].	**Cybersecurity:** Increased attack surface for malicious actors [3, 45].
Improved Traffic Efficiency: Reduced congestion and travel times through optimized routing and traffic flow.	**Data Privacy:** Collection and use of vast amounts of personal and location data.
Increased Accessibility: Greater mobility for the elderly, disabled, and those unable to drive.	**Ethical Dilemmas:** Programming "trolley problem" scenarios and ensuring fairness in AI decision-making.
New Business Models: Emergence of new services in areas like in-vehicle commerce, entertainment, and logistics [8].	**Regulatory Hurdles:** Lack of standardized regulations and liability frameworks for autonomous vehicles.
Environmental Benefits: Optimized driving patterns and platooning can reduce fuel consumption and emissions.	**Infrastructure Investment:** Significant investment required in V2X infrastructure and 6G networks.
Enhanced User Experience: Personalized and intuitive in-vehicle experiences [1].	**Public Trust and Acceptance:** Overcoming scepticism and building confidence in the safety and reliability of AI-driven systems.

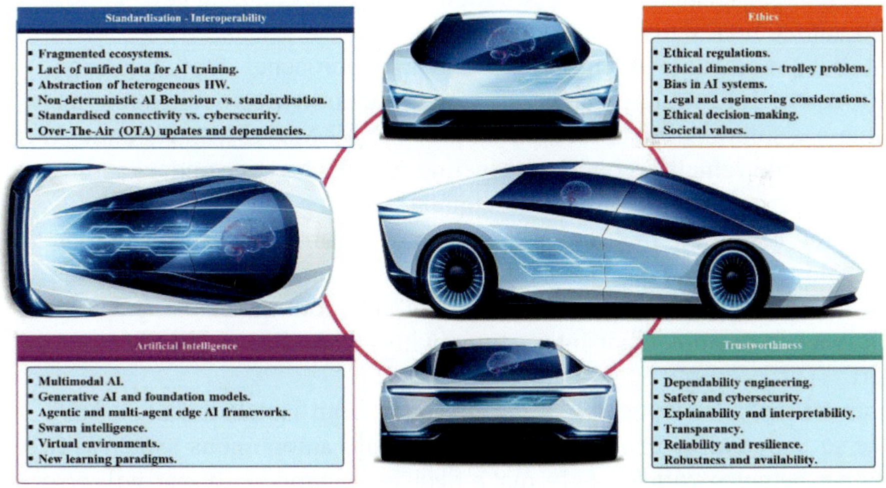

Figure 1.6 Self-evolving vehicles opportunities and challenges.

concepts and architectures, and their evolution will transform every aspect of the automotive value chain.

Future developments in AIDVs are likely to focus on improved perception through multimodal sensing, combining cameras, radar, LiDAR, and contextual data for better situational awareness. Advances in real-time decision-making and edge computing allow vehicles to process information faster and operate safely without relying heavily on cloud connectivity. AI models become more efficient, reducing power consumption while increasing reliability.

V2X-connected intelligence can reduce congestion, improve safety, and enable coordinated driving behaviours. Continuous learning systems may allow fleets to share knowledge, so improvements made by one vehicle can benefit others almost instantly.

The advantages of autonomous vehicle development include increased road safety by reducing human error, which is a leading cause of accidents. AI-driven vehicles can react faster, maintain consistent attention, and make data-driven decisions under pressure. They also offer improved mobility for people who cannot drive, such as the elderly or disabled.

Autonomous vehicles can optimise traffic flow, reduce fuel consumption, and lower emissions by enabling smoother driving and more efficient route planning. Over time, they may reshape urban design by reducing the need for parking and enabling more efficient transportation systems. Economically, they can reduce logistics and transportation costs while enabling new services such as autonomous delivery and ridesharing.

As both modular and end-to-end driving approaches face challenges such as causal confusion, explainability, interpretability, generalization, and robustness, a solution is to embed LLMs [41, 42], VLMs [19], and agentic AI [40, 43] into the vehicle architecture pipeline, alongside scene understanding, reasoning, zero-shot recognition, in-context learning, and interpretability. The use of a unified multimodal input and vocabulary for vision, language, and action can unify vision- and action-related tasks, including, among others, scene understanding, planning, and control, by using agentic AI approaches to implement interactions with the vehicle decision-making support.

The concept of agentic AI shifts the focus from isolated vehicle intelligence to cooperative behaviour among multiple autonomous systems. In the future, vehicles will not only make decisions individually but will also coordinate with each other through multi-agent learning systems and swarm intelligence frameworks. This cooperation is particularly essential for managing dense traffic situations, achieving efficient route planning, and ensuring collective safety during complex manoeuvres.

Developing robust multi-agent frameworks involves research into FL paradigms, where each vehicle processes local data while contributing to a shared global model without compromising data privacy. Moreover, integrating these intelligent agents with V2X communication networks enables real-time information exchange, enhancing overall traffic management and coordination. The challenges lie in ensuring system scalability, reducing latency, and safeguarding cybersecurity across distributed platforms [27].

These research directions open the door to a future in which urban mobility is revolutionised by interconnected, cooperative vehicle systems.

Swarm intelligence involves the coordination of multiple autonomous vehicles working together as a collective to optimise traffic flow and reduce congestion. Future research in this domain should focus on developing algorithms that facilitate cooperative behaviour among vehicles, enabling them to make joint decisions in real time. Such systems must be robust enough to handle dynamic changes in traffic and varying environmental conditions. The development of cooperative multi-agent systems will rely on novel RL techniques and advanced communication protocols that enable vehicles to reliably share sensor data and decision-making parameters. Leveraging swarm intelligence could revolutionise urban mobility by enabling distributed coordination among vehicles, reducing travel times, lowering emissions, and enhancing overall traffic stability. Research should also evaluate the potential cybersecurity risks inherent in large-scale inter-vehicle communication and develop protocols to mitigate these risks [27].

The prospect of a future dominated by AIDVs is both stimulating and challenging, given the profound societal implications of this technological shift. The potential of AI to dramatically improve road safety is perhaps the most significant benefit, as the World Health Organization estimates that over 1.3 million deaths occur each year from road traffic crashes [44]. Preliminary data for the first half of 2024, which covers 26 countries, show an improvement compared to the same period in 2023. Road fatalities decreased in 16 countries, while increasing in ten. On average, road deaths across these countries declined by 2% [45]. It is expected that by removing the human element, which is a factor in most accidents, AIDVs have the potential to save many lives.

1.3.2 Trust

Trust in AI-driven vehicles is grounded in the belief that the autonomous systems behave safely, predictably, and in alignment with human expectations. For users and regulators, trust develops when the vehicle consistently demonstrates correct decisions across a wide range of driving conditions, including rare and uncertain situations.

Trustworthiness is closely tied to dependability properties such as reliability, safety, availability, and robustness. Reliability refers to the system performing its intended functions without failure over time. Safety ensures that even when failures occur, the system minimises harm. Availability means the vehicle can operate when needed without unexpected downtime, while robustness reflects its ability to handle noise, uncertainty, and changing environments.

Research into robust, resilient autonomous systems focuses on reducing cumulative error propagation within multi-module architectures and ensuring redundancy across critical components. By integrating emergency response protocols and actively learning from near-miss incidents, these systems can improve overall reliability and public trust.

The emerging of new safety concepts emphasises deep world understanding and introspective AI models that simulate human-like intuition. Traditional scenario modelling, which relies on rigid safety frameworks, falls short in addressing the "long-tail" of rare and complex emergencies. Future research must develop adaptive, introspectable models that align with international safety standards such as ISO 26262 [29] and SOTIF [46]. The challenge is not only to predict and prevent injuries but also to implement fail-safe measures that allow vehicles to respond gracefully to unexpected conditions. Recent studies indicate that leveraging GenAI for predictive world modelling can enhance vehicle safety, reduce accidents, and improve situational awareness in densely populated or challenging environments [47].

Other key aspects of trustworthiness are transparency, explainability, and interpretability. Users are more likely to trust AI-driven vehicles if they can understand, at least at a high level, why certain decisions are made. This is particularly important in situations involving sudden manoeuvres or accident avoidance, where opaque behaviour can reduce confidence even if the outcome is safe.

XAI has emerged as a crucial requirement for the next generation of autonomous vehicles. The inherent "black-box" nature of many DL models challenges the ability of engineers, regulators, and end-users to understand AI-driven decisions. Techniques that combine vision, language, and action (such as LLMs and VLMs) offer potential solutions by providing interpretable narratives that can be monitored both during operation and through post-trip analysis. Developing robust XAI frameworks is also critical for regulatory compliance and user accountability. With nearly 94% of road accidents attributed to human error, a significant motivation for the adoption of autonomous vehicles, the need for clear, interpretable AI decisions is essential to bridging the trust gap between AI systems and human stakeholders [48].

Validation and verification are central to building trust. Unlike traditional SW, AI systems learn from data, which makes their behaviour harder to predict and formally verify. Ensuring that models perform safely across diverse real-world scenarios, including rare edge cases, remains a major challenge.

One of the main challenges in developing trust is handling uncertainty in complex environments. Weather conditions, unpredictable human behaviour, and incomplete sensor data can all affect decision-making. AI systems must not only perform well under ideal conditions but also degrade gracefully when conditions worsen.

Another challenge is bias and data limitations. If the training data does not adequately represent all driving environments or populations, the system may perform unevenly, posing safety risks and eroding trust. Continuous data collection and updating are necessary, but they introduce further complexity in maintaining consistency and safety.

Human-machine interaction plays a significant role in AIDVs. Misunderstandings about system capabilities, overreliance, or lack of proper user awareness can lead to misuse. Building intuitive interfaces and clearly communicating system limits is necessary to ensure that trust is appropriate and not misplaced.

Cybersecurity is a paramount concern for AIDVs. AI-driven vehicles are connected systems that can be vulnerable to attacks, potentially compromising safety and eroding public trust. Ensuring secure communication, resilient architectures, and rapid response to threats is essential.

As vehicles become more connected and reliant on SW, they also become more vulnerable to cyberattacks. A successful attack could have devastating consequences, ranging from data theft to remote control of vehicles. Comprehensive surveys highlight the multi-layered security and privacy challenges in V2X systems that must be addressed [39, 49].

When addressing security vulnerabilities in an AIDV, several approaches can be employed to strengthen data exchange against common threats. Trust Execution Environments (TEEs), both SW- and HW-based, and secure enclaves, more HW-oriented, can be used to isolate sensitive code or data from the main OS and applications [50]. These measures can enhance system robustness against potentially compromised applications, thereby addressing one of the major V2X threats: OTA update manipulation. Additional security risks arise from man-in-the-middle and side-channel attacks, which can be mitigated using advanced cryptographic approaches such as secure multi-party computation or homomorphic encryption [51].

In scenarios utilising heterogeneous sensor analytics, e.g., different kinds of cameras, privacy-preserving protection is essential [52]. Anonymisation algorithms can be deployed to de-identify faces of individuals, household interiors or license plates of cars detected around moving AIDVs. FL offers another solution by sharing only model updates (gradients) rather than raw data, dramatically reducing privacy exposure in communications [53].

1.3.3 Ethics

Regulatory and ethical challenges further complicate the development of trust. There is still no universal agreement on safety standards, liability in case of accidents, or acceptable risk levels. These uncertainties make it harder for the public to fully trust the introduction of new technologies.

AIDVs' concept and the implementation of autonomous functions that allow the vehicles to operate independently raise questions about how much control should remain with humans and when the system should override human decisions. These issues are interlinked with the AIDV data and AI models' dependence, since these vehicles rely on massive amounts of data from cameras, Global Navigation Satellite System (GNSS), and other sensors, as well as AI models that process the data to enable the vehicles to function safely.

Safety is a central ethical issue. While AI can reduce human error, it can also fail in unpredictable ways. Determining who is responsible in the event of an accident (the manufacturer, the SW developer, or the user) is a complex legal and moral challenge.

Bias in AI systems is another concern. If the data used to train these systems is incomplete or skewed, the vehicle may make unfair or unsafe decisions, such as misidentifying pedestrians or behaving differently in certain environments.

Privacy is also at stake. AIDVs collect and process large amounts of personal and location data, raising concerns about surveillance, data misuse, and consent. Users may not fully understand how their data is being stored or shared.

AIDVs' deployment can have broader societal impacts as widespread adoption could affect jobs in driving professions and change urban infrastructure. Ensuring that these technologies are accessible and beneficial to all, rather than only to a privileged group, is an ongoing ethical challenge.

The ethical dimensions of AI in autonomous vehicles are a subject of intense debate. The "trolley problem," where the vehicle must make a split-second decision in an unavoidable accident; the thorny issue of liability attribution; the primary concern of data privacy; the chilling prospect of hacking vulnerabilities; and the potential for overall job displacement are well-known examples [54]. SDVs and AIDVs must make decisions that carry ethical dimensions that are increasingly significant and safety-critical, as choosing a specific trajectory determines how risks are distributed among traffic participants [55].

Programming these ethical choices into machines is a complex and contentious issue that requires broad societal input and careful consideration by developers. Policymakers, standardisation organizations and vehicle producers must conceptualize what (shall) constitute(s) ethical decision-making for SDVs and AIDVs and integrate ethical, legal and engineering considerations into the development process by defining approaches on computational ethics (particularly in autonomous driving) while offering practitioners in the automotive sector a decision-making process for SDVs and AIDVs that is technically viable, legally permissible, ethically grounded and adaptable to societal values [55].

1.3.4 Architecture

The vehicle architecture has evolved from the domain architecture, a distributed system defined by function, to the zonal architecture, which addresses the limitations of the domain approach and provides the physical backbone for SW-defined mobility, to the SDV architecture, which is a paradigm shift that leverages zonal architecture to decouple SW from underlying HW opening the way for AI-defined architecture that builds upon the SDV and zonal foundation by deeply integrating AI, ML, DL, GenAI (SLMs, LLMs, VLMs, etc.) and agentic AI into core operations.

The evolution of computing platform design in the ITS domain is ideally based on the chiplets concept and RISC-V architectures, as these are two key ingredients that can foster faster productisation, lower costs, and quicker market adoption of newly developed solutions, especially those devised within the European market.

Chiplet architectures facilitate heterogeneous integration and high-bandwidth interconnects, such as the Universal chiplet interconnect express (UCIe), enabling higher processing density and improved power efficiency for demanding applications like ADAS and AI-driven electronic units. The flexibility inherent in Chiplet designs helps facilitate the transition towards centralised, zonal E/E architectures emerging in the AIDV, which can be upgraded and improved over the lifespan of a vehicle [56, 57, 58].

The feasibility of the AIDV architecture relies heavily on an open, scalable HW foundation, a role increasingly filled by RISC-V, which has reached a level of industrial maturity sufficient for safety-critical automotive applications, including those requiring the highest ISO 26262 ASIL-D integrity levels. The AIDV functions are defined by SW and AI, and the underlying HW must ensure the necessary foundation. RISC-V brings openness and flexibility to HW and offers standardisation and an ecosystem to support development toward certified-ready RISC-V Microcontroller Units (MCUs) for multiple Automotive Safety Integrity Levels (e.g., ASIL-B, ASIL-D) and toward compliance with automotive security standards (e.g., ISO21434) [59, 60].

The introduction of heterogeneous platforms incorporating conventional processing units (CPUs and GPUs) and more energy efficient and effective architectures (TPUs, NPUs, HW accelerators, neuromorphic computing-based devices) has the potential to drastically reduce energy consumption, e.g., an order of magnitude in the case of neuromorphic-based applications, and improve the capability to deliver complex real-time value-added services running on dedicated HW (HW accelerators), capable of processing the needed AI workloads at the edge.

1.3.5 Job transformation

The transition to AIDVs will have a significant impact on the workforce as well. Jobs in areas such as trucking, taxi services, and delivery will be impacted. Proactive measures, such as retraining programs and social safety nets, will be needed to mitigate the social and economic consequences of this shift.

Engineering careers will also be transformed by AIDVs, requiring a re-focus of skills: mechanical engineers will evolve into mechatronics specialists, electrical engineers into SW-HW integration experts, and service technicians into SW diagnostics and remote troubleshooting specialists, among other role transformations. In summary, most of the required skills will have to be based on AI-focused methods, combining elements of SW and HW design, AI frameworks and Data [61].

1.3.6 Regulation and Standardisation

The fragmented global regulatory landscape is a hindrance to the broader development of AIDVs. Alignment among regulatory agencies and agreements on world-recognised legislation, such as the EU AI Act, will enable a much smoother and more effective deployment of AIDVs [62]. Similar fragmentation exists within standardisation bodies, where multiple international entities develop technical specifications that often overlap and occasionally conflict on key aspects [63]. Greater alignment and clearer responsibility distribution are essential to tackle the complex challenge of AIDV standardisation.

Finally, it is worth noting that a balance between regulation and free-market rules, and between safety and security, is to be found; otherwise, the market entry of potentially breakthrough innovations and life-saving new features may be hindered by overly strict rules required to fulfil the regulations.

The convergence of AI and advanced communication is steering the automotive industry into an era of innovation. The AIDV, with its promise of enhanced safety, efficiency, and personalisation, represents a transformative vision for the future of both personal mobility and ITSs. Realising this vision will require a concerted effort from researchers, technologists, policymakers, and society to address the significant technical, ethical, and societal challenges that lie ahead. The road to the AI-defined future is still under construction, but its direction is clear [64].

1.4 Future Research Directions

The evolution of DTs into immersive triplets offers a transformative approach for predictive modelling and real-time operations in AIDVs. Future research should prioritise creating highly accurate, scalable virtual representations that seamlessly integrate vehicles with edge devices and cloud platforms. Establishing interoperability standards for these simulations is essential to ensure they function across various manufacturers. This enables rigorous AI testing in virtual environments, significantly reducing costs and the need for physical prototypes while accelerating development timelines.

As AIDV's architecture becomes more complex, new research is needed to develop virtual validation, verification, and benchmarking pipelines. This involves developing AI-based development tools that combine SW workflows with GenAI and agentic AI to safely implement automotive functions. High-fidelity simulations must be advanced to recreate rare, hazardous, or complex traffic scenarios, enabling automakers to train and validate integrated systems spanning HW, SW, and AI algorithms without the risks of real-world testing.

GenAI and synthetic data approaches are expected to accelerate the training and evaluation of AIDVs' autonomy across diverse scenarios, while multi-agent systems and collaborative frameworks foster cooperative behaviour among autonomous fleets, optimising urban mobility. Improvements in operational workflows that facilitate human–machine collaboration, along with robust V2X communications and distributed predictive maintenance systems, enhance overall vehicle performance. Further research on swarm intelligence is needed to develop scalable, coordinated transportation systems that ultimately redefine how future cities and vehicles interact.

End-to-end AI models that integrate RL and imitation learning will strengthen decision-making and planning. These approaches allow systems to learn both from experience and from observed behaviour, improving adaptability in complex situations. GenAI and synthetic data are increasingly important for training robust systems. They enable the simulation of rare edge cases that are difficult to capture in real-world datasets. Agentic AI and multi-agent systems will support cooperative driving and swarm intelligence. These capabilities can help optimise traffic flow and improve overall urban mobility.

To address the growing energy demands of intensive AI models, energy efficiency and sustainability must become central research areas. This includes developing energy-efficient algorithms using model compaction techniques and optimising edge computing to process data locally rather than in the cloud. Future investigations should conduct full AI life-cycle assessments and explore renewable energy integration to minimise the ecological footprint of AIDVs.

Interdisciplinary collaboration is crucial for addressing challenges in interoperability, cybersecurity, explainability, and ethics. Research must extend beyond technical specifications to address the ethical decision-making of AI, focusing on bias and accountability, while also safeguarding data privacy across the V2X ecosystem. Partnerships between automakers, semiconductor companies, edge, and cloud providers are necessary to standardise edge computing communications and create lightweight, scalable architectures that can operate efficiently on resource-constrained devices.

The development of end-to-end unified AI compute platforms and safety-certified operating systems is vital for the autonomy continuum. Future work envisions advancing vehicle architectures through RISC-V System-on-Chips (SoCs), heterogeneous chiplets interfaces, safety-certified MCUs, and the integration of neuromorphic, quantum sensing, and communication technologies.

Future research is needed to define and develop AIDV's full technology stack, a comprehensive safety system that unifies vehicle architecture, AI models, chips, SW, tools, and services to ensure the safe development of autonomous vehicles across the computing and communication continuum from vehicle to edge and cloud.

Finally, research must focus on interdisciplinary approaches to develop components, systems, tools, workflows, and platforms to be integrated into a robust AIDV ecosystem that supports the entire design, training, simulation, and in-vehicle processing loop, ensuring that real-time AI operates with end-to-end reliability from the vehicle to the edge and the cloud.

Acknowledgements

This publication has received funding through the Chips JU MOSAIC project. The Chips JU MOSAIC "A MOSAIC of Essential Electronic Components and Systems (ECS) for our Automated Digital Future in Industry and Mobility" project is supported by the Chips Joint Undertaking and its members, including top-up funding by Austria, Belgium, Denmark, France, Germany, Greece, Israel, Italy, Latvia, Netherlands, Norway, Poland and Turkey under Grant Agreement No. 101194414.

References

[1] B. Zheng *et al.*, "Online Location Planning for AI-Defined Vehicles: Optimizing Joint Tasks of Order Serving and Spatio-Temporal Heterogeneous Model Fine-Tuning," *IEEE Transactions on Mobile Computing*, vol. 25, no. 2, pp. 1777-1794, Feb. 2026, https://www.doi.org/10.1109/TMC.2025.3608179.

[2] L. Zhao *et al.*, "Vehicular Communications: Standardization and Open Issues," *IEEE Communications Standards Magazine*, vol. 2, no. 4, pp. 74-80, Dec. 2018, https://doi.org/10.1109/MCOMSTD.2018.1800027.

[3] S. E. Shladover, "Connected and automated vehicle systems: Introduction and overview," *Journal of Intelligent Transportation Systems*, vol. 22, no. 3, pp. 190–200, Jun. 2018, https://doi.org/10.1080/15472450.2017.1336053.

[4] A. Mohanty *et al.*, "Age of Computational AI for Autonomous Vehicles," *Artificial Intelligence for Autonomous Vehicles: The Future of*

Driverless Technology, Wiley, 2024, pp. 25-54, https://doi.org/10.1002/9781119847656.ch2.

[5] T. Gong *et al.*, "Edge Intelligence in Intelligent Transportation Systems: A Survey," *IEEE Transactions on Intelligent Transportation Systems*, vol. 24, no. 9, pp. 8919–8944, Sep. 2023, https://doi.org/10.1109/tits.2023.3275741.

[6] D. Greenbaum, "Autonomous vehicles: innovations, challenges, and implications for society and law," *Oxford University Press eBooks*, May 2025, https://doi.org/10.1093/9780198972877.003.0034.

[7] K. Yadav *et al.*, "Design Considerations and Framework Analysis for Software-Defined Autonomous Vehicles," in *2024 IEEE 99th Vehicular Technology Conference (VTC2024-Spring)*, Singapore, 2024, pp. 1-5, https://doi.org/10.1109/VTC2024-Spring62846.2024.10683354.

[8] Morgan Stanley. "Software-Defined Vehicles: The Future of Cars," *Morgan Stanley Research*. https://www.morganstanley.com/ideas/software-defined-vehicles-outlook, 2024.

[9] W. Tong *et al.*, "Artificial Intelligence for Vehicle-to-Everything: A Survey," *IEEE Access*, vol. 7, pp. 10823-10843, 2019, https://doi.org/10.1109/ACCESS.2019.2891073.

[10] O. Vermesan *et al.*, "Automotive Intelligence Embedded in Electric Connected Autonomous and Shared Vehicles Technology for Sustainable Green Mobility," *Frontiers in Future Transportation*, vol. 2, Aug. 2021, https://doi.org/10.3389/ffutr.2021.688482.

[11] P. Koopman *et al.*, "Ethics, Safety, and Autonomous Vehicles", Virtual roundtable. Computer. Dec. 2021. pp 28-37. [Online] Available: https://users.ece.cmu.edu/~koopman/pubs/koopman21_Ethics_Safety_AVs_IEEE_Roundtable.pdf.

[12] Y. Mao *et al.*, "A Survey on Spatio-Temporal Prediction: From Transformers to Foundation Models," *ACM Computing Surveys*, Sep. 2025, https://doi.org/10.1145/3766546.

[13] A. Kuznietsov *et al.*, "Explainable AI for Safe and Trustworthy Autonomous Driving: A Systematic Review," *IEEE Transactions on Intelligent Transportation Systems*, vol. 25, no. 12, pp. 19342-19364, Dec. 2024, https://doi.org/10.1109/TITS.2024.3474469.

[14] E. Haque *et al.*, "Towards an Interpretable AI Framework for Advanced Classification of Unmanned Aerial Vehicles (UAVs)," in *2024 IEEE 21st Consumer Communications & Networking Conference (CCNC)*, Las Vegas, NV, USA, 2024, pp. 644-645, https://doi.org/10.1109/CCNC51664.2024.10454862.

[15] J. Huang *et al.,* "Reinforcement Learning Based Resource Management for 6G-Enabled mIoT With Hypergraph Interference Model," *IEEE Transactions on Communications*, vol. 72, no. 7, pp. 4179-4192, July 2024, https://doi.org/10.1109/TCOMM.2024.3372892.

[16] S. Atakishiyev *et al.,* "Explainable Artificial Intelligence for Autonomous Driving: A Comprehensive Overview and Field Guide for Future Research Directions," *IEEE Access*, vol. 12, pp. 101603-101625, 2024, https://doi.org/10.1109/ACCESS.2024.3431437.

[17] E. Peltonen *et al.,* "Towards Data-Centric and Context-Aware Decision Making in Software-Defined Vehicles," in *2025 IEEE 22nd International Conference on Software Architecture Companion (ICSA-C)*, Odense, Denmark, 2025, pp. 574-577, https://doi.org/10.1109/ICSA-C65153.2025.00085.

[18] E. Yurtsever *et al.,* "A Survey of Autonomous Driving: Common Practices and Emerging Technologies," *IEEE Access*, vol. 8, pp. 58443-58469, 2020, https://doi.org/10.1109/ACCESS.2020.2983149.

[19] X. Zhou *et al.*, "Vision Language Models in Autonomous Driving: A Survey and Outlook," *IEEE Transactions on Intelligent Vehicles*, pp. 1–20, 2024, https://www.doi.org/10.1109/TIV.2024.3402136.

[20] L. Chen *et al.*, "End-to-End Autonomous Driving: Challenges and Frontiers," *IEEE Transactions on Pattern Analysis and Machine Intelligence*, vol. 46, no. 12, pp. 10164-10183, Dec. 2024, https://www.doi.org/10.1109/TPAMI.2024.3435937.

[21] A. Tampuu *et al.*, "A Survey of End-to-End Driving: Architectures and Training Methods," *IEEE Transactions on Neural Networks and Learning Systems*, vol. 33, no. 4, pp. 1364-1384, April 2022, https://doi.org/10.1109/TNNLS.2020.3043505.

[22] N. Hameed Hussein *et al.*, "SDN-Based VANET Routing: A Comprehensive Survey on Architectures, Protocols, Analysis, and Future Challenges," *IEEE Access*, vol. 13, pp. 126801-126861, 2025, https://doi.org/10.1109/ACCESS.2024.3355313.

[23] S. D. A. Shah, M. A. Gregory, F. Bouhafs and F. D. Hartog, "Artificial Intelligence-Defined Wireless Networking for Computational Offloading and Resource Allocation in Edge Computing Networks," *IEEE Open Journal of the Communications Society*, vol. 5, pp. 2039-2057, 2024, https://doi.org/10.1109/OJCOMS.2024.3382265.

[24] E. Kartsakli *et al.*, "AI-Powered Edge Computing Evolution for Beyond 5G Communication Networks," in *2023 Joint European Conference on*

Networks and Communications & 6G Summit (EuCNC/6G Summit), Gothenburg, Sweden, 2023, pp. 478-483, https://doi.org/10.1109/EuCNC/6GSummit58263.2023.10188371.

[25] O. Vermesan and V. Frascolla, Eds., "Edge IoT Industrial Immersive Technologies and Spatial Computing Continuum," AIOTI White Paper, Alliance for Internet of Things Innovation, Brussels, Belgium, 2024. [Online]. Available: https://aioti.eu/wp-content/uploads/AIOTI-Paper-Edge-AI-IoT-Immersive-Technologies-Published.pdf.

[26] J. Hwang, K. -W. Lim and D. Kim, "What If Vehicles are Controlled by the Road?," *IEEE Transactions on Intelligent Vehicles*, vol. 10, no. 4, pp. 2219-2233, Apr. 2025, https://doi.org/10.1109/TIV.2024.3372007.

[27] K. Kandali and S. Nouh, "AI-Native V2X and Internet of Vehicles Systems: Architectures, Learning Paradigms, and Open Challenges," Feb. 2026, https://doi.org/10.36227/techrxiv.177006069.92717813/v1.

[28] Xu et al., "A Low-Latency and Massive-Connectivity Vehicular Fog Computing Frame-work for 5G," in *2018 IEEE Globecom Workshops (GC Wkshps)*, Abu Dhabi, United Arab Emirates, 2018, pp. 1-6, https://doi.org/10.1109/GLOCOMW.2018.8644428.

[29] ISO 26262:2018, "Road vehicles — Functional safety," International Organization for Standardization, Geneva, Switzerland, 2018. [Online]. Available: https://www.iso.org/publication/PUB200262.html.

[30] D. Hepp and M. Harrysson. "Beyond CES 2025: How gen AI is revolutionizing vehicle tech." *McKinsey & Company*. [Online]. Available: https://www.mckinsey.com/featured-insights/themes/beyond-ces-2025how-gen-ai-is-revolutionizing-vehicle-tech.

[31] Jesus Gutierrez *et al.*, "Seamless Integration of Efficient 6G Wireless Technologies for Communication and Sensing Enabling Ecosystems," *IFIP advances in information and communication technology*, pp. 190–201, Jan. 2024, doi: https://doi.org/10.1007/978-3-031-63227-3_13.

[32] X. Li *et al.,* "MultiX: Advancing 6G-RAN Through Multi-Technology, Multi-Sensor Fusion, Multi-Band and Multi-Static Perception," *IEEE Wireless Communications*, 2025, https://doi.org/10.1109/mwc.2025.3629589.

[33] D. Firmani *et al.,* "INTEND: Intent-Based Data Operation in the Computing Continuum," in *International Conference on Advanced Information Systems Engineering (CaiSE) 2024*, Limassol, Cyprus, 03-07.07.2024, pp. 43-50.

[34] Z. Xi *et al.,* "The rise and potential of large language model based agents: a survey," *Science China Information Sciences*, vol. 68, no. 2, Jan. 2025, https://doi.org/10.1007/s11432-024-4222-0.

[35] W. Raslan *et al.*, "Smart Vehicle Safety: AI-Driven Driver Assistance and V2X Communications," in *2024 International Telecommunications Conference (ITC-Egypt)*, Cairo, Egypt, 2024, pp. 787-792, https://doi.org/10.1109/ITC-Egypt61547.2024.10620463.

[36] K. Agrawal *et al.*, "Advancing Software-Defined Vehicles: An End-to-End Framework with Digital Twin Based Attestation for OTA Updates," in *2025 17th International Conference on COMmunication Systems and NETworks (COMSNETS)*, Bengaluru, India, 2025, pp. 514-522, https://doi.org/10.1109/COMSNETS63942.2025.10885560.

[37] M. Eskandari *et al.*, "Visual GANs for End-to-End UAV Trajectory Generation in RIS-Assisted Energy-Efficient Wireless Vehicular Networks," *Green Energy and Intelligent Transportation*, pp. 100365–100365, Sep. 2025, https://doi.org/10.1016/j.geits.2025.100365.

[38] L. Zhang *et al.*, "Integrated Motion Planning for On-Ramp Merging Based on Stackelberg Game Modeling Considering Interactive Characteristics," *IEEE Transactions on Vehicular Technology*, vol. 74, no. 8, pp. 11762-11776, Aug. 2025, https://doi.org/10.1109/TVT.2025.3554978.

[39] T. Yoshizawa *et al.*, "A Survey of Security and Privacy Issues in V2X Communication Systems," *ACM Computing Surveys*, Aug. 2022, https://doi.org/10.1145/3558052.

[40] Satyabrata Pradhan, "Agentic AI for Software-Defined Vehicles: A Generative Testing Framework for Autonomous Feature Assurance," *Journal of Electrical Systems*, vol. 21, no. 01, pp. 993–1001, Apr. 2025, https://doi.org/10.52783/jes.9181.

[41] Mao *et al.*, "GPT-Driver: Learning to Drive with GPT," in *37th Annual Conference on Neural Information Processing Systems (NeurIPS)*, New Orleans, Dec. 2023, https://doi.org/10.48550/arXiv.2310.01415.

[42] J. Wei *et al.*, "OccLLaMA: An Occupancy-Language-Action Generative World Model for Autonomous Driving," *arXiv (Cornell University)*, Sep. 2024, https://doi.org/10.48550/arxiv.2409.03272.

[43] J. Mao, J. Ye, Y. Qian, M. Pavone, and Y. Wang, "A Language Agent for Autonomous Driving," *arXiv (Cornell University)*, Nov. 2023, https://doi.org/10.48550/arxiv.2311.10813.

[44] World Health Organization. *Global status report on road safety 2023.* https://assets.bbhub.io/dotorg/sites/64/2023/12/WHO-Global-status-report-on-road-safety-2023.pdf.

[45] International Transport Forum. Road Safety Annual Report 2024. https://www.itf-oecd.org/sites/default/files/docs/irtad-road-safety-annual-report-2024.pdf.

[46] ISO/PAS 21448:2019, "Road vehicles-Safety of the intended functionality," International Organization for Standardization, Geneva, CH, 2019. [Online]. Available: https://www.iso.org/standard/70939.html.

[47] Wayve. "Pioneering a New Paradigm in AV Safety: Solving Long-Tail Challenges," Jul., 2024. https://wayve.ai/technology/safety-framework/

[48] S. Atakishiyev *et al.*, "Explainable Artificial Intelligence for Autonomous Driving: A Comprehensive Overview and Field Guide for Future Research Directions," *IEEE Access*, vol. 12, pp. 101603-101625, 2024, https://doi.org/10.1109/ACCESS.2024.3431437.

[49] S. E. Shladover, "Connected and automated vehicle systems: Introduction and overview," *Journal of Intelligent Transportation Systems*, vol. 22, no. 3, pp. 190–200, Jun. 2018, https://doi.org/10.1080/15472450.2017.1336053.

[50] Y. Bai *et al.*, "SecPaging: Secure Enclave Paging with Hardware-Enforced Protection against Controlled-Channel Attacks," pp. 1–6, Jun. 2024, https://doi.org/10.1145/3649329.3658241.

[51] Y. Liang *et al.*, "Secure Multi-Party Computation on the Encrypted Network: a Lattice-based Multi-Party Homomorphic Encryption Protocol," in *2024 9th International Conference on Communication, Image and Signal Processing (CCISP)*, Gold Coast, Australia, 2024, pp. 112-117, https://doi.org/10.1109/CCISP63826.2024.10765563.

[52] W. Abbasi *et al.*, "Privacy vs Accuracy Trade-Off in Privacy Aware Face Recognition in Smart Systems," *2022 IEEE Symposium on Computers and Communications (ISCC)*, Rhodes, Greece, 2022, pp. 1–8, doi:10.1109/ISCC55528.2022.9912465.

[53] L. Skovajsova *et al.*, "A Review of Multi-Objective and Multi-Task Federated Learning Approaches," in *2025 IEEE 23rd World Symposium on Applied Machine Intelligence and Informatics (SAMI)*, Stara Lesna, Slovakia, 2025, pp. 000035-000040, https://doi.org/10.1109/SAMI63904.2025.10883172.

[54] K. Shah and E. Guven, "Exploring Ethical Issues and Challenges of Autonomous Vehicles in Different Countries and Cultures," in *2025 59th Annual Conference on Information Sciences and Systems (CISS)*, pp. 1–6, Mar. 2025, https://doi.org/10.1109/ciss64860.2025.10944682.

[55] F. Poszler *et al.*, "Ethical Decision-Making for Self-Driving Vehicles: A Proposed Model & List of Value-Laden Terms that Warrant (Technical)

Specification," *Science and Engineering Ethics*, vol. 30, no. 5, Oct. 2024, https://doi.org/10.1007/s11948-024-00513-0.

[56] P. Onufryk and S. Choudhary, "UCIe: Standard for an Open Chiplet Ecosystem," *IEEE Micro*, vol. 45, no. 1, pp. 16-25, Jan.-Feb. 2025, https://doi.org/10.1109/MM.2024.3451532.

[57] M. Odema *et al.*, "Performance Implications of Multi-Chiplet Neural Processing Units on Autonomous Driving Perception," in *2025 Design, Automation & Test in Europe Conference (DATE)*, Lyon, France, 2025, pp. 1-7, https://doi.org/10.23919/DATE64628.2025.10993228.

[58] T. Uehling *et al.*, "Chiplet Package for Automotive and Edge Processors," in *2025 IEEE 75th Electronic Components and Technology Conference (ECTC)*, Dallas, TX, USA, 2025, pp. 1259-1263, https://doi.org/10.1109/ECTC5168.

[59] S. Roy et al., "Exception Coverage on Automotive Processors," *IEEE Embedded Systems Letters*, vol. 18, no. 1, pp. 27–30, Feb. 2026, https://doi.org/10.1109/LES.2025.3571040.

[60] L. Cuomo *et al.,* "Towards a RISC-V Open Platform for Next-generation Automotive ECUs," in *2023 12th Mediterranean Conference on Embedded Computing (MECO)*, 2023, pp. 1-8, https://doi.org/10.1109/MECO58584.2023.10154913.

[61] K.-H. Wang and W.-C. Lu, "AI-induced Job impact: Complementary or substitution? Empirical Insights and Sustainable Technology Considerations," *Sustainable Technology and Entrepreneurship*, vol. 4, no. 1, 2024, https://doi.org/10.1016/j.stae.2024.100085.

[62] European Parliament and Council of the European Union, "Regulation (EU) 2024/1689 of the European Parliament and of the Council of 13 June 2024 laying down harmonised rules on artificial intelligence (Artificial Intelligence Act) and amending Regulations (EC) No 300/2008, (EU) No 167/2013, (EU) No 168/2013, (EU) 2018/858, (EU) 2018/1139 and (EU) 2019/2144 and Directives 2014/90/EU, (EU) 2016/797 and (EU) 2017/2394," *Official Journal of the European Union*, vol. L 1689, July 12, 2024. [Online]. Available: https://artificialintelligenceact.eu/the-act/.

[63] B. Raaf *et al.,* "Key technology advancements driving mobile communications from generation to generation," *Intel Technology Journal*, vol. 18, no. 1, 2014.

[64] U. Rajasekaran *et al.,* "Artificial Intelligence in Autonomous Vehicles - A Survey of Trends and Challenges," pp. 1–24, Feb. 2024, https://doi.org/10.1002/9781119847656.ch1.

2

From Complexity to Efficiency: Pruning Vision Transformers in Practice

Martyna Poreba, Ahmed Soulmani, Victor Bercy, and Michal Szczepanski

Université Paris-Saclay, CEA, List, France

Abstract

Vision Transformers (ViTs) achieve state-of-the-art performance in semantic segmentation. However, their high computational cost, especially when processing high-resolution images, remains a major obstacle for real-time and embedded applications. In this work, we provide a taxonomy of existing pruning approaches and observe that many efficient methods overlook fine-grained hardware and latency characteristics. We further investigate selected pruning strategies that merge redundant information at the patch or token level to effectively reduce computational complexity. To assess their practical relevance, we evaluate deployment performance on an NVIDIA Jetson Orin AGX platform, analysing trade-offs between latency, computational workload, and accuracy. While token pruning is commonly motivated by the assumption that fewer tokens lead to lower latency, our results reveal that this relationship is often non-linear due to GPU workload scheduling, framework overhead, and kernel design constraints.

Keywords: Vision Transformer, Semantic Segmentation, Token Pruning, Model Compression, Embedded AI.

2.1 Introduction and Background

Recent advances in Vision Transformers (ViTs) have reshaped the landscape of computer vision by introducing attention-based architectures capable of

DOI: 10.1201/9788743815273-2

capturing global context. In semantic segmentation, this capacity to model long-range dependencies has translated into substantial accuracy gains on complex datasets. However, this efficiency comes at a high computational and memory costs, which grows dramatically for high-resolution inputs. Such constraints hinder the deployment of ViTs in real-time or embedded settings, where latency, memory footprint, and energy efficiency are critical. To mitigate these limitations, several approaches have been explored, including model quantization, distillation, or architectural redesign. In parallel, a family of techniques referred to as pruning has been gaining popularity. These methods primarily target Transformer blocks, attention heads, linear layers, or tokens. While pruning blocks or heads modifies the model's architecture, token pruning distinguishes itself by shortening the sequence length during forward pass. The underlying premise is intuitive: by identifying and removing redundant or non-informative tokens at various stages of the network, the computational workload can be substantially reduced, thereby decreasing inference latency. A growing body of literature has proposed various pruning criteria applied either before the encoder or within its shallow layers. Their effectiveness is typically reported through reductions in Floating Point Operations (FLOPs), along with the corresponding impact on accuracy, for example mean Intersection over Union (mIoU) in segmentation. While many pruning approaches succeed in reducing theoretical FLOPs, they often overlook key aspects of practical deployment.

This paper presents a practical study of token pruning for semantic segmentation, emphasizing the gap between theoretical efficiency and real-world deployable performance. We first categorize existing methods and then empirically evaluate selected approaches that prune tokens at the patch level and within shallow encoder layers. Our central contribution is a comprehensive assessment of their end-to-end deployability, which encompasses not only accuracy but also TensorRT exportability and inference latency on an NVIDIA Jetson Orin platform. Our results demonstrate that the theoretical reductions in FLOPs from token pruning do not always translate linearly into latency gains on embedded GPUs, as actual runtime performance is influenced by factors such as memory access patterns, parallelization efficiency, and framework or kernel-level overheads. This highlights the practical trade-offs between pruning ratio, accuracy, and real-world performance that must be considered for efficient model design at the edge. The real technical bottleneck is exportability. We observe, that pruned models are often not compatible with standardized deployment formats such as ONNX, preventing their efficient execution on hardware-optimized runtimes like TensorRT.

2.2 Related Work

The success of Vision Transformers (ViTs) in image classification [1, 2] has quickly extended to dense prediction tasks such as semantic segmentation. However, adapting the Transformer paradigm to dense prediction required the design of novel architectures capable of mapping sequences to pixel-level representations. Pioneering works like SETR [3, 4] demonstrated this feasibility by employing a pure Transformer encoder followed by a CNN-style decoder. The focus then shifted towards improving efficiency and accuracy. SegFormer [5] introduced a hierarchical Transformer encoder that eliminates the need for positional encoding and was combined with a simple MLP decoder. The Segmenter [6] model adopted a more symmetrical encoder-decoder Transformer architecture, using mask tokens to directly predict semantic classes. More recently, SegViT [7] and SegViT2 [8] argued for a powerful decoder, introducing a lightweight ViT decoder with an attention-to-mask mechanism to enhance fine-grained detail.

Despite their high accuracy, the computational cost of these models, driven by the self-attention mechanism on a large number of patches, remains a significant bottleneck for real-world deployment. To mitigate this cost, token pruning reduces computational load by shortening the input sequence through the removal or merging of redundant or less informative tokens. The design of these approaches involves critical choices regarding both the scoring metrics (e.g., based on attention, similarity, or confidence) used to rank tokens, and the stage of application. Some techniques apply early pruning at the patch embedding level to maximize workload reduction, while others employ progressive pruning within the encoder layers to base decisions on more refined features (Figure 2.1). Pruning methods diverge also significantly in their adaptability to input content. While static pruning applies a uniform compression rate across all images, dynamic pruning tailors the number of preserved tokens to the specific complexity of each input.

Early approaches focused on attention-based scoring, exploiting the observation that tokens receiving little attention from the *[CLS]* token contribute marginally to the final representation and can therefore be safely discarded. EViT [9] and Evo-ViT [10] use the attentiveness value as a criterion to identify the top-k relevant tokens for classification and fuse the inattentive ones. EViT aggregates these scores across heads within each layer, while Evo-ViT accumulates class attention across layers to capture global token contributions. This concept was later refined by methods introducing more sophisticated attention mechanisms. For instance, SPViT [11] incorporates a saliency prediction module to guide token pruning, aiming to preserve semantically important regions by leveraging attention distributions. ATS [12], in contrast, introduces a parameter-free sampling module that adaptively retains tokens based on *[CLS]*-attention scores through soft sampling, so less informative tokens are down-weighted. AS-ViT [13] employs head-weighted attention scores with learnable thresholds for instance-wise pruning to permanently discard non-informative tokens.

A recent breakthrough in ViT optimization lies in token merging techniques, which depart from traditional pruning by offering a softer alternative. Instead of permanently discarding tokens deemed redundant or non-informative, these methods progressively merge them, preserving information. The foundational work on ToMe [14] demonstrated that applying similarity-based fusion between consecutive Transformer layers provides an effective way to reduce token redundancy while maintaining model performance. Specifically, ToMe leverages the attention keys to compute token similarity and employs a fast bipartite matching algorithm to identify pairs of redundant tokens. These tokens are merged through weighted averaging, while proportional attention further ensures that the merging process reflects each token's relative contribution. This idea was subsequently adopted in other approaches [15–20], or [31].

Another line of work exploits confidence-based criteria to guide token pruning. The underlying intuition is that tokens with high predictive certainty can be safely removed from further computation. DToP [21] implements this idea through a multi-stage early-exit mechanism, where the maximum softmax probability from intermediate segmentation heads is used as a confidence score to halt tokens deemed sufficiently processed. STEP [22] extends this idea by systematically analysing the placement of intermediate pruning heads and demonstrates that their positioning plays a crucial role in overall effectiveness. DoViT [23] adopts a similar principle but adds a reconstruction module to preserve spatial consistency, which requires dedicated training and makes it less plug-and-play. PAUMER [24] further refines this direction by leveraging entropy over class probabilities as a confidence score, halting tokens with the highest certainty and thereby reducing redundant computation.

Although token pruning has demonstrated strong results in image classification, it does not always generalize to dense prediction tasks. In classification, preserving the *[CLS]* token is often sufficient for accurate global predictions, whereas segmentation requires maintaining fine-grained spatial information across all tokens, making token removal inherently problematic. Consequently, merging tokens too aggressively or permanently discarding

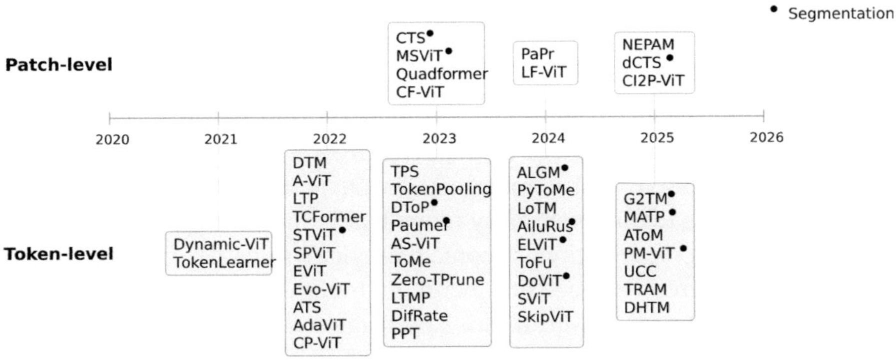

Figure 2.1 Overview of pruning techniques in ViT. The diagram distinguishes between patch-level and token-level approaches.

them leads to the loss of critical details required for accurate segmentation. To date, only a limited number of works have directly addressed token pruning in ViT-based segmentation models [16, 19, 21–29, 31].

Some of these methods employ patch-level pruning that adapts the tokenization process to the image content before the Transformer encoder. This results in a non-uniform token grids from the very beginning. Two complementary directions can be distinguished. First, top-down adaptive tokenization, where a mixed-scale patch grid allocates fine resolution to salient regions while coarsening homogeneous areas [25]. Second, bottom-up merging, where adjacent patches are grouped into larger semantic units after the initial tokenization like in CTS [26] or dCTS [22]. For instance, CTS merges tokens within fixed 2×2 patch groups, guided by a lightweight CNN-based policy network that decides whether the patches should share a token. dCTS extends this approach by allowing multi-scale merging across variable window sizes.

STViT [27] introduces a super-token mechanism to reduce redundancy in early layers of ViTs. Local tokens are first aggregated into super-tokens through sparse attention within limited neighbourhoods, then a compact self-attention is applied among super-tokens, before redistributing the information back to the original tokens. In contrast, AiluRus [28] applies an adaptive resolution strategy. Instead of processing all tokens at a uniform resolution, the method employs a spatial-aware density-based clustering algorithm at intermediate layers to identify representative tokens. Tokens in less informative regions (e.g., object interiors or homogeneous backgrounds) are merged into lower-resolution clusters, while tokens near boundaries or salient regions are preserved at high resolution. ELViT [29] inserts a token clustering layer that aggregates locally redundant tokens into compact super-tokens, followed by a token reconstruction layer that restores high-resolution representations before the prediction head. More recently, building on ToMe's global bipartite matching, ALGM [16], introduces a hierarchical strategy. Instead of relying solely on progressive global merging, it first performs local merging within small windows to eliminate early redundancy, and then applies global merging once token representations become more discriminative. G2TM [31] proposes a more aggressive one-shot merging strategy that can be applied as early as the first encoder layer. In this approach, tokens are grouped into large graph-based super-tokens using a breadth-first search over the similarity graph.

2.3 Benchmark Setup

We benchmark two baseline architectures, SegViT and Segmenter, together with several state-of-the-art token merging mechanisms that reduce the token count at complementary levels. Specifically, we evaluate two patch-level merging methods: CTS, which performs a fixed 30% token merging, and dCTS, a dynamic variant that applies size-dependent thresholds (0.6, 0.8, 0.9, and 0.9) for 2×2, 4×4, 8×8, and 16×16 patch groups, respectively. We further consider DToP, an early-stopping module inserted after the 8th layer with a confidence threshold of 0.9, as well as STEP, a hybrid method that combines patch merging via dCTS with DToP, using the same configurations as their respective base methods. We also evaluate two recent token-level methods: ALGM, which uses a two-stage dynamic merging strategy (local at the first layer, global at the fifth) with a 0.95 threshold, and G2TM, which applies graph-based token merging at the second layer with the same threshold. For all these methods, we adopt the parameter configurations proposed in the original papers to ensure a fair and reproducible comparison.

Backbone. All methods are evaluated with a ViT-Base backbone. This model has 12 transformer layers, 12 attention heads, and a hidden embedding dimension of 768, resulting in about 86M parameters. This choice enables fair comparison across methods while keeping a suitable scale for embedded deployment and a balanced trade-off between accuracy and efficiency.

Dataset. We use the Cityscapes dataset [30], a standard benchmark for evaluating urban scene segmentation methods. To analyse how the models scale with input resolution, we report results at both 768×768 and 1024×1024.

Metrics. We assess the models in terms of both segmentation quality and computational efficiency. For accuracy, we report the mIoU, which is the standard metric in semantic segmentation. To capture runtime performance under real-time constraints, we measure the throughput in frames per second (FPS) with a batch size of one. Finally, we estimate the intrinsic computational complexity of each model in GFLOPs, computed using the fvcore library.

Implementation. All models are implemented in PyTorch. As none of the methods could be exported to ONNX, inference was conducted directly in PyTorch. Section 1.5 discusses the likely causes of these export failures.

Hardware. Experiments are conducted on the NVIDIA Jetson AGX Orin with 64 GB LPDDR5 and an Ampere GPU (2,048 CUDA cores, 64 Tensor Cores), operated in its maximum power mode (MaxN, 60 W).

2.4 Results

To provide an initial qualitative assessment, we illustrate the token partitioning obtained with different merging-based pruning strategies (Figure 2.2). At the patch level, we compare CTS and its dynamic variant dCTS, while at the token level, we show ALGM and G2TM. These visualizations highlight how merging operates at different granularities and serve as a reference point for contrasting patch-based and token-based pruning approaches. In general, all methods reduce the number of active tokens by approximately 40% on average, except for CTS, which removes a fixed 30% of tokens.

Figure 2.2 Visual examples of pruning with selected SOTA methods (from left to right): regular grid partitioning, CTS, dCTS, ALGM, and G2TM.

In terms of segmentation accuracy, Segmenter consistently outperforms SegViT, achieving higher mIoU across both resolutions. However, as shown in Figure 2.3, SegViT tends to better capture small or thin structures, whereas Segmenter provides more accurate and spatially consistent segmentation overall. SegViT is also notably more efficient, requiring fewer FLOPs and achieving higher FPS. While all evaluated pruning approaches demonstrate clear theoretical efficiency gains, their practical acceleration is mainly determined by the pruning method's design and its implementation efficiency (Table 2.1 and Table 2.2). For SegViT, when assessed at a resolution of 768×768, pruning achieves up to a 50% reduction in computational cost while preserving segmentation accuracy with only about a one-point

Figure 2.3 Segmentation results (top to bottom): SegViT with STEP, Segmenter with G2TM, and ground truth.

Table 2.1 Performance evaluation on Cityscapes (768×768) of state-of-the-art token reduction methods integrated into a ViT-Base backbone with different decoders

Method	mIoU [%]	GFLOPs	FPS
SegViT	73.7	301	8.0
+CTS	72.9	190	15.2
+DToP	73.5	233	6.6
+dCTS	72.8	182	15.0
+STEP	72.7	149	7.3
Segmenter	77.6	348	2.9
+CTS	77.6	172	5.3
+ALGM	76.4	199	4.7
+G2TM	76.0	230	4.0

decrease. At 1024×1024, the reduction in GFLOPs is even more pronounced, reaching about 70%, though this comes with a larger accuracy drop of up to three mIoU points. CTS and dCTS provide the best trade-off. In contrast, STEP achieves the largest reduction in computational cost across resolutions but shows limited runtime gains. Figure 2.4 illustrates the per-layer behavior of the model, revealing that throughput does not scale linearly with FLOP savings. Although fewer tokens are processed in deeper layers, each layer takes more time to execute, revealing the overhead introduced by the dynamic masking and control operations of the early-exit mechanism (as in DToP), which create bottlenecks due to irregular control flow and memory access patterns.

Table 2.2 Performance evaluation on Cityscapes (1024×1024) of state-of-the-art token reduction methods integrated into a ViT-Base backbone with different decoders

Method	mIoU [%]	GFLOPs	FPS
SegViT	75.2	670	3.1
+CTS	74.9	403	5.5
+DToP	74.6	500	3.4
+dCTS	72.7	247	9.8
+STEP	72.0	200	6.8
Segmenter	77.1	776	1.2
+CTS	72.2	448	1.9
+ALGM	76.6	381	2.2
+G2TM	75.1	424	2.0

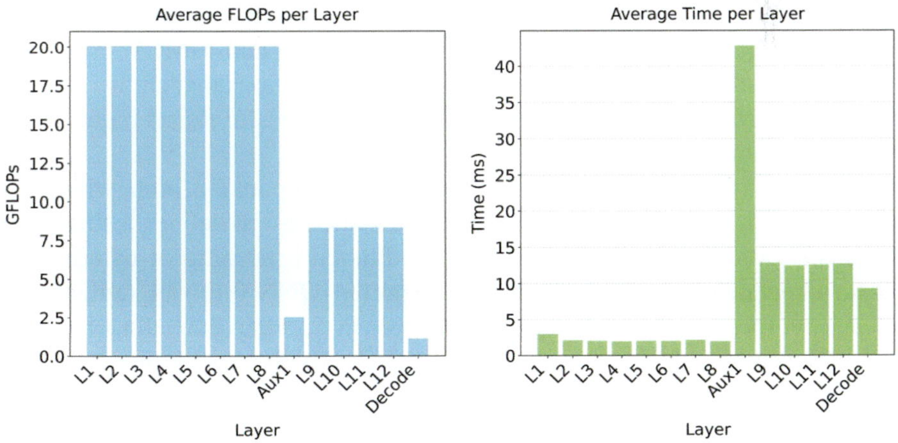

Figure 2.4 Per-layer complexity (GFLOPs) and throughput (FPS) at 1024×1024 for SegViT+STEP, comparing encoder and auxiliary pruning heads.

With the Segmenter, similar trends are observed: although pruning reduces the theoretical cost by nearly half, the real-time performance remains low, particularly at higher resolutions. At 768×768, CTS achieves the best trade-off, delivering both the largest FLOP reduction and the highest throughput. At 1024×1024, it remains efficient but achieves smaller FLOP reductions than G2TM and ALGM, yielding similar FPS.

2.5 Deployment Challenges in Practice

Deploying optimized TensorRT-based ViT models on the NVIDIA Jetson Orin platform presents several practical challenges, primarily related to model conversion into the ONNX format. While ONNX provides a standardized representation of computational graphs across different frameworks and hardware platforms, TensorRT uses ONNX as an intermediate format to enable GPU-accelerated inference through NVIDIA's optimized libraries. In practice, the export process often exposes inconsistencies when applied to complex model architectures. Empirical validation indicates that exporting all SegViT-based models (the baseline and pruned variants, including CTS, DToP, dCTS, and STEP) is technically feasible. However, the ONNX runtime outputs fail to numerically match those of the original PyTorch model, indicating a fundamental corruption of the computation graph. This issue already originates from the SegViT architecture itself, even before applying any pruning. In fact, exporting SegViT to ONNX is challenging due to its additional dependencies on MMSegmentation [32] and the MMCV operator set. The main issues come from operator incompatibilities and dynamic tensor shapes coded in the library itself. Some PyTorch and MMCV layers in the attention and decoding stages use reshaping operations that are hard to represent in the static ONNX graph. Consequently, successful export requires manual graph modifications.

In contrast to SegViT, Segmenter is implemented in pure PyTorch, which simplifies ONNX export process. Its clean and static design defines a single deterministic computation graph without conditional branching or external metadata dependencies. As a result, the exported ONNX model remains stable and reproduces the PyTorch outputs. However, when extending Segmenter with pruning blocks, none of the selected methods allow a successful ONNX export. Although CTS and G2TM can be exported, the generated ONNX graphs are found to be incorrect or incomplete. In contrast, ALGM systematically fails during export. This issue is probably due to non-static control flow, unsupported custom operations, variable tensor shapes, and

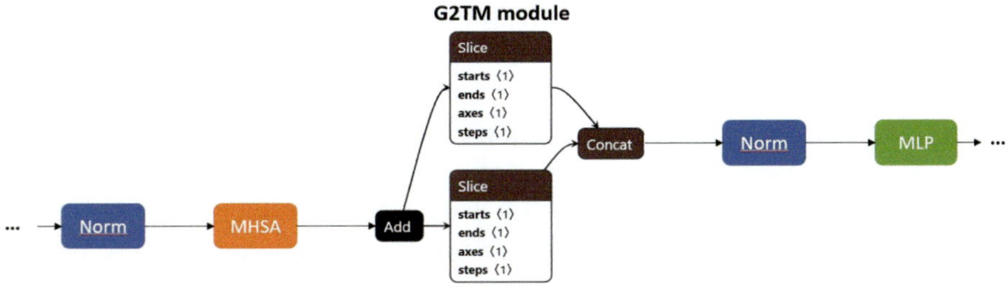

Figure 2.5 Wrong ONNX export of the G2TM module. G2TM is reduced to two brown Slice blocks, which separate the *[CLS]* token from the rest of the tokens, and a Concat operation. The internal computations responsible for the token merging behavior of G2TM are not translated at all and therefore do not appear in the ONNX graph.

in-place operations (e.g., *scatter_reduce*) used to save memory, which disrupted ONNX graph generation. For instance, the G2TM module is exported using only three ONNX blocks (Figure 2.5), corresponding to a simple slicing operation on the token sequence to separate the *[CLS]* token from the remaining tokens. It represents the first step of G2TM, which prevents this special token from being merged with others. The two groups are then directly concatenated with no token reduction applied. In practice, the G2TM module becomes transparent in the ONNX computation graph. This behavior indeed arises because G2TM relies on control-flow constructs such as *if–else* statements conditioned on runtime values or tensor shapes, as well as *for* loops whose iteration ranges are determined by computed values. Additionally, it also relies on third-party libraries (e.g., NetworkX) and performs operations that convert tensors into Python objects such as lists. These conversions cause data to leave the tensor computation graph, thereby preventing ONNX from tracing and representing the corresponding operations.

Overall, the ONNX exporter attempts to freeze the model into a single tensor-based computation graph. However, dynamic control flow, data structures such as lists or dictionaries, and unsupported operators prevent a full conversion, often leading to incomplete graphs or numerical discrepancies compared to PyTorch outputs.

2.6 Conclusions

Numerous pruning strategies based on token merging or discarding have been explored in the literature, but only a handful have been adapted or validated for semantic segmentation. While all selected pruning methods achieve substantial theoretical gains with up to a twofold reduction in FLOPs, they do not always exhibit corresponding improvements in real throughput. Real-time performance often shows limited improvement because compute units are underutilized and batching is inefficient. Dynamic operations such as masking, token selection, and re-indexing are rarely optimized for specific hardware, adding extra runtime overhead. This issue is further amplified in dynamic pruning methods, where the number of active tokens varies per sample. Since modern accelerators are optimized for fixed-size and dense tensor operations, such variability leads to irregular memory access patterns and thread divergence. More fundamentally, these inefficiencies stem from a lack of algorithm–hardware co-design, as most token pruning strategies are developed under idealized computational assumptions, such as FLOPs reduction, without considering the behavior and limitations of actual deployment hardware.

A major challenge lies in deploying pruned models for optimized inference. In particular, exporting ViT architectures to TensorRT via ONNX often proves difficult due to compatibility and graph conversion issues. For many existing pruning methods, dynamic control flow remains one of the most significant obstacles to seamless ONNX export. Operations involving conditional branching (e.g., pruning rules that apply different thresholds depending on activation magnitude or token importance) and iterative loops (e.g., progressive token merging or pruning functions that stop once a confidence target is reached) introduce runtime variability that conflicts with ONNX's static computational graph representation. In fact, ONNX needs all execution paths and tensor shapes to be fixed when the graph is created. As a result, any operation that depends on dynamic values like *if–else* conditions based on tensor data or loops whose range is decided at runtime cannot be properly exported. Consequently, achieving a successful conversion requires either removing these dynamic behaviours altogether or introducing workarounds such as conditional masking, tensor-based indexing, or custom operators that preserve the model's functionality while adhering to ONNX's static graph constraints.

Acknowledgements

This work was conducted within the NEUROKIT2E project, funded by the EU Horizon Europe programme (Grant Agreement No. 101112268).

References

[1] A. Vaswani, *et al.,* "Attention is All you Need," in *Proceedings of the 31st International Conference on Neural Information Processing Systems (NeurIPS)*, vol. 30, pp. 6000–6010, 2017.

[2] A. Dosovitskiy, *et al.,* "An Image is Worth 16×16 Words: Transformers for Image Recognition at Scale," in *International Conference on Learning Representations (ICLR)*, 2021.

[3] S. Zheng, *et al.,* "Rethinking Semantic Segmentation from a Sequence-to-Sequence Perspective with Transformers," in *Proceedings of the IEEE/CVF Conference on Computer Vision and Pattern Recognition (CVPR)*, 2021.

[4] L. Zhang, *et al.,* "Vision transformers: From semantic segmentation to dense prediction," in *Proceedings of the International Journal of Computer Vision*, pp. 1–21, 2024.

[5] E. Xie, W. Wang, Z. Yu, A. Anandkumar, J. M. Alvarez, and P. Luo, "SegFormer: Simple and Efficient Design for Semantic Segmentation with Transformers," in *Proceedings of the 35th International Conference on Neural Information Processing Systems*, no. 924, pp. 12077–1209, 2021.

[6] R. Strudel, R. Garcia, I. Laptev, and C. Schmid, "Segmenter: Transformer for Semantic Segmentation," in *Proceedings of the IEEE/CVF International Conference on Computer Vision (ICCV)*, pp. 7242–7252, 2021.

[7] B. Zhang, *et al.,* "SegViT: Semantic Segmentation with Plain Vision Transformers," in *Proceedings of the 36th International Conference on Neural Information Processing Systems (NeurIPS)*, 2022.

[8] B. Zhang, L. Liu, M. H. Phan, et al., "SegViT v2: Exploring Efficient and Continual Semantic Segmentation with Plain Vision Transformers," *International Journal of Computer Vision*, vol. 132, pp. 1126–1147, 2024.

[9] Y. Liang, C. Ge, Z. Tong, Y. Song, J. Wang, and P. Xie, "Not All Patches are What You Need: Expediting Vision Transformers via Token Reorganizations," in *International Conference on Learning Representations (ICLR)*, 2022.

[10] Y. Xu, *et al.*, "Evo-ViT: Slow-fast token evolution for dynamic vision transformer," in *Proceedings of the AAAI Conference on Artificial Intelligence*, vol. 36, pp. 2964–2972, 2022.

[11] Z. Kong, *et al.*, "SPViT: Enabling Faster Vision Transformers via Latency-Aware Soft Token Pruning," in *Computer Vision – ECCV 2022: 17th European Conference, Tel Aviv, Israel, October 23–27, Proceedings, Part XI*, pp. 620–640, 2022.

[12] M. Fayyaz, *et al.*, "Adaptive Token Sampling for Efficient Vision Transformers," in *Computer Vision – ECCV 2022*, S. Avidan, G. Brostow, M. Cissé, G. M. Farinella, and T. Hassner, Eds. Cham: Springer Nature Switzerland, pp. 396–414, 2022.

[13] X. Liu, T. Wu, and G. Guo, "Adaptive Sparse ViT: Towards Learnable Adaptive Token Pruning by Fully Exploiting Self-Attention," in *Proceedings of the Thirty-Second International Joint Conference on Artificial Intelligence (IJCAI-23)*, pp. 1222–1230, 2023.

[14] D. Bolya, C.-Y. Fu, X. Dai, P. Zhang, C. Feichtenhofer, and J. Hoffman, "Token Merging: Your ViT but Faster," in *International Conference on Learning Representations (ICLR)*, 2023.

[15] M. Bonnaerens and J. Dambre, "Learned Thresholds Token Merging and Pruning for Vision Transformers," *Transactions on Machine Learning Research*, 2023.

[16] N. Norouzi, S. Orlova, D. De Geus, and G. Dubbelman, "ALGM: Adaptive Local-then-Global Token Merging for Efficient Semantic Segmentation with Plain Vision Transformers," in *Proceedings of the IEEE/CVF Conference on Computer Vision and Pattern Recognition (CVPR)*, pp. 15773–15782, 2024.

[17] M. Kim, S. Gao, Y.-C. Hsu, Y. Shen, and H. Jin, "Token fusion: Bridging the gap between token pruning and token merging," in *Proceedings of the IEEE/CVF Winter Conference on Applications of Computer Vision (WACV)*, pp. 1383–1392, 2024.

[18] D. H. Lee and S. Hong, "Learning to Merge Tokens via Decoupled Embedding for Efficient Vision Transformers," in *Advances in Neural Information Processing Systems (NeurIPS)*, 2024.

[19] J. Mao, Y. Shen, J. Guo, Y. Yao, X. Hua, and H. Shen, "Prune and Merge: Efficient Token Compression for Vision Transformer with Spatial Information Preserved," *IEEE Transactions on Multimedia*, pp. 1–14, 2025.

[20] Y. Yang, Y. Zhou, X. Hu, and S. Duan, "KFF: K-feature fusion token merging for vision transformer," *Expert Systems with Applications*, vol. 288, Art. no. 128206, 2025.

[21] Q. Tang, B. Zhang, J. Liu, F. Liu, and Y. Liu, "Dynamic Token Pruning in Plain Vision Transformers for Semantic Segmentation,"

in *Proceedings of the IEEE/CVF International Conference on Computer Vision (ICCV)*, pp. 777–786, 2023.

[22] M. Proust, M. Poreba, M. Szczepanski, and K. Haroun, "STEP: SuperToken and Early-Pruning for efficient semantic segmentation," in *Proceedings of the 20th International Joint Conference on Computer Vision, Imaging and Computer Graphics Theory and Applications (VISIGRAPP)*, vol. 3, Porto, Portugal, pp. 56–61, 2025.

[23] Y. Liu, *et al.*, "Dynamic Token-Pass Transformers for Semantic Segmentation," in *Proceedings of the IEEE/CVF Winter Conference on Applications of Computer Vision (WACV)*, pp. 1816–1825, 2024.

[24] E. Courdier, P. T. Sivaprasad, and F. Fleuret, "PAUMER: Patch Pausing Transformer for Semantic Segmentation," *arXiv preprint arXiv:2311.00586*, 2023.

[25] J. D. Havtorn, A. Royer, T. Blankevoort, and B. E. Bejnordi, "MSViT: Dynamic Mixed-Scale Tokenization for Vision Transformers," in *Proceedings of the IEEE/CVF International Conference on Computer Vision (ICCV) Workshops*, pp. 838–848, 2023.

[26] C. Lu, D. de Geus, and G. Dubbelman, "Content-aware Token Sharing for Efficient Semantic Segmentation with Vision Transformers," in *Proceedings of the IEEE/CVF Conference on Computer Vision and Pattern Recognition (CVPR)*, 2023.

[27] H. Huang, X. Zhou, J. Cao, R. He, and T. Tan, "Vision Transformer with Super Token Sampling," in *Proceedings of the IEEE/CVF Conference on Computer Vision and Pattern Recognition (CVPR)*, pp. 22690–22699, 2023.

[28] J. Li, *et al.*, "AiluRus: A Scalable ViT Framework for Dense Prediction," in *Advances in Neural Information Processing Systems (NeurIPS)*, vol. 36, pp. 30979–30996, 2023.

[29] Y. Yuan, W. Liang, H. Ding, Z. Liang, C. Zhang, and H. Hu, "Expediting Large-Scale Vision Transformer for Dense Prediction Without Fine-Tuning," *IEEE Transactions on Pattern Analysis and Machine Intelligence*, vol. 46, no. 1, pp. 250–266, 2024.

[30] M. Cordts, *et al.*, "The Cityscapes Dataset for Semantic Urban Scene Understanding," in *Proceedings of the IEEE Conference on Computer Vision and Pattern Recognition (CVPR)*, 2016.

[31] V. Bercy, M. Poreba, M. Szczepanski, and S. Bouchafa, "G2TM: Single-Module Graph-Guided Token Merging for Efficient Semantic Segmentation," in *Proceedings of the 21st International Conference on*

Computer Vision Theory and Applications (VISAPP 2026), Marbella, Spain, pp. 43–54, 2026.

[32] MMSegmentation Contributors, "MMSegmentation: OpenMMLab Semantic Segmentation Toolbox and Benchmark," *GitHub repository*, 2020.

3

GStreamer Plugin for RDMA Offload on BlueField-3 for Edge Applications

Raphael Frantz[1], Romain Pouillard[2], Idelfonso Tafur Monroy[3], Juan Jose Vegas Olmos[4], and Salvatore Di Girolamo[5]

[1]NVIDIA, Italy / Eindhoven University of Technology, The Netherlands
[2]Université Clermont Auvergne, France / Scuola Superiore Sant'Anna, Italy
[3]Eindhoven University of Technology, The Netherlands
[4]NVIDIA, Denmark
[5]NVIDIA, Switzerland

Abstract

Edge computing enables running applications without the added latency of transferring data to datacenters. With an application processing a video stream, an AI agent can operate near the end user using these decentralized servers. Remote Direct Memory Access (RDMA) is a high-speed network transport protocol (100Gbps and more) that can be run at the edge to facilitate communication between different systems. This allows processing the video stream in Data Processing Units (DPUs), instead of running on servers, where CPU usage is a scarce resource. To demonstrate, we implement a demo application of a virtual try-on by leveraging RDMA and DPUs, allowing a better usage of hardware resources. We leverage GStreamer, an industry-standard framework for processing media streams, and implement an RDMA network plugin for BlueField DPUs.

Keywords: RDMA, DOCA, BlueField, DPU, SmartNIC, GStreamer, Video Streaming, Edge Computing.

DOI: 10.1201/9788743815273-3

3.1 Introduction and Background

Applications based on video processing, such as those required by media streaming platforms, need to perform various operations on the video stream, including decompression, image extraction, AI agent execution, and image compression before sending it back to the viewer. Frameworks such as GStreamer can be used as a middleware to interface these independent operations, allowing a pipeline architecture that can run on multiple servers. To communicate between the hosts, network protocols such as UDP or TCP can be used natively in GStreamer. However, these protocols are processed by the kernel, utilizing precious CPU resources and running memory copies, which wastes memory bandwidth. In contrast, RDMA is a zero-copy protocol that bypasses the kernel. The packets are directly processed by the network card, which places data in memory at the proper virtual address using the PCIe bus. In addition to offloading the network stack, RDMA offers ultra-high bandwidth, which enables transferring raw images of a video stream, offering the possibility to offload encoding and decoding to specialized hardware. GStreamer does not support RDMA out of the box, but can be extended via plugins. Therefore, we implement an RDMA plugin for BlueField DPUs. It uses RDMA over Converged Ethernet (RoCE) to be easily integrated into IP networks.

BlueField is a DPU that integrates an RDMA-capable network card for both InfiniBand and RoCE networks, and lightweight ARM cores that can be used to accelerate the application. To run the demo, we use the BlueField-3 that integrates eight ARMv8.2 A78 cores along with 32 GB of on-board memory.

Recent research has demonstrated the potential of BlueField DPUs to offload servers in distributed architectures. For instance, the study by Kashyap et al. provides a comprehensive performance analysis of BlueField generations 1 through 3, identifying key trade-offs related to integration mode (off-path vs. on-path). Notably, we observe a 30% increase in RDMA latency in on-path mode on BlueField-3 [9]. Additionally, Li et al. show that computational loads such as compression can be efficiently offloaded to DPUs using frameworks like PEDAL [10], significantly reducing host CPU usage. These findings reinforce the relevance of leveraging the hardware acceleration capabilities of BlueField DPUs for edge video processing.

GStreamer is widely used in embedded systems due to its modularity and extensibility. In the GOTE architecture, Robaina and Fiorese demonstrate how it enables a low-latency edge gaming pipeline by integrating NVENC hardware encoding [11]. Similarly, the work of Primo da Silva et al. integrates a hardware JPEG encoder into a GStreamer pipeline running on an FPGA, confirming that GStreamer adapts well to real-time applications in constrained environments [12].

3.2 Virtual Try-On Application

We base the virtual try-on application architecture on previous work [1], integrating it with GStreamer and RDMA to enable real-time feedback. A virtual try-on enables users to virtually test clothes using a camera and a feedback screen, while running multiple AI model inferences on the backend to replace the client's clothes. The camera captures the video stream and sends it to the preprocessing edge server via UDP. The preprocessing server runs the first AI tasks (*OpenPose* [3–6], *HumanParsing* [7]), enabling segmentation

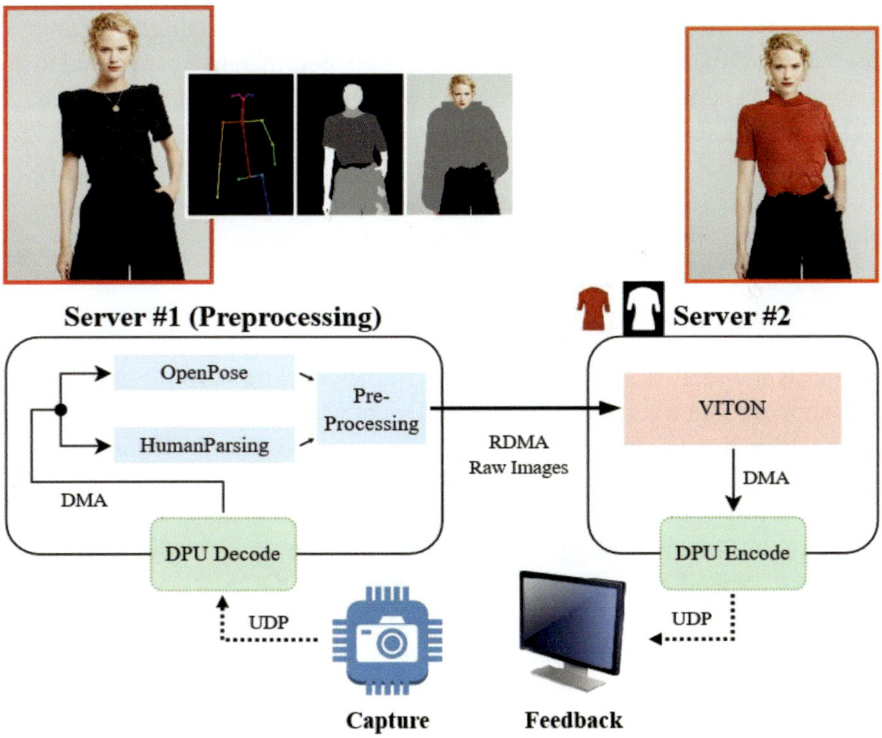

Figure 3.1 Architecture of the virtual try-on application with the two edge servers running the AI inference, and their DPU encoding/decoding the video.

of the human body. The proposed approach follows a distributed pipeline architecture inspired by initiatives like VideoPipe [13], which dynamically maps video processing tasks across multiple edge nodes based on workload and network conditions. This allows pose estimation (e.g., OpenPose) to run on lightweight devices, while the final image generation is offloaded to more powerful nodes. We adopt a similar split: pose detection and semantic parsing are executed on the first server, while the virtual try-on rendering (using VITON) is performed on the second. The original VITON model [14] introduced a two-stage synthesis pipeline to achieve photo-realistic try-on results without requiring 3D information and remains foundational to modern virtual try-on applications. The output of this stage is used as input to the *VITON* model [8] in the second server, which generates the final image from a human mask and the new cloth mask.

We use RDMA to communicate between the two edge servers. Raw images are sent to eliminate one encoding/decoding step, but increase drastically the bandwidth requirements of the video stream, which can be fulfilled thanks to RDMA. In addition, we offload image decoding/encoding to BlueField-3 DPUs. Indeed, RDMA works between distant hosts but also between the DPU and its attached host by leveraging Direct Memory Access (DMA) via the PCIe bus.

To have seamless operation between servers, parts of the application are integrated into a GStreamer pipeline. RDMA is integrated into GStreamer via our plugin, which allows zero-copy transfer between hosts.

3.3 RDMA Plugin

GStreamer is a widely adopted multimedia framework; however, it does not natively support data transport via Remote Direct Memory Access (RDMA). RDMA enables direct memory access between systems without CPU involvement, providing extremely low latency and high throughput, characteristics that make it well-suited for real-time multimedia workloads. We present here a novel GStreamer plugin designed to transfer multimedia streams using RDMA. Specifically, the plugin leverages the DOCA RDMA API to enable RDMA-based communication within GStreamer pipelines. It supports both inter-host RDMA transfers and host-to-DPU DMA communication. The proposed RDMA plugin integrates seamlessly with existing GStreamer pipelines, serving as a drop-in replacement for traditional transport elements such as TCP or UDP.

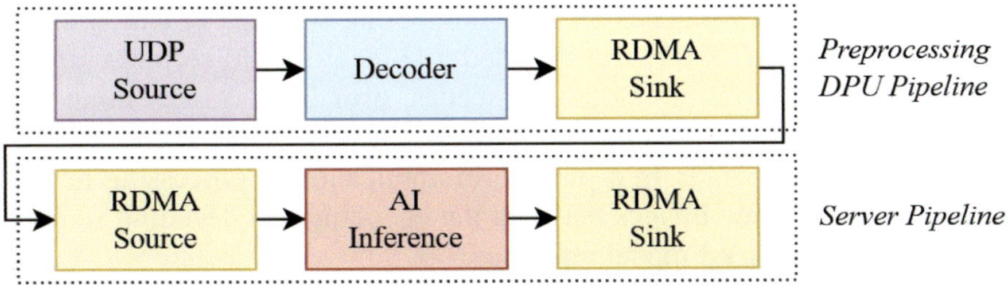

Figure 3.2 RDMA plugin integrated in GStreamer. Each operation is independent, and pipelines communicate via "sources" and "sinks". The DPU decodes the video while the server runs the AI inference.

While GStreamer includes native support for TCP, this protocol consumes significant CPU resources, particularly when handling large data volumes such as uncompressed video streams. UDP provides better performance but suffers from reliability issues and payload size limitations. The maximum UDP payload is restricted to a single MTU (typically less than 8 KiB), whereas a single raw video frame may occupy several megabytes. In contrast, RDMA combines high performance with reliability and supports message sizes up to 1 GB, effectively eliminating this constraint.

The RDMA plugin is implemented in C and C++. Its core is a C++ communication layer built on top of DOCA RDMA, responsible for reliable transmission and reception of media streams as well as credits-based flow control. A C interface bridges this layer with the GStreamer framework. The plugin provides two elements, a source for sending and a sink for receiving, as shown in Figure 3.2, similarly to how other protocols are implemented, adhering to GStreamer standards and permitting smooth integration. It enables zero-copy data transfer, allowing buffers to move directly between hosts without CPU intervention. Furthermore, the plugin ensures reliability by blocking the sending pipeline when the receiver cannot keep up, thereby avoiding data loss. The design remains fully transparent to applications and requires no changes to existing pipeline configurations.

3.4 Experimental Results

3.4.1 Offloading Scenarios

To evaluate the benefits of offloading video processing tasks to BlueField-3 DPUs, we conducted experiments on a dual-socket Intel Xeon Silver 4416+ server (80 cores), with 128 GB of RAM and two BlueField-3

DPUs. The experiment simulates an edge computing scenario in which the server receives a 1920×1080 H.264-encoded, pre-recorded, 30-second video stream, composed of different landscape scenes, over UDP (representing a camera), decodes it, re-encodes it, and transmits the re-encoded stream back to the final client over UDP. In a real-world application, a processing task would operate on the raw images between the encoding and decoding steps on the server, such as an AI model inference.

As shown in Figure 3.3, we compare four configurations, each reflecting whether the encoding step, the decoding step, or both are offloaded. As a baseline, in the "No Offloading" scenario, the entire decoding and encoding pipelines are handled by the host server CPU. For "Full Offloading", decoding and encoding are handled by separate DPUs, with the server managing only data transfer.

Figure 3.4 reports the server CPU usage over time for each scenario, measured as the number of logical cores actively used, averaged over multiple runs. As expected, the "No Offloading" case imposes the highest computational burden on the host, with CPU usage peaking at around four

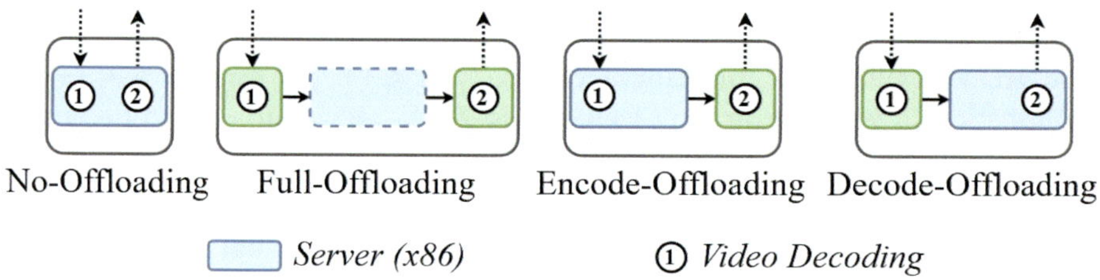

Figure 3.3 Tested scenarios to measure the impact of offloading specific algorithms to the BlueField-3 DPUs.

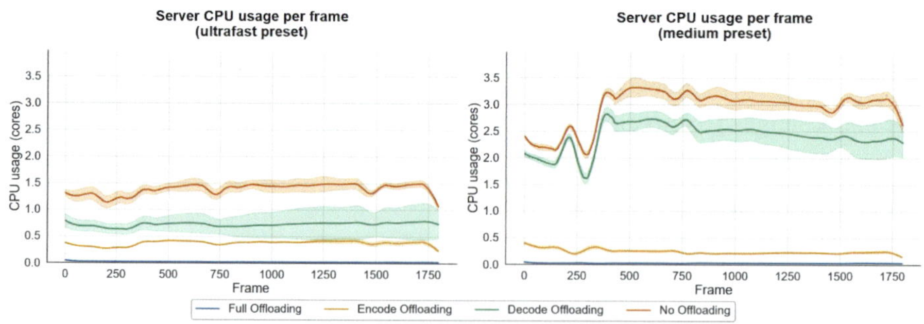

Figure 3.4 CPU usage of the server under different offloading scenarios for two H.264 encoder preset configurations: *ultrafast* and *medium*.

full cores. The "Decode Offloading" case slightly reduces the load, and the "Encode Offloading" case significantly reduces it. We observe that most of the computational cost is in video encoding. In the "Full Offloading" scenario, where both tasks are delegated to the BlueField-3 DPUs, server CPU usage drops consistently to near-zero levels, demonstrating a substantial gain in computational efficiency.

These results highlight the clear advantage of leveraging DPUs to offload media processing in high-throughput, low-latency edge environments. By freeing up CPU resources, such offloading strategies enable the server to host additional applications or scale to handle more concurrent streams (especially for the decoding step, which is a light computation with data movement, making it the ideal task for a DPU), without compromising real-time performance.

In addition to CPU utilization, we measured the end-to-end latency of the video-processing pipeline across the same set of offloading scenarios. Figure 3.5 reports the latency distribution observed between the transmission of a video frame to the remote server and its reception after decoding, re-encoding, and retransmission. The results show that offloading strategies not only affect server resource usage but also directly impact end-to-end latency.

For the *medium* preset, the results show that *Decode Offloading* achieves lower latency than the *No Offloading* configuration. This indicates that offloading the decoding stage to the DPU already provides tangible latency benefits, even when the encoding remains on the host. Since decoding is largely dominated by data movement and control operations, delegating this task to the DPU reduces host-side contention and scheduling overhead, resulting in improved end-to-end latency. In contrast, performing both

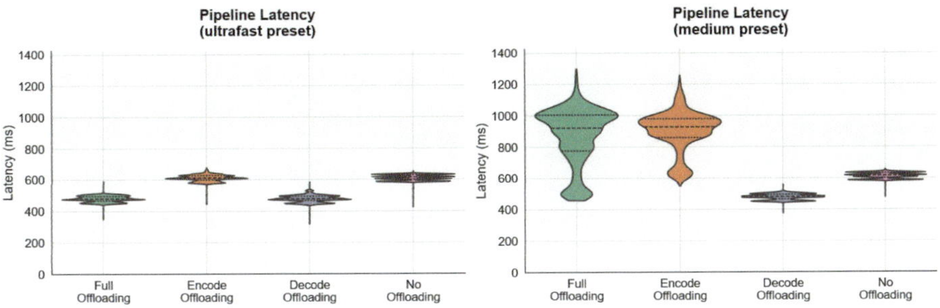

Figure 3.5 Latency of the end-to-end video stream under different offloading scenarios for the two H.264 encoder preset configurations.

decoding and encoding on the server increases latency despite comparable encoder settings.

In the *ultrafast* preset, the relative differences between scenarios are reduced, as the encoding complexity is significantly lower. In this case, *Full Offloading* achieves the lowest latency, while *Encode Offloading* and *Decode Offloading* exhibit similar distributions, and *No Offloading* remains slightly higher. This suggests that when encoding complexity is minimized, host-side processing becomes less dominant, and the benefit of partial offloading is less pronounced.

Overall, these results demonstrate that the impact of offloading on latency strongly depends on the encoder configuration. While full offloading is most effective for latency-critical scenarios with relaxed quality constraints, selectively offloading decoding can already yield meaningful latency reductions when higher-quality encoder presets are required.

3.4.2 TCP vs RDMA

While both TCP and RDMA are viable transport protocols for DPU offloading, RDMA delivers significantly higher performance and is well-suited to this edge datacenter environment. To demonstrate this advantage, we compare the CPU usage of TCP and RDMA implementations, as shown in Figure 3.6.

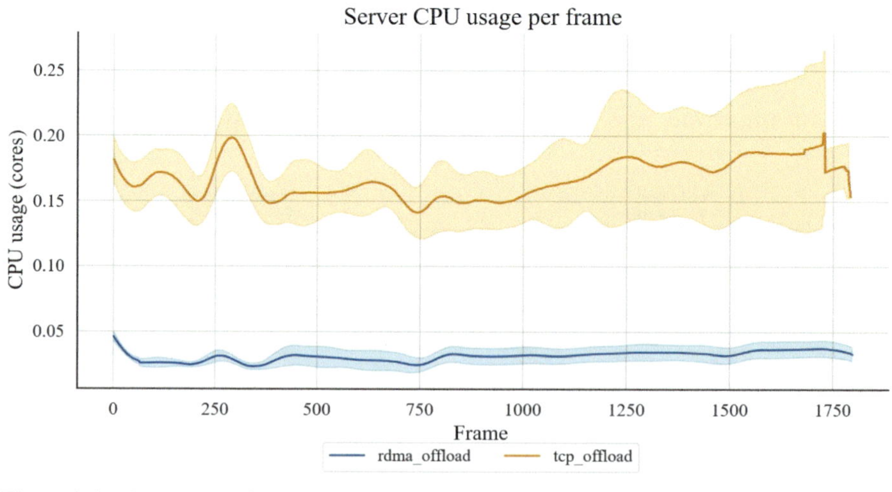

Figure 3.6 CPU usage of the "Full Offloading" scenario over multiple runs, comparing when RDMA or TCP is used as a network protocol.

The results demonstrate a high contrast: TCP transport exhibits high CPU consumption with significant fluctuations, whereas RDMA imposes negligible computational overhead on the server. This near-zero CPU burden makes RDMA the preferred choice for resource-constrained edge environments where server CPU cycles must be preserved for application workloads.

3.5 Conclusion

In conclusion, we show that RDMA can be transparently integrated into GStreamer pipelines via our custom plugin, rather than relying on TCP. This makes it easier to leverage external accelerators, thereby reducing server CPU usage in controlled environments, such as edge datacenters, as shown in our benchmarks. On the other hand, we demonstrate this use case by leveraging BlueField-3 DPUs to offload video decoding and encoding for a virtual try-on application.

Beyond the reduction in server CPU usage demonstrated in our benchmarks, our results highlight the importance of adapting the offloading strategy to the target application requirements. When low end-to-end latency is the primary objective and visual quality can be relaxed, fully offloading both decoding and encoding to DPUs represents an efficient solution, as it minimizes host involvement and reduces processing delay. Conversely, for use cases where output quality is critical, keeping the encoding stage on the host while offloading decoding to the DPU appears to be a better trade-off. In this configuration, the computationally intensive but quality-sensitive encoding process can leverage more advanced encoder settings on the server, while the DPU efficiently handles decoding, which is largely dominated by data movement rather than computationally intensive tasks.

These observations suggest that DPU-based media pipelines should not rely on a single fixed offloading configuration but instead dynamically adapt encoding and offloading strategies according to application-level constraints, such as latency, visual quality, and available computational resources. This flexibility is particularly relevant for edge deployments, where heterogeneous workloads and fluctuating requirements are common.

Acknowledgements

This work was partly funded by the QUARC project by the European Union Horizon Europe research and innovation program within the framework of Marie Skłodowska-Curie Actions with grant number 101073355, and by the grant PID2021-123041OB-I00 funded by MCIN/AEI/10.13039/501100011033 and by "ERDF A way of making Europe".

The demo application was tested in the CNIT testbed located in Pisa, Italy, which allowed us to use their RoCE infrastructure

References

[1] M. Guaitolini, A. Khan, E. Rouzic, F. Paolucci, and F. Cugini, "Virtual Try-On Application leveraging RoCE in Low-latency Edge Computing Networks," in Proc. 2024 24th International Conference on Transparent Optical Networks (ICTON), Bari, Italy, Jul. 2024, pp. 1–4, doi: 10.1109/ICTON62926.2024.10647389.

[2] GStreamer Project, "GStreamer Multimedia Framework," [Online]. Available: https://gstreamer.freedesktop.org/. Accessed: Nov. 2025.

[3] Z. Cao, G. H. Martinez, T. Simon, S. Wei, and Y. A. Sheikh, "OpenPose: Realtime Multi-Person 2D Pose Estimation using Part Affinity Fields," *IEEE Transactions on Pattern Analysis and Machine Intelligence*, 2019.

[4] T. Simon, H. Joo, I. Matthews, and Y. Sheikh, "Hand Keypoint Detection in Single Images using Multiview Bootstrapping," 2017.

[5] Z. Cao, T. Simon, S.-E. Wei, and Y. Sheikh, "Realtime Multi-Person 2D Pose Estimation using Part Affinity Fields," 2017.

[6] S.-E. Wei, V. Ramakrishna, T. Kanade, and Y. Sheikh, "Convolutional Pose Machines," 2016.

[7] B. Wu and F. Zhao, "2D-Human-Parsing," 2021. [Online]. Available: https://github.com/fyviezhao/2D-Human-Parsing.

[8] J. Kim, G. Gu, M. Park, S. Park, and J. Choo, "StableVITON: Learning semantic correspondence with latent diffusion model for virtual try-on," in Proc. *IEEE/CVF Conference on Computer Vision and Pattern Recognition*, 2024, pp. 8176–8185.

[9] A. Kashyap, Y. Li, D. Ng, and X. Lu, "Understanding the Idiosyncrasies of Emerging BlueField DPUs," Proc. *39th ACM International Conference on Supercomputing*, 2025, pp. 807–821. doi: 10.1145/3721145.3725780.

[10] Y. Li, A. Kashyap, W. Chen, Y. Guo, and X. Lu, "Accelerating Lossy and Lossless Compression on Emerging BlueField DPU Architectures," in *2024 IEEE International Parallel and Distributed Processing Symposium (IPDPS)*, May 2024, pp. 373–385. doi: 10.1109/IPDPS57955.2024.00040.

[11] G. Robaina and A. Fiorese, "GOTE: An Edge Computing Architecture for Mobile Gaming," Proc. *25th International Conference on Enterprise Information Systems - Volume 1: ICEIS*, 2023, pp. 721–730. doi: 10.5220/0011962000003467.

[12] H. Lee and J. Jeon, "Accelerating Image Processing on FPGAs using HLS and PYNQ," 2020, pp. 1–2. doi: 10.1109/ICCE-Asia49877.2020.9277085.

[13] M. Salehe, Z. Hu, S. H. Mortazavi, I. Mohomed, and T. Capes, "VideoPipe: Building Video Stream Processing Pipelines at the Edge," Proc. *20th International Middleware Conference Industrial Track*, 2019, pp. 43–49. doi: 10.1145/3366626.3368131.

[14] X. Han, Z. Wu, Z. Wu, R. Yu, and L. S. Davis, "VITON: An Image-Based Virtual Try-on Network," in 2018 IEEE/CVF Conference on Computer Vision and Pattern Recognition, 2018, pp. 7543–7552. doi: 10.1109/CVPR.2018.00787.

4

On-Device Continual Learning for Unsupervised Visual Anomaly Detection in Dynamic Manufacturing

Haoyu Ren[1,2], Kay Köhle[1,2], Kirill Dorofeev[2], and Darko Anicic[2]

[1]Technical University of Munich, Germany
[2]Siemens AG, Germany

Abstract

In modern manufacturing, Visual Anomaly Detection (VAD) is essential for automated inspection and consistent product quality. Yet, increasingly dynamic and flexible production environments introduce key challenges: First, frequent product changes in small-batch and on-demand manufacturing require rapid model updates. Second, legacy edge hardware lacks the resources to train and run large AI models. Finally, both anomalous and normal training data are often scarce, particularly for newly introduced product variations. We investigate on-device continual learning for unsupervised VAD with localization, extending the PatchCore to incorporate online learning for real-world industrial scenarios. The proposed method leverages a lightweight feature extractor and an incremental coreset update mechanism based on k-center selection, enabling rapid, memory-efficient adaptation from limited data while eliminating costly cloud retraining. Evaluations on an industrial use case are conducted using a testbed designed to emulate flexible production with frequent variant changes in a controlled environment. Our method achieves a 12% AUROC improvement over the baseline, an 80% reduction in memory usage, and faster training compared to batch retraining. These results

DOI: 10.1201/9788743815273-4

confirm that our method delivers accurate, resource-efficient, and adaptive VAD suitable for dynamic and smart manufacturing.

Keywords: Edge AI, TinyML, Continual Learning, Visual Anomaly Detection, On-device Learning, Industry 4.0.

4.1 Introduction and Background

With the advent of Industrial 4.0, manufacturing is undergoing a shift from long-term, high-volume production towards short-term, small-batch, and flexible operations [1]. The increasing demand for customization is encouraging factories to accommodate frequent changeovers and product families with many variants. However, traditional quality assurance frameworks, which are typically optimized for stable, large-scale production, can struggle to maintain performance under such variability. Visual Anomaly Detection (VAD), a core element of automated inspection in industry made possible by advances in computer vision and deep learning, exemplifies this challenge. In dynamic manufacturing scenarios, each new product variant or revision can introduce subtle visual differences (e.g., shapes, textures, or coatings), resulting in a distributional shift in feature space. This can degrade the accuracy of pre-trained static VAD models, a problem known as data drift. It is necessary to have VAD systems capable of quickly and continuously learning new product variations to sustain reliability. While cloud-based retraining is feasible in theory, it is often impractical due to limited network bandwidth, data privacy concerns, and factory IT policies that restrict external connectivity. These constraints highlight the need for modern VAD systems to not only perform inference, but also learn and update directly at the source where the data is generated.

In practice, most VAD systems are deployed on constrained hardware on the shop floor, such as industrial PCs, embedded systems, or camera-integrated processors, which have limited memory, computational power, and energy budgets. These systems are generally not designed for model training which requires significant computational power. Growing interest is being shown in Edge Artificial Intelligence (Edge AI) and Tiny Machine Learning (TinyML) to enable continual learning directly on constrained devices [2]. These two paradigms aim to make machine learning (ML) more accessible to devices with limited capabilities and shift the ML workload from the cloud to the edge. There have been advancements in hardware [3, 4], software [5, 6], and the ecosystem [7, 8]. For industrial anomaly detection, the implications are transformative. Edge AI and TinyML enable VAD systems to execute efficient inference and on-device model adaptation without relying on cloud infrastructure. This reduces latency, enhances system robustness in the event of intermittent connectivity, and mitigates privacy concerns by keeping sensitive production data within the factory. Furthermore, by fitting the model architecture and learning strategy to the capabilities of existing shop floor hardware, factories can avoid modifying the current hardware topology. This minimises the complexity of integration, the cost of hardware upgrades, and the risk of disrupting established infrastructure.

Despite the recent development of Edge AI and TinyML, a substantial gap remains between research and the practical implementation of applying adaptive VAD on the industrial shop floor. Many existing frameworks, such as [9–11], depend on large pre-trained backbones or offline batch training pipelines. These approaches are computationally intensive and data-hungry, making them poorly suited for the resource-constrained hardware typically found on the shop floor. Furthermore, edge-oriented methods such as [12] and [13], primarily aim to achieve high detection accuracy in static conditions using benchmark datasets such as MVTec AD [14] and VisA [15]. They do not reflect the variability and continuous change in customized and dynamic production. As a result, such methods require costly retraining whenever new product variants are introduced. Although continual learning has been studied in the supervised domain [16, 17], its application in unsupervised domain, especially under edge hardware constraints, still lacks discussion. While recent work [18, 19] has evaluated several VAD methods within a continual learning setup, their task designs involve large domain shifts, such as transitioning from detecting anomalies in screws to bottles and cables, or from brain MRIs to liver CTs and chest X-rays. Consequently, their primary focus lies in mitigating catastrophic forgetting, where model performance on earlier tasks drops after adapting to new ones [20]. Nevertheless, these approaches remain relatively naïve, as they rely on offline subsampling that assumes full access to the entire dataset of new tasks. Moreover, the extracted features are simply appended to the memory bank, without considering how knowledge can be transferred or shared across related tasks to enhance subsequent learning. This limitation becomes particularly critical in small-batch production settings, where product variants often exhibit subtle differences and only limited training samples are available. In such cases, leveraging shared representations and inter-task relationships could enhance adaptability and detection performance.

Moreover, as noted by [21], much of the existing research overlooks the operational realities of the industrial environment, often assuming the availability of abundant and diverse training data such as that in the MVTec AD dataset. In practice, however, production environments are tightly controlled, with fixed inspection hardware configurations, including camera, inspection position, and lighting condition. Consequently, all normal images (i.e. images without anomalies) of the same product can appear visually identical, regardless of how many are captured. Collecting additional normal data, therefore, offers little benefit, as it contributes minimal new information. This takes the learning scenario into a one-shot setting, where only a single representative normal sample exists for each product variant. Under these constraints, leveraging prior knowledge across tasks becomes essential to support adaptation to new variants. Furthermore, obtaining anomalous samples, especially labelled ones, is even more challenging while the production plant is operational, particularly when new product variants are introduced. These challenges underscore the need for an efficient, resource-aware continual learning paradigm that can run directly on edge devices using limited training data, while maintaining consistent inspection accuracy in dynamic industrial environments.

To tackle these challenges, we extend PatchCore [22] by integrating efficient on-device continual learning. PatchCore achieves state-of-the-art performance in unsupervised VAD with pixel-level localization across many benchmarks [23, 24]. It leverages pre-trained feature extractors to encode images into a high-dimensional memory bank, known as coreset, which captures the statistical distribution of normal samples without requiring defect samples. During inference, test images are compared against the coreset to determine their similarity using nearest-neighbour search, which enables both detection and localization. Our framework builds on this concept by incorporating incremental and resource-efficient adaptation mechanism. Specifically, we employ a compact feature extractor suitable for constrained hardware and redesign the coreset update mechanism using an incremental k-center selection strategy. This allows the system to perform online, memory-efficient updates by exploiting relationships between embeddings from previous and new tasks. As a result, the model can efficiently adapt to new tasks with minimal data and without the need for full retraining.

We evaluate the proposed method on an industrial use case for dynamic manufacturing using a controlled experimental setup with diverse and interchangeable workpieces that emulate real-world production scenarios. The setup maintains consistent product positioning, camera configurations, and lighting conditions to accurately reflect practical inspection environments. We compare our method with a baseline continual learning approach adopted in [18] that performs coreset subsampling and appends embeddings from new tasks to the existing memory bank. To assess the feasibility of our approach on edge hardware, we deploy and benchmark our method on an NVIDIA Jetson Orin Nano board, using CPU-only execution. The device features an Arm Cortex-A78AE processor and 8 GB of memory, representing a realistic low-power industrial edge computing platform. Experimental results demonstrate that our proposed method delivers substantial gains in both performance and resource efficiency. Specifically, it achieves a 12% increase in AUROC compared to the coreset-subsampling baseline, while reducing memory consumption by over 80% and providing faster learning against the batch training with a batch size of 10.

The rest of the paper is structured as follows: Section 1.2 introduces our method. Section 1.3 covers the use case, describes the experimental settings, and analyzes the results. Finally, Section 1.4 concludes the paper and presents future research directions.

4.2 Approach

We propose an on-device continual learning framework that extends PatchCore for fast, localized model adaptation. The method is designed to operate efficiently on resource-constrained edge devices deployed in dynamic environments, enabling a pre-trained PatchCore model to continuously acquire inspection capabilities for new tasks (e.g., product variants) using very limited data, while maintaining performance on previously learned tasks.

PatchCore is a state-of-the-art, memory-bank-based approach for unsupervised VAD that provides pixel-level localization. It leverages pre-trained feature extractors to transform images into high-dimensional embeddings stored in a memory bank, or coreset. This coreset effectively models the statistical characteristics of normal samples without the need for defective examples during training. At inference, PatchCore computes the similarity between test image features and those in the coreset using a nearest-neighbor search. This allows the system to quantify how "unfamiliar" each local feature is relative to the learned normal distribution, thereby identifying not only whether an image is anomalous but also where anomalies occur with high spatial precision.

While traditional PatchCore is effective, its coreset subsampling is typically performed offline, assuming access to the complete dataset and lacking

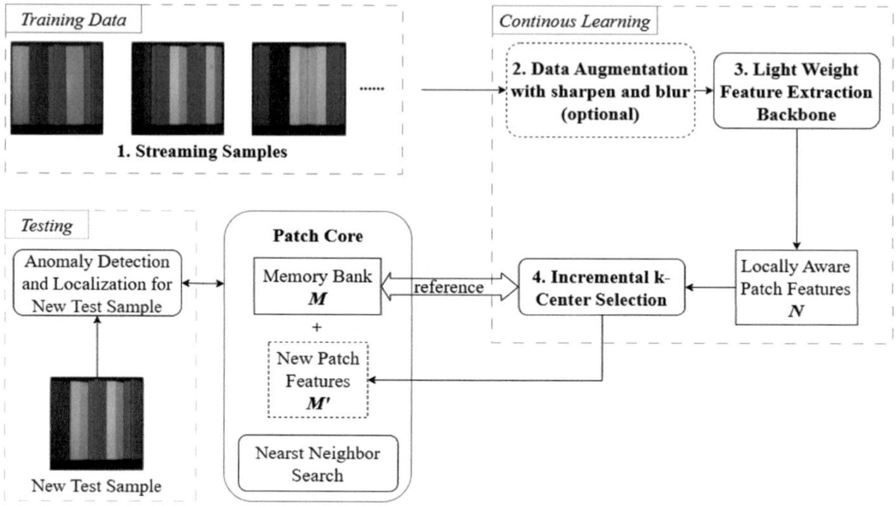

Figure 4.1 Illustration of our framework extending PatchCore for incremental and resource-efficient adaptation using limited data.

the ability to handle continual updates without full retraining. As illustrated in Figure 4.1, our framework integrates four key components into PatchCore to enable incremental and resource-efficient adaptation, reducing latency and eliminating the need for a full offline dataset or the transfer of sensitive data beyond the local network. These components are:

- Streaming data consumption in an online learning manner,
- A data augmentation mechanism,
- A lightweight feature extraction backbone, and
- An incremental coreset update mechanism based on k-center selection, incorporating the principles of online learning.

Each component is described in detail below.

4.2.1 Streaming Samples

With the concept of online learning, data arrives sequentially, one sample at a time, which aligns well with industrial scenarios where new data, such as samples from new product variants, are continuously captured and provided. Rather than assuming access to large offline datasets, our framework operates in a streaming data setting, where normal samples are processed as they arrive during operation. This paradigm updates the model using one sample per iteration and then discards it, ensuring that only a single data instance is held in memory at any given time. Consequently, this approach significantly reduces memory overhead and enables efficient training even on resource-constrained devices.

4.2.2 Data Augmentation

Each incoming image sample undergoes optional data augmentation operations, such as sharpening and blurring, to generate additional samples that enhance the diversity of local texture patterns without altering the overall appearance. Although the original PatchCore method does not employ data augmentation, prior studies [25] have demonstrated that augmentation is crucial for achieving state-of-the-art performance, particularly in scenarios with limited training data. This strategy improves the model's robustness to minor visual variations, such as camera noise, and enhances its generalization to unseen conditions.

4.2.3 Lightweight Feature Extractor

After the optional data augmentation step, each image is passed through a lightweight feature extraction backbone. The backbone converts the image into a set of patch-level embeddings that capture its local feature information with normal visual distribution. In this work, a pre-trained lightweight image model, such as MobileNetV3 [26] trained on ImageNet-1K, is employed as the feature extractor. MobileNetV3 contains approximately 3.9 million parameters and is specifically designed to meet the computational and memory constraints of edge hardware, reducing inference latency while maintaining strong representational capacity. Compared to the default Wide-ResNet backbone used in PatchCore, which has approximately 69 million parameters, it offers a more resource-efficient alternative that achieves a balance between efficiency and performance. Depending on the available hardware resources, larger or smaller backbones may also be selected to further optimize feature extraction.

4.2.4 Incremental k-Center Selection and Memory Bank Update

Traditional PatchCore constructs a coreset memory bank $M{=}m^1, m^2, \ldots, m_{\mathrm{k}}$ from normal patch features using offline subsampling, which represents the statistical distribution of normal appearances. While effective, this process assumes access to the entire dataset and cannot accommodate continual learning.

To overcome this problem, we introduce an incremental k-center selection strategy that enables memory-efficient coreset updates incorporating the concept of online learning. Compared to existing continual learning approaches in [18] and [19], where the memory bank is updated in a single step by subsampling standalone patch features from all available data of a new task, our method updates the memory bank continuously by comparing each new data sample with the existing memory bank, one sample at a time. When each new data arrives, a set of locally aware patch features $\boldsymbol{N}$ is extracted using the lightweight backbone. The incremental k-center selection algorithm then identifies the most informative subset of features M' in $\boldsymbol{N}$ by comparing it with the existing memory bank M based on their distances in feature space. Mathematically, each candidate feature $\boldsymbol{p} \in N$ is evaluated using the distance metric

$$d\,(p, M) = min_{m_i \in M} \|p - m_i\|^2.$$

Features with the highest distance scores are incrementally added to $M\prime$, which are in the end appended to the memory bank M. By referencing prior feature distributions, this continual coreset growth mechanism has two major advantages:

- It maintains representational knowledge from previously seen samples, and
- It efficiently selects diverse new representations with high information content, consuming minimal computational and memory overhead.

During inference, a test sample is processed through the same lightweight feature extractor to generate patch embeddings $t_i \in T$. These embeddings are then compared against the updated coreset using nearest-neighbour search in the feature space

$$s_i = \min_{m_j \in M} |\, t_i - m_j|_2.$$

The resulting distance s_i represents the anomaly score for patch i. Higher scores indicate greater deviation from the learned normal feature distribution. By mapping these patch-level scores back to their spatial positions, a pixel-level anomaly map is obtained, highlighting potential defect regions. The overall image-level anomaly score is computed as either the maximum or average of all patch-level scores, providing a comprehensive measure of the sample's abnormality.

4.3 Experiments and Evaluation

We quantitatively evaluate our method using an experimental setup that simulates a dynamic manufacturing scenario with frequent product variations. We compare our approach against a continual learning baseline regarding various metrics, such as AUPR, AUROC, memory overhead, and inference latency. To examine the performance at the edge, the method is deployed and benchmarked on an NVIDIA Jetson Orin Nano (CPU-only), representative of low-power industrial edge hardware.

4.3.1 Use Case

Our use case focuses on VAD of five workpieces representing manufactured products. The inspection setup, shown in Figure 4.2, consists of a fixed industrial camera (Siemens SIMATIC MV500) mounted above a holder designed to accommodate five workpiece positions. Multiple workpieces with five different shapes are used in the experimental setup. Each workpiece can be freely placed in any of the five positions, with possible repetition

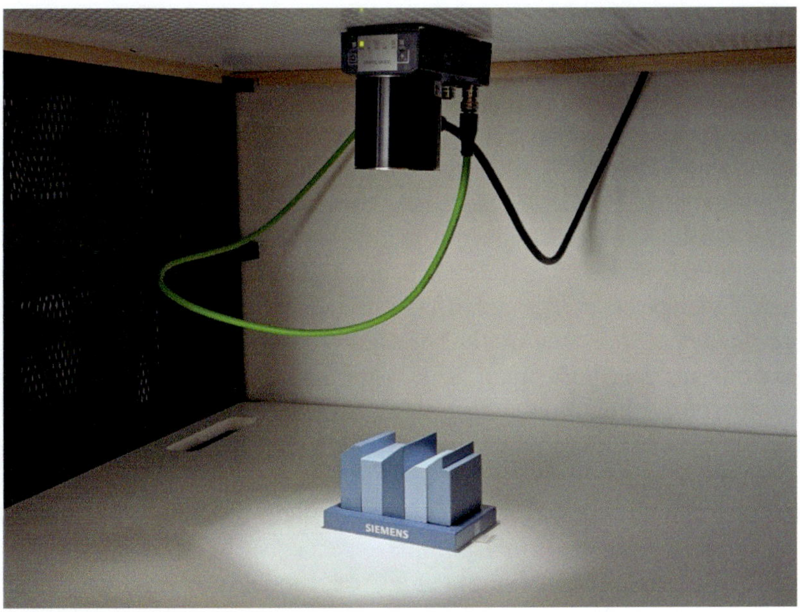

Figure 4.2 Testbed with a Siemens SIMATIC MV540 camera and five different workpieces on the holder.

Figure 4.3 A collection of normal samples of various workpiece combinations.

and 180° yaw rotation, resulting in more than 50,000 unique combinations. These variations effectively emulate the diversity of product configurations encountered in dynamic, small-batch manufacturing environments.

Figure 4.3 and Figure 4.4 illustrate representative normal and abnormal workpiece configurations captured by the camera. Given the vast number of potential configurations, training a single VAD model that generalizes across all of them is impractical for edge deployment. Furthermore, collecting extensive image datasets per variant offers limited benefit in this unsupervised setting, as images of the same product variant under such controlled inspection conditions are nearly identical aside from minor camera noise. The key challenge, therefore, lies in enabling rapid on-device continual learning of a pre-trained VAD model to new combinations using only a few, or even a single, normal image per variant.

Figure 4.5 and Figure 4.6 illustrate the prediction results of a trained model on normal and abnormal samples, respectively. These examples demonstrate the capability of the PatchCore model not only to detect abnormal images but also to accurately localize defective regions through anomaly maps, thereby enhancing interpretability and explainability in visual inspection.

Figure 4.4 A collection of abnormal samples of various workpiece combinations.

Figure 4.5 Example of the model prediction on a normal sample.

4.3.2 Experiments Design

We investigate the continual learning capability of a pre-trained PatchCore model when adapting to new workpiece combinations. All experiments start with the same model, trained using the traditional PatchCore method on 117 images, each corresponding to a distinct workpiece configuration. These 117 variants represent standard product lines and already pose a considerable challenge for a single inspection model. Throughout the experiments,

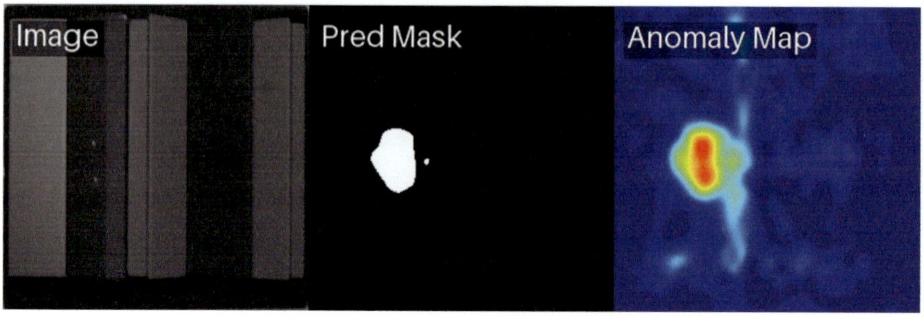

Figure 4.6 Example of the model prediction on an abnormal sample with highlighted defective region.

the lightweight MobileNetV3 backbone is employed to extract patch-level features.

Subsequently, the model is presented with new workpiece configurations that were not included in the initial training set, where a degradation in detection performance is expected due to data shifts. To address this, we enable continual adaptation by fine-tuning the model online using only a single normal image per new variant. During this process, both the model's performance and the associated hardware requirements are monitored. Here, model performance is evaluated on a fixed dataset comprising 35 unseen workpiece variants, each containing one normal image and multiple abnormal images. The evaluation metrics include the AUPR and the AUROC, which together capture the model's ability to discriminate between normal and abnormal samples under class imbalance, an inherent characteristic of anomaly detection tasks. Hardware efficiency is assessed in terms of memory consumption and inference latency to evaluate the practicality of the approach for edge deployment. We compare our method against a baseline continual learning algorithm from [18], which applies coreset subsampling to extract patch features of given data and append them to the memory bank. Additionally, ablation study is conducted to analyze the impact of key components of our approach, including online adaptation and data augmentation. All experiments are repeated multiple times, and average results are reported to ensure reliability. Hyperparameters are tuned for stable performance rather than for maximal optimization.

4.3.3 Evaluation

Figure 4.7 shows the learning progress across different training configurations, showing that the AUPR increases as more normal samples are used

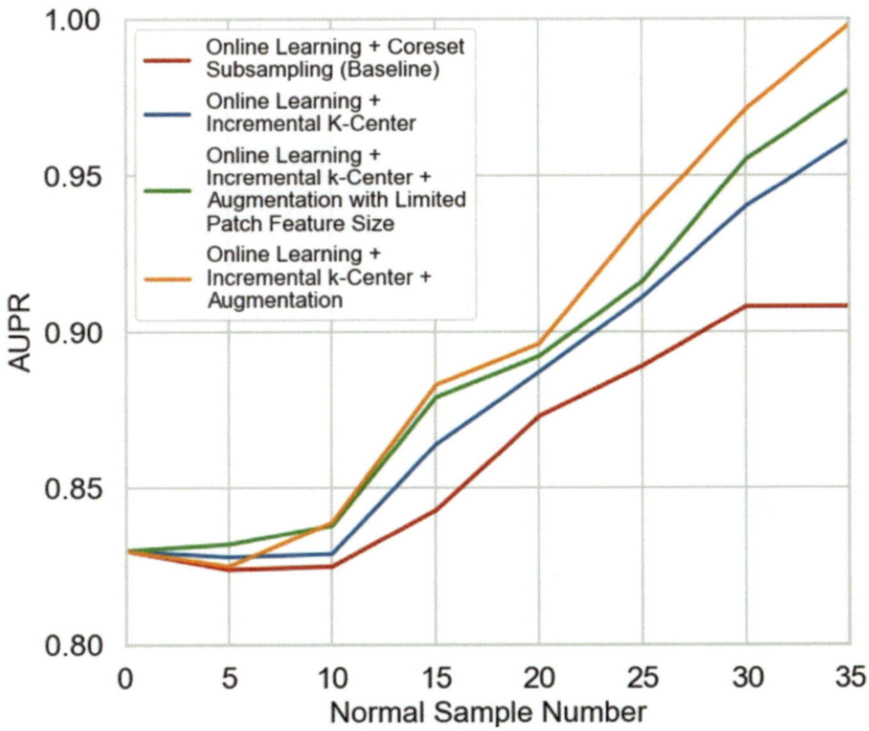

Figure 4.7 Learning progress of different configurations: AUPR vs. number of normal samples used for finetuning.

for continual learning. A higher AUPR indicates stronger capability in correctly identifying anomalies while reducing false alarms. Here, the baseline shows the slowest improvement, suggesting limited adaptation efficiency. In contrast, our approach incorporating incremental k-center selection achieve faster and more stable performance gains. Also, in the last two configurations, we compare the performance of data augmentation with and without a constraint on the patch feature size. Data augmentation naturally increases the amount of training data, resulting in more features to extract. In the third training configuration, we restrict the number of extracted features added to the memory bank to match that of the second configuration, which does not use augmentation. The results demonstrate that data augmentation can substantially improve model performance, even when the number of extracted features is constrained, effectively balancing accuracy gains with memory overhead.

Figure 4.8 shows the AUROC as a function of the number of normal samples used for fine-tuning. AUROC reflects the model's ability to distinguish normal from abnormal samples across various thresholds. A similar trend is observed: methods incorporating incremental k-center sampling and data augmentation achieve the best performance, confirming their effectiveness in improving detection accuracy with limited fine-tuning data.

Table 4.1 summarizes the final detection performance under different training configurations. The "Pre-trained (Lower Bound)" represents the model's initial performance without any fine-tuning, serving as the minimum reference point. The "Pre-trained + BL (Upper Bound)" corresponds to the batch learning setting, where the model is trained with full access to all normal samples, establishing the performance ceiling. Among the online learning configurations, the baseline approach shows moderate improvement

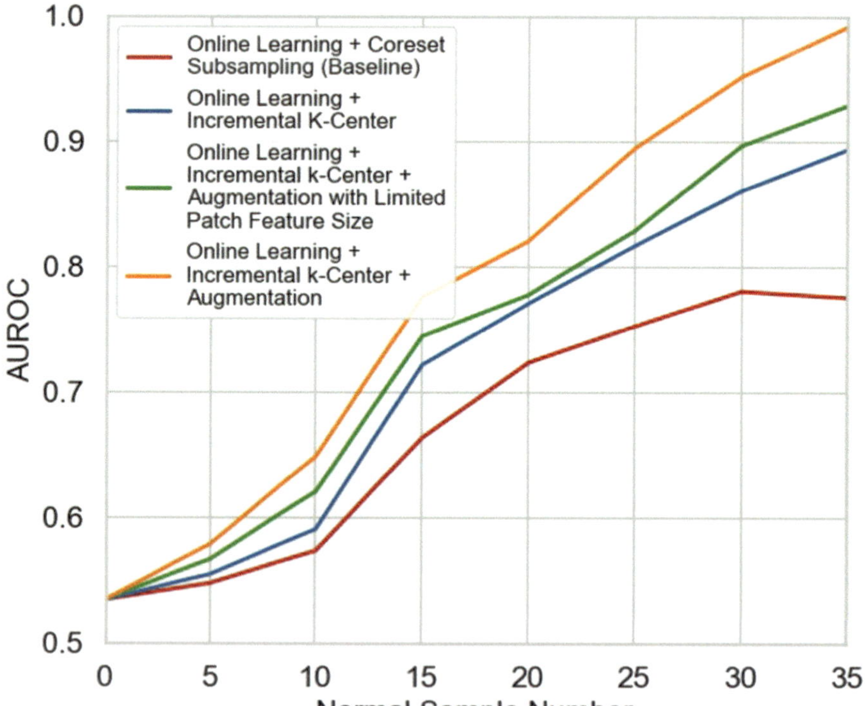

Figure 4.8 Learning progress of different configurations: AUROC vs. the number of normal samples used for finetuning.

over the lower bound. Incorporating incremental k-center selection further narrows the gap. With data augmentation, the performance surpasses that of batch training, even when using a limited patch feature size.

Table 4.2 shows that our online learning methods require significantly less memory than batch learning, reducing usage from around 221 MB to 23 MB for training. The inference stage demands only 0.56 MB, demonstrating that the proposed online learning framework enables efficient training and deployment on memory-constrained devices.

As shown in Table 4.3, our method requires minimal memory for feature storage thanks to the lightweight feature backbone combined with incremental k-center selection. Overhead increases linearly with the number of samples. This demonstrates an efficient balance between memory usage and performance, enabling scalability under constrained resources.Table 4.4 compares the average training and inference latency across two platforms. Our

Table 4.1 Comparison of final detection performance under different configurations, OL: Online Learning, BL: Batch Learning

	Pre-trained (Lower Bound)	**Pre-trained + BL (Upper Bound)**	**Pre-trained + OL + Coreset Subsampling (Baseline)**	**Pre-trained + OL + Incremental K-Center**	**Pre-trained + OL + Incremental k-Center + Augmentation**	**Pre-trained + OL + Incremental k-Center + Augmentation with Limited Patch Feature Size**
AUPR	0.829	0.972	0.908	0.961	**0.998**	0.977
AUROC	0.535	0.912	0.776	0.890	**0.992**	0.929

Table 4.2 Comparison of memory overhead for training and inference under different configurations, OL: Online Learning, BL: Batch Learning

	Training: OL + Coreset Subsampling (baseline)	**Training: BL with Batch Size 10 + Incremental K-Center (baseline)**	**Training: OL + Incremental K-Center**	**Inference: OL + Incremental K-Center**
Memory Overhead (MB)	24.1	227.1	**23.1**	**0.56**

Table 4.3 Comparison of memory overhead for storing different numbers of the training samples

	One Image	**Three Images**	**Ten Images**
Memory Overhead (MB)	0.06	0.18	0.62

Table 4.4 Comparison of average latency for training under different configurations on two platforms

	Training (ours vs. batch learning)	Inference (ours vs. batch learning)
Laptop – Intel Ultra 5 235U (seconds per epoch)	**0.18** vs. 1.97	**0.19** vs. 2.02
Jetson Nano - Cortex-A78AE (seconds per epoch)	**0.45** vs. 5.08	**0.57** vs. 6.34

method achieves substantially lower latency than batch learning, enabling efficient operation even on constrained devices. Moreover, the minimal gap between training and inference times demonstrates the framework's consistency and suitability for real-time applications.

4.4 Conclusion and Outlook

We presented a novel on-device continual learning framework for unsupervised VAD in dynamic manufacturing environments. Our approach integrates online learning, a lightweight feature backbone, and incremental k-center memory updates into the standard PatchCore algorithm to achieve strong performance under tight resource budgets. Experimental results show that our method outperforms the coreset subsampling baseline in both accuracy and efficiency. It achieves a 12% improvement in AUROC, reduces memory usage by 80%, and enables significantly faster training. Furthermore, evaluation on a Jetson Nano (CPU-only) confirms its suitability for industrial edge deployment, providing an order-of-magnitude speedup over batch learning and maintaining a minimal training–inference latency gap, with memory overhead below 25 MB for training and below 1 MB for inference.

Looking forward, several avenues can be further explored to strengthen our work. From a practical perspective, future efforts can focus on deploying the framework across additional industrial use cases to validate its generality and robustness. Methodologically, integrating more advanced continual learning mechanisms, such as enhanced knowledge retention, is a promising way to improve long-term adaptability. In parallel, exploring memory bank optimization techniques such as dimension reduction and quantisation can further reduce the resource requirements of our method. These future advancements aim to broaden the applicability of our approach as an on-device continual learning solution for adaptive VAD in flexible industrial environments.

Acknowledgements

This work is partially supported by the NEPHELE (ID: 101070487) and SMARTEDGE (ID: 101092908) projects that have received funding from the European Union's Horizon Europe research and innovation program.

References

[1] C. Schmitz, A. Tschiesner, C. Jansen, S. Hallerstede and F. Garms, "Industry 4.0: Capturing value at scale in discrete manufacturing," McKinsey & Company, 2019.

[2] V. Tsoukas, A. Gkogkidis, E. Boumpa and A. Kakarountas, "A Review on the emerging technology of TinyML," ACM Computing Surveys, vol. 56, p. 1–37, 2024.

[3] A. Khajooei, M. Jamshidi and S. B. Shokouhi, "A super-efficient TinyML processor for the edge metaverse," Information, vol. 14, p. 235, 2023.

[4] A. Krishna, S. R. Nudurupati, D. G. Chandana, P. Dwivedi, A. van Schaik, M. Mehendale and C. S. Thakur, "Raman: A reconfigurable and sparse TinyML accelerator for inference on edge," IEEE Internet of Things Journal, vol. 11, p. 24831–24845, 2024.

[5] V. J. Reddi, "Generative AI at the Edge: Challenges and Opportunities: The next phase in AI deployment," Queue, vol. 23, p. 79–137, 2025.

[6] H. Ren, D. Anicic, X. Li and T. Runkler, "On-device online learning and semantic management of TinyML systems," ACM Transactions on Embedded Computing Systems, vol. 23, p. 1–32, 2024.

[7] R. David, J. Duke, A. Jain, V. Janapa Reddi, N. Jeffries, J. Li, N. Kreeger, I. Nappier, M. Natraj, T. Wang and others, "Tensorflow lite micro: Embedded machine learning for tinyml systems," Proceedings of machine learning and systems, vol. 3, p. 800–811, 2021.

[8] R. Kallimani, K. Pai, P. Raghuwanshi, S. Iyer and O. L. A. López, "TinyML: Tools, applications, challenges, and future research directions," Multimedia Tools and Applications, vol. 83, p. 29015–29045, 2024.

[9] K. Batzner, L. Heckler and R. König, "Efficientad: Accurate visual anomaly detection at millisecond-level latencies," in Proceedings of the IEEE/CVF winter conference on applications of computer vision, 2024.

[10] V. Zavrtanik, M. Kristan and D. Skočaj, "Draem-a discriminatively trained reconstruction embedding for surface anomaly detection," in

Proceedings of the IEEE/CVF international conference on computer vision, 2021.

[11] X. Du, J. Chen, J. Yu, S. Li and Q. Tan, "Generative adversarial nets for unsupervised outlier detection," Expert Systems with Applications, vol. 236, p. 121161, 2024.

[12] M. Barusco, F. Borsatti, D. D. Pezze, F. Paissan, E. Farella and G. A. Susto, "Paste: Improving the efficiency of visual anomaly detection at the edge," in Proceedings of the Computer Vision and Pattern Recognition Conference, 2025.

[13] Y. Long, Z. Ling, S. Brook, D. McFarlane and A. Brintrup, "Leveraging unsupervised learning for cost-effective visual anomaly detection," in IET Conference Proceedings CP885, 2024.

[14] P. Bergmann, M. Fauser, D. Sattlegger and C. Steger, "MVTec AD–A comprehensive real-world dataset for unsupervised anomaly detection," in Proceedings of the IEEE/CVF conference on computer vision and pattern recognition, 2019.

[15] Y. Zou, J. Jeong, L. Pemula, D. Zhang and O. Dabeer, "Spot-the-difference self-supervised pre-training for anomaly detection and segmentation," in European conference on computer vision, 2022.

[16] R. Mohandas, M. Southern, E. O'Connell and M. Hayes, "A survey of incremental deep learning for defect detection in manufacturing," Big Data and Cognitive Computing, vol. 8, p. 7, 2024.

[17] W. Sun, R. Al Kontar, J. Jin and T.-S. Chang, "A continual learning framework for adaptive defect classification and inspection," Journal of Quality Technology, vol. 55, p. 598–614, 2023.

[18] N. Bugarin, J. Bugaric, M. Barusco, D. D. Pezze and G. A. Susto, "Unveiling the anomalies in an ever-changing world: A benchmark for pixel-level anomaly detection in continual learning," in Proceedings of the IEEE/CVF Conference on Computer Vision and Pattern Recognition, 2024.

[19] M. Barusco, F. Borsatti, N. Beda, D. D. Pezze and G. A. Susto, "Towards Continual Visual Anomaly Detection in the Medical Domain," arXiv preprint arXiv:2508.18013, 2025.

[20] W. Li, J. Zhan, J. Wang, B. Xia, B.-B. Gao, J. Liu, C. Wang and F. Zheng, "Towards continual adaptation in industrial anomaly detection," in Proceedings of the 30th ACM International Conference on Multimedia, 2022.

[21] A. Alzarooni, E. Iqbal, S. U. Khan, S. Javed, B. Moyo and Y. Abdulrahman, "Anomaly detection for industrial applications, its

challenges, solutions, and future directions: A review," arXiv preprint arXiv:2501.11310, 2025.
[22] K. Roth, L. Pemula, J. Zepeda, B. Schölkopf, T. Brox and P. Gehler, "Towards total recall in industrial anomaly detection," in Proceedings of the IEEE/CVF conference on computer vision and pattern recognition, 2022.
[23] Y. Zheng, X. Wang, Y. Qi, W. Li and L. Wu, "Benchmarking unsupervised anomaly detection and localization," arXiv preprint arXiv:2205.14852, 2022.
[24] G. Xie, J. Wang, J. Liu, J. Lyu, Y. Liu, C. Wang, F. Zheng and Y. Jin, "IM-IAD: Industrial Image Anomaly Detection Benchmark in Manufacturing," IEEE Transactions on Cybernetics, vol. 54, pp. 2720-2733, 2024.
[25] J. Santos, T. Tran and O. Rippel, Optimizing PatchCore for Few/many-shot Anomaly Detection, 2023.
[26] A. Howard, M. Sandler, G. Chu, L.-C. Chen, B. Chen, M. Tan, W. Wang, Y. Zhu, R. Pang, V. Vasudevan and others, "Searching for mobilenetv3," in Proceedings of the IEEE/CVF international conference on computer vision, 2019.

5

In-GPU GNN-based Intrusion Detection System

Ahmed Salah Tawfik Ibrahim[1], Emilio Paolini[2], Filippo Cugini[1], and Francesco Paolucci[1]

[1]CNIT, Italy
[2]Scuola Superiore Sant'Anna, Italy

Abstract

Graph Neural Networks (GNNs) have proven effective for intrusion detection by modeling the relational structure of network traffic. However, the high cost of graph construction often dominates the overall prediction time, limiting real-time applicability. In this work, we propose a GPU-accelerated framework that speeds up not only GNN inference but also the graph construction phase. Unlike traditional approaches that build the adjacency matrix from scratch for each input graph, our method introduces a precomputed default adjacency matrix, generated in parallel on the GPU, which is then selectively modified for each graph instance. Node features are also computed using GPU threads, enabling end-to-end graph generation and inference entirely within GPU memory. Experimental results on the 5G-NIDD dataset show a consistent speedup of approximately 1.22× over CPU execution, while preserving detection accuracy. This work demonstrates the feasibility of deploying GNN-based intrusion detection systems in time-sensitive environments by optimizing both algorithmic design and hardware utilization.

Keywords: Graph Neural Networks (GNN), GPU Acceleration, Intrusion Detection, Cybersecurity, CUDA.

DOI: 10.1201/9788743815273-5

5.1 Introduction and Background

The interest in graph neural networks (GNNs) has been growing in recent years. This is thanks to their outstanding ability to model and learn from non-Euclidean data [1] like graphs, allowing them to incorporate relational information into the learning [2]. In fact, GNNs have proven useful in intrusion detection in computer networks as highlighted in [3].

Nonetheless, real-time deployment is challenged by the prediction time $T_{Prediction}$, defined as the summation of the graph construction time T_{Graph} and the inference time $T_{Inference}$, which is almost entirely dependent on T_{Graph} because $T_{Inference}$ is negligible as shown in Figure 5.1.

This paper proposes utilizing the GPU to accelerate the graph construction, reducing $T_{Prediction}$. Following the Single Instruction Multiple Data (SIMD) paradigm, the GPU executes the same instruction on multiple data items in parallel using threads [4].

As key enablers to deep learning (DL), GPUs are particularly suitable for the acceleration of matrix operations, which constitute the backbone of neural network training and inference [5]. Since matrices are used to model graphs [6], GPUs can be used to accelerate their computations.

A graph $G = (V, E)$ is defined by a set of nodes V and a set of edges E. To model this graph, two matrices are required: the feature matrix X and the adjacency matrix A [7]. Constructing X involves organizing the features of the nodes in V such that each row of X contains the features of one node, resulting in a matrix of size $|V| \times n$ where n is the number of features. The matrix A, instead, is a binary square matrix of size $|V|$ x $|V|$ with entries reflecting the existence of edges between nodes.

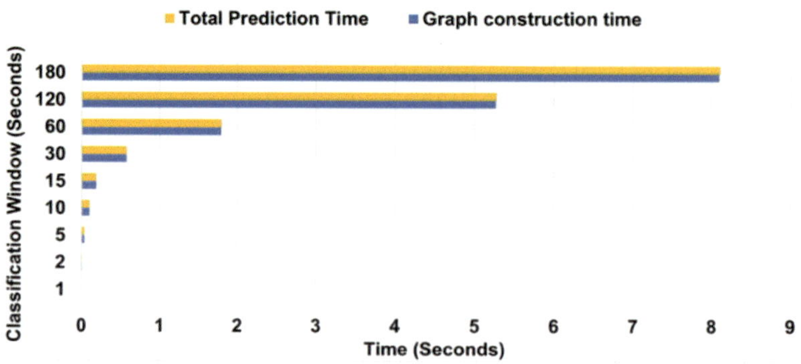

Figure 5.1 Total Prediction Time vs Graph Construction Time.

Several GPU Graph libraries exist; however, they are mostly general purpose and they do not provide the flexibility needed to construct a graph from incoming packets. For instance, systems such as cuSTINGER [8] and Hornet [9] support inserting and deleting edges while keeping the vertex set unchanged. cuSTINGER offers a flexible, dynamic adjacency-list structure on GPUs and was one of the earliest demonstrations of high-throughput GPU updates. However, its memory layout is not well suited for fine-grained, real-time insertions. Network telemetry commonly arrives as numerous small, time-ordered events rather than large, uniform batches, and cuSTINGER's dependence on batch-oriented processing can cause substantial latency increases and update stalls—problems that are especially detrimental for intrusion detection or online flow tracking.

GNNs learn from graphs by performing two operations: (i) message passing and (ii) embedding update [10]. That way, nodes aggregate their own embeddings with those of their neighbors. The aggregation can be executed in a number of ways, including graph convolutional networks (GCNs) and graph attention networks (GATs). Usually, the final aim of graph learning is node classification, edge prediction or graph classification.

In any case, choosing how to accelerate a graph algorithm depends on the application at hand. So, one must consider the patterns and trends in the application and decide how to apply GPU acceleration accordingly.

5.2 Main Text

Recalling some of the concepts in [3] is needed before outlining the proposed methodology. In [3], Raw packets are transformed into a traffic graph $G = (V, E)$ whose nodes are identified by a flow id. The flow id is defined by the source IP, the source port, the destination IP, the destination port and the protocol. Each node contains a set of packets of the node's flow id.

The construction of the graph is completed by connecting the nodes via edges. Two nodes v_1 and v_2 have an edge if:

- **R1:** the flow ids of the two nodes are different but $Src(v_1) = Dst(v_2)$ or $Src(v_2) = Dst(v_1)$.

Hence, constructing the graph can be summarized in 4 steps: (i) collecting packets; (ii) extracting features; (iii) filling the nodes; and (iv) constructing the adjacency matrix.

The initial two steps are straight-forward, so the last two steps are suitable candidates for the GPU acceleration. Adding a packet to a node involves extracting the packet's flow id. Upon the existence of a node with the same flow id, the packet gets inserted into that node where its features are aggregated with the existing ones. Otherwise, a new node is created where the packet can be inserted. Neglecting the complexity of the aggregation, the complexity of the node creation process is linear in the number of packets ($O(|P|)$).

To construct the adjacency matrix, nodes are ordered chronologically. Then, the edge condition is checked by comparing each node with all the subsequent ones. If it holds, then the two nodes get connected by an undirected edge. This means setting the corresponding entry in the adjacency matrix to 1. Clearly, this algorithm has a quadratic complexity in the number of nodes ($O(|V|^2)$).

Upon successfully terminating these steps, the constructed matrices are passed to the GPU where the GNN inference gets performed. This transfer has an overhead that can be eliminated by constructing the graph directly on the GPU. That way, the GPU parallelization capabilities can be further utilized in speeding up the entire process.

However, achieving this paradigm shift requires handling two main practical challenges. First of all, memory pre-allocation is required in GPU programming, meaning that the number of nodes must be decided in advance. Furthermore, the adjacency matrix construction requires a unique mapping between actual IP addresses and adjacency matrix indices.

Fortunately, a classification window of 75 packets is sufficient to make accurate predictions according to [3]. In that case, the session may have up to 150 unique addresses. With this, the default adjacency matrix, defined to be the matrix corresponding to the case where there are packets between all pairs of addresses in the session, can be constructed. The size of this matrix will be $150^2 \times 150^2$ This solves the first challenge related to the pre-allocated memory.

The default matrix is invariant for all sessions of size N, so it can be built only once in the beginning. The procedure that highlights building the default matrix using the GPU is shown in Alg. 1. Each thread considers one node and fills its corresponding row and column in the matrix according to the edge condition (R1).

The second challenge requires finding a bijective function whose bijectivity holds only within the session. This means that the output of the mapping must correspond to one and only one address in the session and, in turn, each address must correspond to one and only one output. So, this bijective function can be defined as $f : x \to N \text{ } where \text{ } x \in \{Src(v), Dst(v) \; \forall v \in V\}$. In

Algorithm 1 Thread to Initialize Default Adjacency Matrix

Input : Adjacency Matrix Adj, Maximum Number of Node Configurations N

Output: Initialized Adjacency Matrix Adj

```
row ← ThreadIdx.x
col ← ThreadIdx.y
if row ≠ col and row < n and col < n then
    NodeIndex ← row * N + col
    Adj[NodeIndex, NodeIndex] ← 1
    for i ← 0 to N do
        if col ≠ i then
            Adj[NodeIndex, col * N + i] ← 1
        if row ≠ i then
            Adj[NodeIndex, i * N + row] ← 1
```

the case where $N = 150$ addresses, the output of f should be a natural number in the set $\{0, 1, 2, ..., 149\}$.

While hashing is the preferred implementation for this mapping, it is very challenging to come up with a hash function that has the desired bijective property due to potential conflicts. Since the address space is much larger than the integers of the mapping, finding such a function is almost impossible. It is, however, possible to use an in-GPU dictionary data structure, but to the best of our knowledge, no such implementation exists in python. Therefore, a GPU-accelerated k-means clustering algorithm with k equal to the number of addresses is used. This guarantees that each address during the session will be mapped to one and only one integer between 0 and k-1, ensuring the bijective property within the session.

The constructed default adjacency matrix may be later modified by each graph, reflecting the actual flows.

To measure the performance brought by the GPU acceleration, a machine with an NVIDIA Tesla T4 GPU[1] is used to execute a number of tests.

A. Graph Initialization Time vs Window Size

The graph initialization outlined in Alg. 1 is executed to measure the time of execution. This is done by considering different classification window sizes

[1] https://www.nvidia.com/en-us/data-center/tesla-t4/

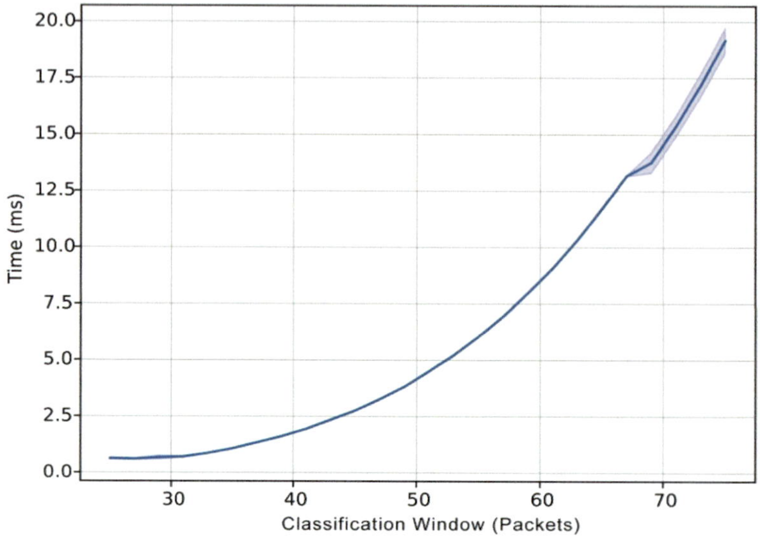

Figure 5.2 Graph Initialization Time.

Table 5.1 CPU vs GPU F1 Score

Metric	CPU	GPU
F1 Score	83.9%	83.78%

(N) and recording the execution times of each. The maximum considered size is 75 due to the GPU memory limitations. Statistical significance is ensured by executing the test 30 times to run a t-score test. Figure 5.2 reports the average of these runs along with the 95% confidence interval.

B. CPU vs GPU

In addition, it is important to measure the actual performance gain upon executing the GPU acceleration with respect to the original CPU implementation. Here, the total time to build n graphs is measured by considering different numbers of constructed graphs and recording the corresponding total construction time. The window size of the constructed graphs is set to 75 packets. They are constructed on the CPU and the GPU showing a GPU speedup of 1.22x with respect to the CPU as shown in Figure 5.3. Furthermore, it can be noted that the average F1 score, measured by averaging the F1 scores of 10,000 classification sessions for each implementation, remains almost identical as shown in Table 5.1. The slight change is attributed to the difference in floating point precision between the CPU and the GPU.

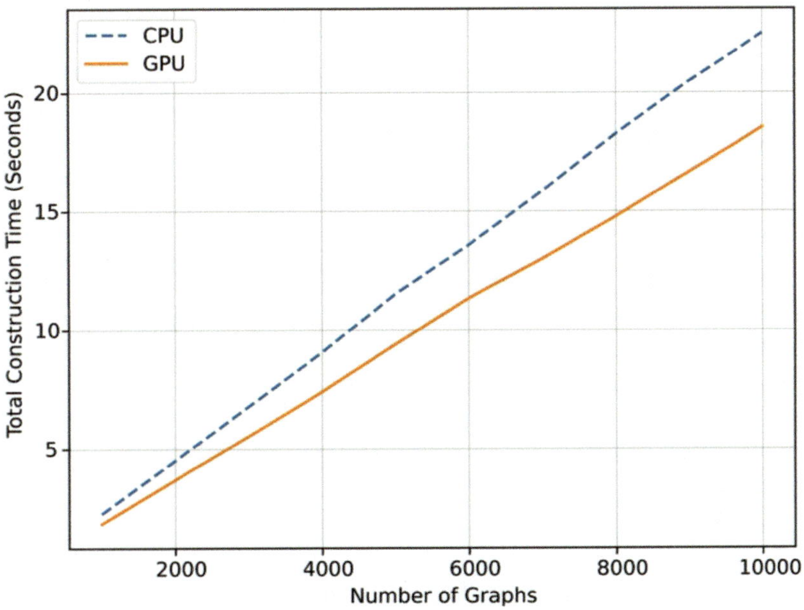

Figure 5.3 CPU vs GPU Graph Construction Time

5.3 Conclusion

In conclusion, this paper introduces GPU acceleration to the GNN intrusion detection system proposed in [3]. This acceleration speeds up the graph construction by constructing the default adjacency matrix using parallel GPU threads. At system startup, this matrix gets computed and stored to be later adjusted by each graph according to its actual edges. The improvement in performance is manifested by the fact that the accelerated system is 1.22 times faster than the original CPU-based system.

In the future, the memory requirements of the system will be considered. This is important to mitigate the exploding space requirements of the default adjacency matrix. A possible direction, therefore, is investigating sparse matrix representations to store it.

Moreover, considering GPU memory access patterns in the outlined algorithms may lead to performance gains. So, a memory-aware design of the algorithms is also another possible future direction.

Finally, to reduce the data size, using a different number representation is useful. So, instead of using 32-bit floating point numbers, 16-bit floating point representations like Bfloat16 [11] may be considered.

Acknowledgements

This work is supported by the Chips Joint Undertaking (JU), European Union (EU) HORIZON-JU-IA, under grant agreement No. 101140087 (SMARTY), including top-up funding by the Italian MUR.

References

[1] Z. Zhu, F. Li, G. Li, Z. Liu, Z. Mo, Q. Hu, X. Liang, and J. Cheng, "Mega: A memory-efficient gnn accelerator exploiting degree-aware mixed-precision quantization," in 2024 IEEE International Symposium on High-Performance Computer Architecture (HPCA). IEEE, 2024, pp. 124–138.

[2] Z. Wu, S. Pan, F. Chen, G. Long, C. Zhang, and P. S. Yu, "A comprehensive survey on graph neural networks," IEEE transactions on neural networks and learning systems, vol. 32, no. 1, pp. 4–24, 2020.

[3] A. S. T. Ibrahim, E. Paolini, F. Cugini, and F. Paolucci, "Real-time graph neural network for malicious traffic detection," in 2025 IEEE International Conference on Machine Learning for Communication and Networking (ICMLCN), 2025, pp. 1–6.

[4] R. Baraglia, G. Capannini, F. M. Nardini, and F. Silvestri, "Sorting using bitonic network with cuda," CEUR Workshop Proceedings, vol. 480, 01 2009.

[5] W. Jeon, G. Ko, J. Lee, H. Lee, D. Ha, and W. W. Ro, "Chapter six - deep learning with gpus," in Hardware Accelerator Systems for Artificial Intelligence and Machine Learning, ser. Advances in Computers, S. Kim and G. C. Deka, Eds. Elsevier, 2021, vol. 122, pp. 167–215. [Online]. Available: https://www.sciencedirect.com/science/article/pii/S0065245820300905

[6] D. Grinberg, "An introduction to graph theory," 2025. [Online]. Available: https://arxiv.org/abs/2308.04512

[7] J. H. Tanis, C. Giannella, and A. V. Mariano, "Introduction to graph neural networks: A starting point for machine learning engineers," 2024. [Online]. Available: https://arxiv.org/abs/2412.19419

[8] O. Green and D. A. Bader, "cuSTINGER: Supporting dynamic graph algorithms for GPUs," *2016 IEEE High Performance Extreme Computing Conference (HPEC)*, Waltham, MA, USA, 2016, pp. 1-6, doi: 10.1109/HPEC.2016.7761622.

[9] F. Busato, O. Green, N. Bombieri and D. A. Bader, "Hornet: An Efficient Data Structure for Dynamic Sparse Graphs and Matrices on GPUs," *2018 IEEE High Performance extreme Computing Conference (HPEC)*, Waltham, MA, USA, 2018, pp. 1-7, doi:10.1109/HPEC.2018.8547541.

[10] W. L. Hamilton, "Graph representation learning," Synthesis Lectures on Artificial Intelligence and Machine Learning, vol. 14, no. 3, pp. 1–159.

[11] N. Burgess, J. Milanovic, N. Stephens, K. Monachopoulos, and D. Mansell, "Bfloat16 processing for neural networks," in 2019 IEEE 26th Symposium osn Computer Arithmetic (ARITH), 2019, pp. 88–91.

6

Vision-language Embeddings in Large Scale LiDAR SLAM for Terrain Segmentation

Pēteris Račinskis, Janis Arents, and Modris Greitans

Institute of Electronics and Computer Science (EDI), Latvia

Abstract

This paper aims to showcase the potential of extending the open-set semantic approach enabled by vision-language model embeddings for autonomous robot perception through the introduction of a vector-valued voxel mapping software package - SLAMVDB, short for "SLAM vector database", capable of terrain segmentation after introducing a lightweight closed-set classifier in the map retrieval stage. This technology integrates point clouds and camera images to construct semantic maps, with a focus on applications in outdoor autonomous robotics. A single neural network inference pass on the image generates pixel-wise embeddings, which are fused into an octree-based spatial data structure. Information in the map is then retrieved by performing vector similarity searches with respect to text or image embeddings, or specific lookup vectors obtained through supervised learning on a discrete class set in the terrain segmentation task. The map is shown to be capable of performing terrain segmentation for robot navigation, with overall accuracy as high as 87.35% on track *00000* of the Rellis-3D data set, with a coarse-grained 5-class ontology. This paper describes the implementation, verification procedure and evaluation results of the system.

Keywords: open-set semantics, vision-language models, edge AI, SLAM, robotics.

DOI: 10.1201/9788743815273-6

6.1 Introduction and Background

In outdoor-focused industries such as agrifood and forestry, demographic shifts as well as the often physically demanding, tedious and even dangerous nature of the work present the looming prospect of labor shortages [1]. While current staffing levels may still be sufficient to maintain productivity, careers in these industries are failing to attract sufficient numbers of replacements as the current workforce retires, resulting in an "aging out" phenomenon. Other industries, such as manufacturing, have for decades successfully employed robotics to both increase productivity and combat labor shortages. In predictable environments the go-to method for deploying robotic systems remains programming by hand. Advances in machine learning, especially in terms of perception, have enabled robots to adapt to their surroundings through object detection and pose estimation [2]. Moreover, when combined with mobile bases, mass adoption of robotic solutions has also reached beyond the static manufacturing line into domains such as warehouse management [3]. However, it must be noted that technology readiness and adoption rapidly decline as the operating environments trend towards the less structured – such as semi-structured farms [4] and unstructured forests.

As soon as a robot departs the confines of a predefined environment, autonomy requires tackling the challenge of Simultaneous Localization and Mapping (SLAM) [5]. However, for a robot to perform complex tasks, its environmental models must be constructed to be not only spatially accurate but also imbued with semantic annotations that encode the meaning and function of objects and surfaces. Prior methodologies in semantic mapping have typically followed a discrete classification paradigm. The discrete semantic mapping approach is exemplified by systems such as *SemanticFusion* [6], which produces surfel cloud maps with class tags. The introduction of Vision-Language embedding Models (VLMs), such as CLIP [7], has paved the way for a new, more flexible approach: open-set semantics. Through self-supervised joint learning of text and image embedding models on large-scale internet-sourced datasets, these models learn to project images and their descriptions to nearby points in a high-dimensional latent vector space. Such a capability enables zero-shot generalization to novel concepts without requiring retraining of the entire vision model. Before this technology can be effectively leveraged in robot control, multiple hurdles need to be overcome. The first involves taking the step from embedding images as a whole, as in the original CLIP model, to producing a latent space embedding for each pixel – resulting in a *feature map*. One approach, as taken by *LSeg* [8], performs end-to-end training using a pre-trained text embedding model. An image segmentation model is directly trained to produce a feature map, using vector embeddings of class names for the final vector similarity comparison. A more involved, two-stage route is taken by *conceptfusion* [9]. They use the Segment Anything Model (SAM) [10] to first partition the image into proposed masks, then individually crop a region around each mask, embed it as a single vector, and add this resulting embedding vector to the feature value of each pixel in the object mask.

With a feature map in hand, the next step is volumetric data association. For example, *conceptfusion* adopts the same surfel approach as taken by the previously described discrete-valued *SemanticFusion* system, producing an unsorted list of surfel elements. Alternatively, one may also construct implicit spatial representations by modifying Neural Radiance Fields (NeRFs) to predict the latent space embedding of each spatial coordinate rather than its appearance [11]. In this case, the "map" is not stored as an explicit data structure, rather being encoded in the weights of the radiance field model. However, one of the classic approaches to building volumetric maps containing arbitrary data is the octree grid map. Indeed, this is also the approach adopted in the authors' previous work [12], where the *OctoMap* [13] software package was extended to permit storing latent space embeddings and allow vector similarity search operations – yielding the *Vectree* system.

The principal goal of the work described in this chapter was demonstrating the applicability of open-set semantics for a different use-case and different information retrieval pattern. The software package introduced here, SLAMVDB [14], is first and foremost designed to accomplish a critical task for autonomous, mobile robotics: terrain segmentation for navigational purposes. Existing approaches to terrain segmentation often rely on models trained specifically for this task on limited datasets, which may not generalize well to novel environments, a challenge addressed by architectures like GANav [15]. This, while achieving substantial improvements over the then-SotA, requires a highly bespoke vision model architecture. The novel contribution outlined here is to instead leverage the open-vocabulary power of VLMs, applying an off-the-shelf, pre-trained *LSeg* vision model with frozen weights to the terrain segmentation problem. We use supervised learning only for creating a specialized set of query vectors, optimized on a small data set to build a discrete classifier operating on latent space embedding features, which can perform retrieval operations in either the image or voxel domain – the latter allowing many observations of a voxel to be fused and averaged over time.

6.2 Approach and Implementation

Before the problem of semantic mapping can be considered, a means of obtaining the robot's position and orientation as well as sufficiently dense distance measurements is required. The already mentioned *Vectree* system did not have to contend with the high intensity ambient lighting often present in outdoor scenery, and therefore relied on depth (RGB-D) images for ranging information. There are multiple advantages inherent in this approach – depth images are, in most systems, synchronized and overlapping with the color image channel by construction. For some cameras, the color image is directly used in constructing the depth cloud, which means their projective parameters are identical. However, this isn't always the case and the cameras deployed for testing *Vectree* require the intrinsic and extrinsic parameters of each channel to be processed separately. A marked disadvantage for both types of depth cameras, however, is their reliance on structured illumination patterns emitted by the device. These limit the camera's effective range and are easily washed out by the sun outdoors. With these limitations in mind, the data modality of choice for large-scale mapping outdoors is a combination of LiDAR for ranging and RGB for performing semantic inference. EDI has developed a portable sensor package for collecting this type of data and already deployed it in collecting the EDI-SLAM data set [16]. Data in a similar format are also available in other public data sets – for example, *RELLIS-3D* [17], which contains not only the raw images and scans, but also high-frequency ground truth pose estimates and highly detailed point-wise discrete semantic labels.

6.2.1 Overall architecture

The sparsity inherent in mechanically scanned LiDAR point clouds renders surface reconstruction-based map formats such as surfel clouds impractical for many applications due to wide gaps between scan lines. Implicit spatial representations such as NRFs do not have straightforward scaling properties and their method of storing data about the volume is entirely opaque, as model parameters. Voxel occupancy grids, which are well understood and widely employed in LiDAR SLAM systems present the most suitable data structure when designing a semantic mapping system for the intended use case. These efficiently store even very large maps, and simplify map update procedures through the log-odds update rule [13].

The sensor modality and fundamental geometric structure of the map motivate the SLAMVDB system architecture, depicted in Figure 6.1. It needs to be able to process images and scans arriving asynchronously, at

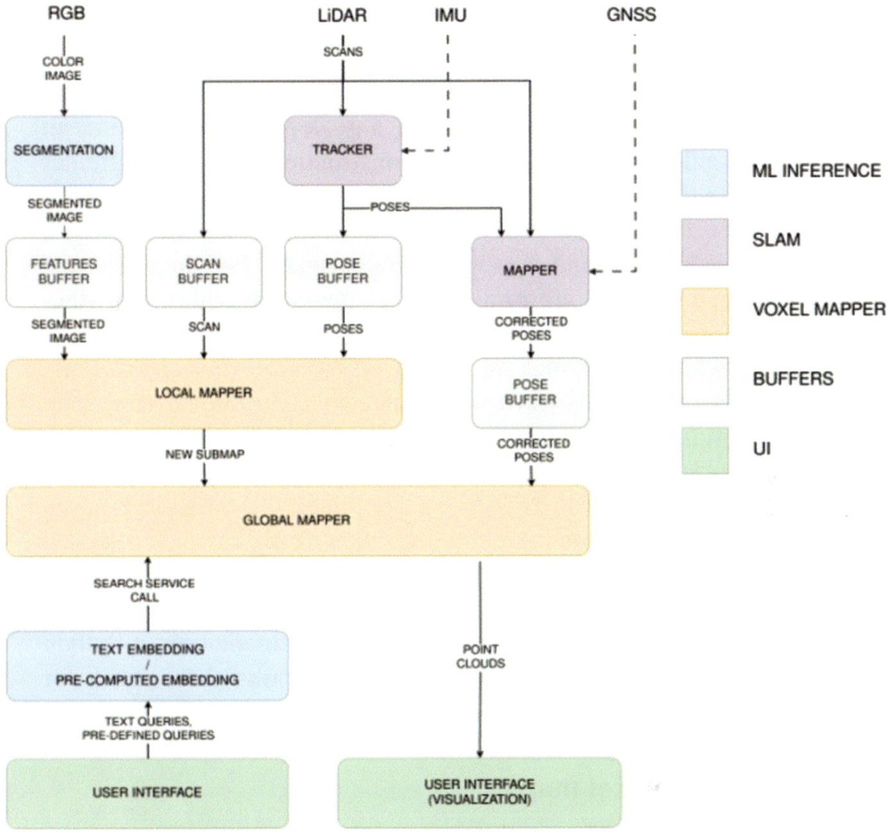

Figure 6.1 Architecture of the SLAMVDB semantic mapping system.

different frequencies, localize the robot, construct a consistent geometric map of the robot's surroundings, and fuse the semantic features extracted from images into this map as they arrive. Hence, the major subsystems in the architecture are the **Tracker** and **Mapper** (loop-closer) for localization; a **Semantic Inference** (image segmentation) module abstracting the neural network-based image processing; and the core of the system – a **Voxel Map**, which stores the environment model and exposes interfaces for lookup operations. Communication between the subsystems – independent software packages in their own right – is implemented using ROS2 [18]. The core voxel mapping application is written in *C++*. The integrated SLAM modules are written in *Python*. ML inference is performed by EDI's fork of *LSeg* [19].

6.2.2 Localization

While purely visual or visual-inertial SLAM systems exist and, under certain circumstances, attain accuracy sufficient to ensure successful robot navigation, LiDAR, which will be available in any deployment or data set SLAMVDB is intended to be used with by construction, still offers greater reliability and tracking accuracy. The SLAMVDB architecture is, in principle, agnostic to the localization provider, but out of the box it ships with two tracker module options and a loop closing mapper. For data sets and deployments where IMU data are available, an integration with the off-the-shelf *fast-lio2* [20] LiDAR-inertial odometry system is provided. No matter what sensor set-up and algorithms are employed for scan-to-scan tracking, error accumulation over time – drift – is expected. To mitigate this, loop closures or position fixes are required. The mapper module exists to accomplish this through pose graph optimization (PGO). This package is decoupled from the tracking module through ROS. It combines the basic ICP-based submap alignment principle employed by *lidarslam_ros2* [21], where a new submap is periodically inserted into a list and compared to previous submaps to detect when the same location has been revisited based on tracker pose estimates, augmented, with a *ScanContext* [22] re-implementation in Python that enables detecting loops even when drift has accumulated too much for raw ICP-based loop detection.

6.2.3 Vector-valued voxel map

The fundamental building block of the semantic voxel map remains the vector-valued octree initially introduced in *Vectree*, though SLAMVDB re-implements it from scratch rather than using an extension of *OctoMap*. The log-odds occupancy update rule remains unchanged. However, the shift from synchronized and co-located RGB-D data for both range and semantics to LiDAR scans combined with RGB from a camera requires a different approach to integrating semantic data. Only a fraction of the points available in every scan will, as a general rule, be directly observed by the camera due to a much more limited field of view and substantial parallax. Hence, during the integration of voxel semantic values $\boldsymbol{v}_{\boldsymbol{x}}$ with the projectively associated image features $\boldsymbol{v}_{\pi(\boldsymbol{x})}$, the existing cell occupancy value reflects the LiDAR observation count, not the visual one, and thus cannot be used directly. Instead, for each visually observed map cell an increment counter $n_{\boldsymbol{x}}$ is implemented, allowing for integration by the rolling average given in Equation 1.1.

$$\boldsymbol{v}_{\boldsymbol{x}} \leftarrow \frac{n_{\boldsymbol{x}} \cdot \boldsymbol{v}_{\boldsymbol{x}} + \boldsymbol{v}_{\pi(\boldsymbol{x})}}{n_{\boldsymbol{x}} + 1} \tag{6.1}$$

Another fundamental difference is in the projective data association algorithm. For depth cameras with identical depth and color projection parameters, there exists a 1:1 mapping between pixels and points, allowing for a trivial data association. When images and range scans are no longer synchronized, and the voxels grow large relative to image pixels, voxel-to-pixel projection and occlusion modeling is required, which has been implemented in *OpenGL* [23], projecting the integer indices of voxels onto the image plane.

For performance reasons, octree maps are typically constrained in their maximum extent by the need to preserve a bijective mapping between system register width integers and the grid cells. While sufficient for small, confined spaces, when combined with practical voxel resolutions on the scale of centimeters, this approach will fail if the robot traverses many kilometers of wilderness. A more immediate concern, however, is the impact of tracker drift accumulation. If a drift compensation mechanism such as loop closing is employed, it may require changing an already fused voxel map after the fact to reflect an updated trajectory estimate. Hence, rather than building a single unified voxel map, we construct smaller submaps, left free-floating to allow subsequent adjustment. SLAMVDB's voxel mapper implements this as a sequence of submaps inserted periodically based on the salient trajectory length since the last submap insertion. If a loop closure is found, and the submaps are sufficiently close, they are merged into a single submap. Another change from *Vectree* is a simplification - no tree data structure is required to store the voxel semantics, so long as a unique correspondence with the grid cells exists. Instead, a simple key-value store is maintained, with values inserted cleared whenever a cell in the voxel grid is observed visually, or a cell is cleared in the tree, since most grid cells are never visually observed and require no semantics. To facilitate lookup operations in a global reference frame, another data structure is maintained – a global lookup index. This contains read-only pointers to submap key-value store entries at their latest position, and is employed during retrieval operations for map visualization and search. During retrieval, all voxel entries in each index grid cell have their vector values averaged, weighted by observation count.

6.2.4 Image-space inference

As with the previous *Vectree* system, the fundamental approach to image segmentation remains producing two-dimensional feature maps where individual features are vectors in the latent text-image embedding space. Analysis of the *conceptfusion* algorithm used in *Vectree* reveals that a significant and non-negotiable contribution to the 2-4 second image processing time is by repeated embedding model invocations on the large number of masks proposed by the first model stage. To obtain higher practical frame rates, a system using a single neural network pass was deemed necessary. SLAMVDB uses *LSeg*, and in all practical tests has been configured to operate at a much lower feature map resolution of 128$\times$192 pixels. The resulting system is able to attain a frame rate of 3-5Hz on a consumer-grade laptop computer. Another performance advantage of using *LSeg* is the lower dimension of the embedding vectors – 512 deep rather than *conceptfusion's* 768. However, this difference also naturally means that the text embedding models used by the respective systems are mutually incompatible, as are any query vectors optimized for lookup operations.

6.2.5 Query vector generation

Vectree, was specifically designed to interface with a natural language instruction parsing framework, and therefore process arbitrary text queries. No additional processing was performed – object descriptions were directly embedded and submitted to the vector map for lookup operations. Moreover, only a single query needed to be considered at time. As shown in Figure 6.2, it is possible to hand-craft sets of positive and negative queries whose vector sum, when compared with the image feature map produced by *LSeg*, clearly distinguishes certain terrain types from the background in an image across multiple resolution scales. However, directly using such text-based queries for terrain segmentation across multiple classes leads to the issue observed in Figure 6.3. The absolute similarity scores w.r.t. one query may completely drown out those computed for other lookup vectors, resulting in essentially random results as a single lookup vector hides results from all the others.

To address this issue, SLAMVDB requires a query vector optimization step, depicted in Figure 6.4. Without altering the image or text embedding model weights, a set of query vectors is initialized with class names drawn from the ontology definition. The vectors are then treated as a model parameter matrix and optimized on a relatively small data set using gradient descent in *PyTorch* [24]. This constitutes a classic supervised learning problem in the image segmentation task, but the number of parameters to be optimized is very small – n x 512 where n is the number of classes in the ontology. For the query vectors used in the evaluations in the next section, tracks *00001* and *00002* from the *RELLIS-3D* data set were sampled – 3234 labelled images,

2911 used for training and the rest for validation. The subsequent evaluations were then performed on the other three tracks in the data set, not present for training the query vectors, performing the lookup operations in voxel space. The loss function used is the same as in *LSeg*. The query vectors shipped with the system and used in the evaluation were trained for two epochs.

In terrain segmentation problems, the approach typically taken to produce the class set involves crafting a coarse ontology – grouping the original class labels in a data set into broad traversability classes [15]. For training the query vectors and testing SLAMVDB, the mapping between the *RELLIS-3D* labels ("fine" labels) and the final ("coarse") classes was:

- Smooth – asphalt, concrete;
- Rough – dirt, grass;
- Bumpy – mud, rubble;
- Obstacle – tree, pole, water, object, building, log, fence, bush, barrier;
- Active – vehicle, person;
- Void – void, sky.

6.3 Experimental Assessment and Results

A number of experimental performance assessments were performed across the various stages of the SLAMVDB semantic mapping pipeline, most of which fall outside the scope of this article. Namely, the localization accuracy tests are summarized in a prior technology report document [25]. This section is concerned with the methods used to estimate terrain segmentation accuracy and results achieved in this domain – independently of the localization provider used.

6.3.1 Data set, deployment platform and performance on the edge

While the EDI-SLAM data set [16], collected by EDI using a portable sensor package, was used extensively during the development of SLAMVDB and in testing the accuracy of the SLAM system, as of the writing of this article no semantic annotations are available. For this reason, the *RELLIS-3D* data set, which contains highly detailed point-wise semantic labels, was used in terrain segmentation accuracy assessment. These labels are available on a per-scan basis – in the sensor-local reference frame – meaning that, for methods like SLAMVDB that perform semantic inference on large-scale fused maps rather than on a per-scan basis, a protocol for associating these local point labels

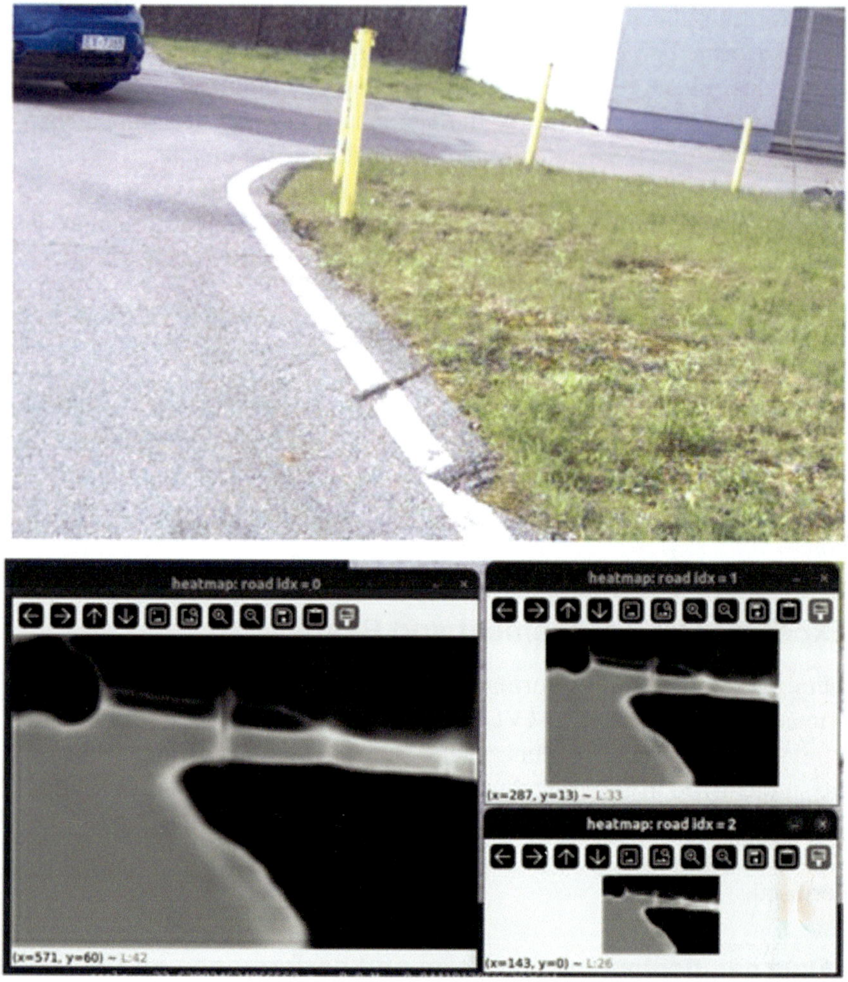

Figure 6.2 Terrain type differentiation using positive and negative text embedding queries.

with global points is required. Since even state of the art LiDAR-inertial tracking systems such as *fast-lio2* accumulate drift on the order of meters over the course of a typical RELLIS-3D track with respect to the provided ground truth trajectory, the pose estimates from such a system cannot be used in measuring the semantic accuracy of the map – the drift will cross voxel boundaries rendering a comparison invalid. Instead, SLAMVDB was configured to use the ground truth trajectory as its localization source. The LiDAR and RGB data were played back in real time using the ROS bag files

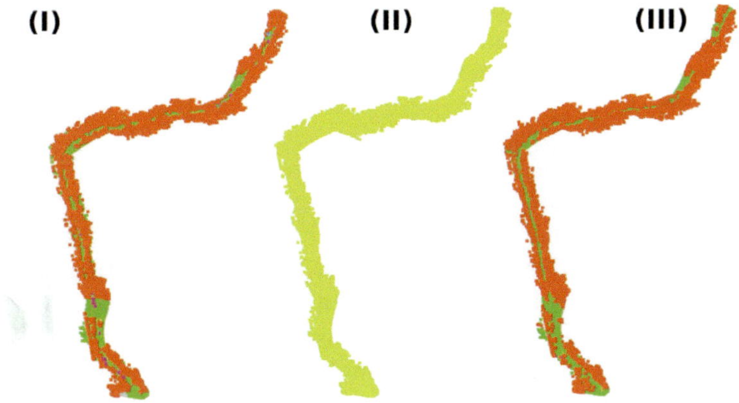

Figure 6.3 (I) The ground truth. (II) Text embeddings. (III) Optimized queries.

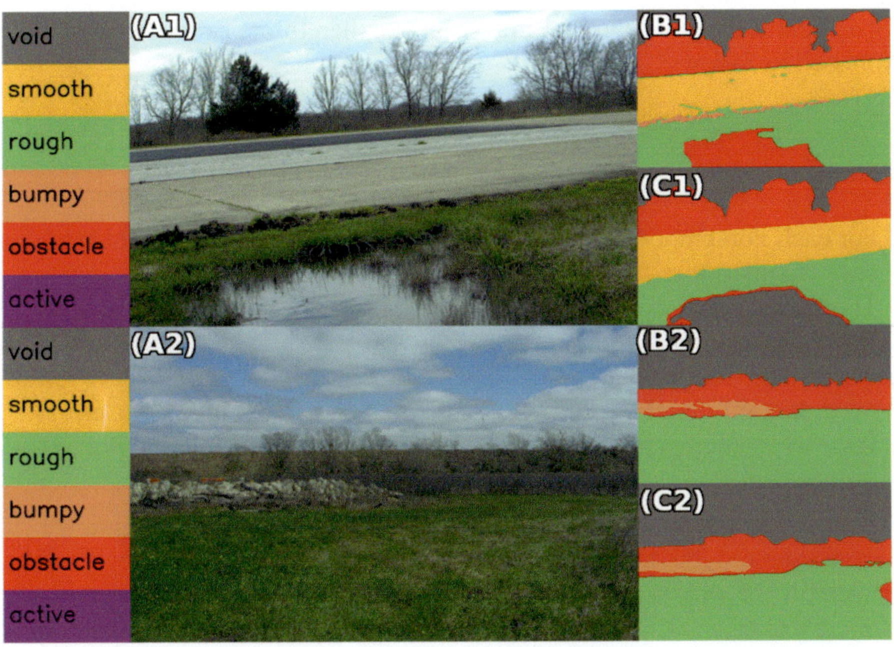

Figure 6.4 (A1-2) RGB images. (B1-2) Ground truth. (C1-2) Inferred classes.

provided as part of the *RELLIS-3D* data set, and the software package was deployed on the same target hardware – a consumer grade laptop: Lenovo Legion 5 with an NVIDIA GeForce RTX 3060m GPU, an AMD Ryzen 5

5600H CPU and 64 GB of RAM. All SLAMVDB software modules were run on this device, which is reflective of the type of deep edge computing hardware commonly found on UGV platforms.

6.3.2 Terrain segmentation accuracy

An issue that must be addressed when comparing a labelled point cloud with a voxel grid map is the choice of discretization. Each point has a theoretically continuously valued set of x,y,z coordinates whereas the voxel map forms a discrete grid with cells of finite size. We have performed two different assessments: point-wise accuracy, which measures the probability that any given point in the ground truth data will be inside a grid cell of the same class, and voxel-wise ground truth class assignment, which attempts to assign each voxel in the global reference frame a "correct" label based on the labels that fall within its confines.

Specifically, the point-wise accuracy statistic (heretofore called "hit rate") is expressed as follows:

$$\rho_{hit}, \% = \frac{|\{\text{labelled points in voxel of the same class}\}|}{|\{\text{labelled points in any non}-\text{empty map voxel}\}|} \cdot 100 \qquad (6.2)$$

For the voxel-wise labelling, we implement the following procedure:

1. For each non-empty voxel in the map, initialize an instance counter for each class;
2. Transform every scan in the labelled data set into the global reference frame using ground truth poses;
3. For every transformed point, if it falls inside a non-empty voxel, increment the counter for the corresponding class label in that voxel;
4. For each non-empty voxel in the map, assign the class with the highest instance count.

The result of this procedure is a voxel map geometrically identical to the one being assessed, but with classes assigned according to the most frequent point label to be observed within each voxel. For this, we compute three typical set partition statistics – recall, precision and intersection over union (IoU).

The results of this evaluation procedure are collated in Table 6.1. The major row blocks in this table – 00000, 00003, 00004 – correspond to the data set tracks used in the evaluation. For each track, the rows correspond to the classes in the coarse ontology, with the "all" row denoting the overall voxel-wise accuracy (in this case equal to recall, precisions and IoU). The

Table 6.1 Terrain segmentation accuracy (ignoring *Void*)

Track	Class	Hit %	Recall %	Prec. %	IoU %	Recalled (x1000)	Relevant (x1000)
00000	*all*	81.26		87.35		108.42	108.42
	smooth	0.00	0.00	0.00	0.00	0.00	0.16
	rough	75.57	80.26	86.60	71.39	38.83	41.90
	bumpy	4.60	5.34	13.00	3.94	0.30	0.73
	obstacle	89.40	93.64	88.11	83.14	69.26	65.17
	active	15.68	2.67	38.71	2.56	0.03	0.45
00003	*all*	80.39		81.37		60.25	60.25
	smooth	67.70	58.60	90.04	55.04	0.26	0.40
	rough	92.76	92.34	81.14	76.02	39.57	34.77
	bumpy	5.08	6.00	7.43	3.43	0.61	0.75
	obstacle	64.56	71.09	84.02	62.62	19.61	23.18
	active	9.85	14.46	81.50	14.00	0.20	1.13
00004	*all*	73.90		76.17		51.40	51.40
	smooth	0.00	0.00	0.00	0.00	0.00	0.51
	rough	90.95	92.03	74.46	69.95	36.19	29.28
	bumpy	10.32	13.27	49.74	11.70	0.96	3.60
	obstacle	58.98	67.09	82.15	58.55	14.13	17.30
	active	6.09	16.97	96.77	16.88	0.12	0.71

rightmost two columns contain the number of voxels recalled (assigned to a class by inference) and relevant (assigned to a class by the ground truth label) for each of the classes, in each of the tracks, expressed in thousands.

The *Void* class, corresponding to concepts not physically observable using a LiDAR sensor, has been neglected in this assessment. Instead, the second highest similarity class is used for voxels initially classified as *Void*. This heuristic was introduced after observing that transparent objects such as tree canopies tend to pick up the semantics of objects visible through them. In most cases this is non-trivial to address but the *Void* class can be eliminated by construction, improving the highest voxel-wise accuracy score from 84.69% to 87.35% on track 00000. Also apparent is that some classes are represented at very low frequencies, and these also tend to have poor recall metrics even if precision is high. Attempts at addressing this particular issue would most likely benefit from increased image feature resolution, reducing the incidence of misclassified voxels in image space or projection error. Differences in accuracy between tracks can sometimes be explained by qualitative observations. Track 00000 is the most uniform. It also features the two terrain types that the system appears to be the most successful at distinguishing – grass and trees. Track 00004, on which the lowest accuracy is observed, features a substantial patch of muddy terrain – belonging to the "bumpy" class – that gets classified as a mix of "smooth" and "rough" terrain.

Figure 6.5 depicts this assessment. Items (III) and (IV) in the figure depict the results for a single scan. Item (V) is the set of voxels that has thus far already been tagged with the most frequent ground truth label. Item (VI) is the semantic map produced by SLAMVDB. Also visible in this last section are the LiDAR points that have not been visually observed (in grey). No semantic assignment is possible for these using image segmentation, so SLAMVDB does not store them in the semantic voxel key-value store. They

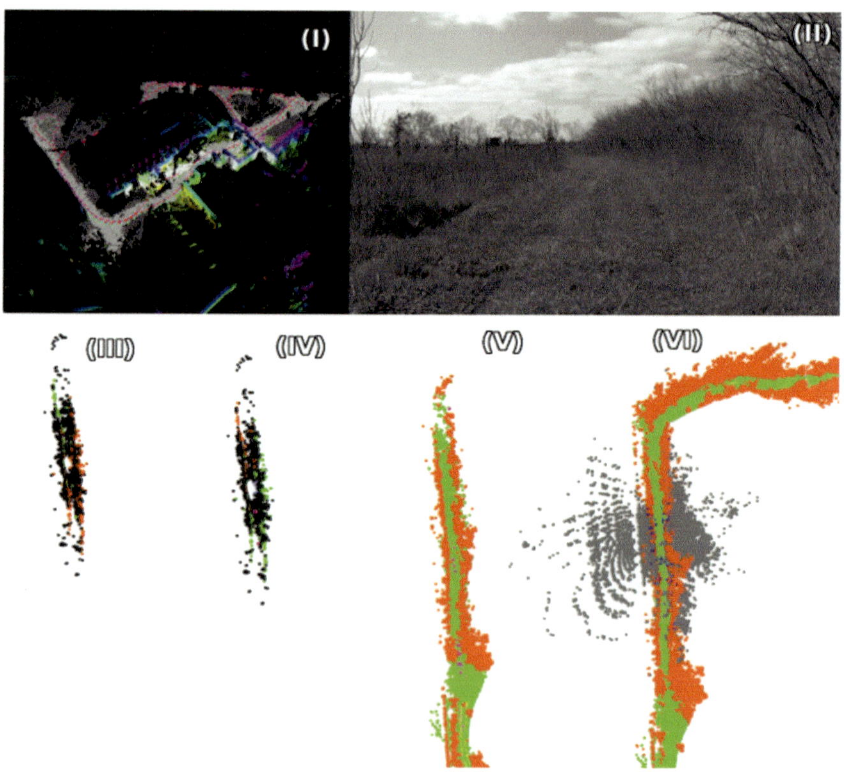

Figure 6.5 Terrain segmentation tests.

do nevertheless contribute to the octree occupancy grid map. Item (I) is a screen capture of SLAMVDB's semantic output on a different data set – the *courtyard_no_gt* track in EDI-SLAM.

6.4 Conclusions

SLAMVDB, the system described in this paper, is a continuation of earlier research in *Vectree*, and successfully demonstrates that the same fundamental approach – storing latent space embeddings in voxel cells and performing search in voxel-space – can be successfully adapted to an entirely different task. Achieving this, however, has (at least so far) taken some adaptations that depart somewhat from the idealized notion of a zero-shot generalizable classifier. Specifically, to address issues with different scaling for similarity distributions of the map semantics w.r.t. different query vectors, a query vector training procedure had to be introduced. This is still substantially less time- and resource-intensive than training a neural network model – requiring only that a handful of vectors be adjusted, and usable with a small data set of labelled images.

Qualitatively, the system appears quite capable of distinguishing between most obstacles and flat, passable terrain, though substantial room for improvement remains. An obvious direction for future work is the integration of newer, more capable image embedding model architectures, such as YOLOE [26]. Other directions already being actively pursued are deployment on real-world UGV platforms for testing in the field, integration of data from multiple UAV, UGV agents, and integration into 3-dimensional scanning software solutions, with one study underway in the space of monitoring and surveying of construction sites.

Acknowledgments

This research was partially supported by: "EdgeAI "Edge AI Technologies for Optimised Performance Embedded Processing", CHIPS JU grant agreement No 10109730".

References

[1] M. Ryan, 'Labour and skills shortages in the agro-food sector', Organisation for Economic Co-operation and Development (OECD), Paris, 2023.

[2] J. Arents and M. Greitans, 'Smart Industrial Robot Control Trends, Challenges and Opportunities within Manufacturing', 2022.

[3] R. Keith and H. M. La, 'Review of Autonomous Mobile Robots for the Warehouse Environment', ArXiv, vol. abs/2406.08333, 2024.

[4] L. F. P. Oliveira, A. P. Moreira, and M. F. Silva, 'Advances in agriculture robotics: A state-of-the-art review and challenges ahead', Robotics, vol. 10, no. 2, p. 52, 2021.

[5] P. Racinskis, J. Ārents, and M. Greitans, 'Constructing Maps for Autonomous Robotics: An Introductory Conceptual Overview', Electronics, 2023.

[6] J. McCormac, A. Handa, A. Davison, and S. Leutenegger, 'SemanticFusion: Dense 3D semantic mapping with convolutional neural networks', in 2017 IEEE International Conference on Robotics and Automation (ICRA), 2017, pp. 4628–4635.

[7] A. Radford et al., 'Learning Transferable Visual Models From Natural Language Supervision', in International Conference on Machine Learning, 2021.

[8] B. Li, K. Q. Weinberger, S. J. Belongie, V. Koltun, and R. Ranftl, 'Language-driven Semantic Segmentation', ArXiv, vol. abs/2201.03546, 2022.

[9] K. M. Jatavallabhula et al., 'ConceptFusion: Open-set Multimodal 3D Mapping', ArXiv, vol. abs/2302.07241, 2023.

[10] N. Ravi et al., 'SAM 2: Segment Anything in Images and Videos', ArXiv, vol. abs/2408.00714, 2024.

[11] K. Mazur, E. Sucar, and A. J. Davison, 'Feature-Realistic Neural Fusion for Real-Time, Open Set Scene Understanding', ArXiv, vol. abs/2210.03043, 2022.

[12] P. Racinskis, O. Vismanis, T. E. Zinars, J. Arents, and M. Greitans, 'Towards Open-Set NLP-Based Multi-Level Planning for Robotic Tasks', Applied Sciences, vol. 14, no. 22, p. 10717, 2024.

[13] A. Hornung, K. M. Wurm, M. Bennewitz, C. Stachniss, and W. Burgard, 'OctoMap: an efficient probabilistic 3D mapping framework based on octrees', Autonomous Robots, vol. 34, pp. 189-206, 2013.

[14] P. Racinskis, 'SLAMVDB - the EDI SLAM Vector Data Base (prerelease version)'. [Online]. Available: https://github.com/edi-administrator/SLAMVDB [Accessed: 15-Oct-2025].

[15] T. Guan, D. Kothandaraman, R. Chandra, and D. Manocha, 'GANav: Group-wise Attention Network for Classifying Navigable Regions

in Unstructured Outdoor Environments', ArXiv, vol. abs/2103.04233, 2021.
[16] P. Racinskis, G. Krasnikovs, J. Arents, and M. Greitans, 'The EDI Multi-Modal Simultaneous Localization and Mapping Dataset (EDI-SLAM)', Data (2306-5729), vol. 10, no. 1, 2025.
[17] P. Jiang, P. R. Osteen, M. B. Wigness, and S. Saripalli, 'RELLIS-3D Dataset: Data, Benchmarks and Analysis', 2021 IEEE International Conference on Robotics and Automation (ICRA), pp. 1110-1116, 2020.
[18] S. Macenski, T. Foote, B. P. Gerkey, C. Lalancette, and W. Woodall, 'Robot Operating System 2: Design, architecture, and uses in the wild', Science Robotics, vol. 7, 2022.
[19] P. Racinskis, 'LSeg: trimmed down fork for use with EDI-SLAMVDB'. [Online]. Available: https://github.com/edi-administrator/langseg-public [Accessed: 15-Oct-2025].
[20] W. Xu, Y. Cai, D. He, J. Lin, and F. Zhang, 'FAST-LIO2: Fast Direct LiDAR-Inertial Odometry', IEEE Transactions on Robotics, vol. 38, no. 4, pp. 2053-2073, 2022.
[21] rsasaki0109, 'lidarslam_ros2'. [Online]. Available: https://github.com/rsasaki0109/lidarslam_ros2 [Accessed: 15-Oct-2025].
[22] G. Kim and A. Kim, 'Scan Context: Egocentric Spatial Descriptor for Place Recognition Within 3D Point Cloud Map', 2018 IEEE/RSJ International Conference on Intelligent Robots and Systems (IROS), pp. 4802-4809, 2018.
[23] Khronos Group, The OpenGL Specification, Version 4.6, July 2017. Available: https://www.khronos.org/registry/OpenGL/index_gl.php [Accessed: 05-Dec-2025]
[24] A. Paszke et al., "Automatic Differentiation in PyTorch," in Proc. NIPS Workshops, 2017. Available: https://openreview.net/pdf?id=BJJsrmfCZ [Accessed: 04-Dec-2025].
[25] M. Greitans et al. "RoLISe T4.1 Published materials". [Online]. Available: https://www.edi.lv/RoLISe_T4_1 [Accessed: 15-Oct-2025].
[26] A. Wang, L. Liu, H. Chen, Z. Lin, J. Han, and G. Ding, 'YOLOE: Real-Time Seeing Anything', arXiv [cs.CV]. 2025.

7

Investigating Target Class Influence on Neural Network Compressibility for Energy-Autonomous Avian Monitoring

Nina Brolich[1,2,3], Simon Geis[1], Maximilian Kasper[1], Alexander Barnhill[4], Axel Plinge[1], and Dominik Seuß[1,5]

[1]Fraunhofer Institute for Integrated Circuits IIS, Germany
[2]Fachhochschule Erfurt, Germany
[3]Universität Erfurt, Germany
[4]Friedrich-Alexander-Universität Erlangen-Nürnberg (FAU), Germany
[5]Center for Artificial Intelligence and Robotics (CAIRO), Technische Hochschule Würzburg-Schweinfurt, Germany

Abstract

Biodiversity loss poses a significant threat to humanity, making wildlife monitoring essential for assessing ecosystem health. Avian species are ideal subjects for this due to their popularity and the ease of identifying them through their distinctive songs. Traditional avian monitoring methods require manual counting and are therefore costly and inefficient. In passive acoustic monitoring, soundscapes are recorded over long periods of time. The recordings are analyzed to identify bird species afterwards. Machine learning methods have greatly expedited this process in a wide range of species and environments, however, existing solutions require complex models and substantial computational resources. Instead, we propose running machine learning models on inexpensive microcontrollers directly in the field. Due to the resulting hardware and energy constraints, efficient Artificial Intelligence (AI) architecture is required.

In this paper, we present our method for avian monitoring on microcontrollers. We trained and compressed models for various numbers of target

DOI: 10.1201/9788743815273-7

classes to assess the detection of multiple bird species on edge devices and evaluate the influence of the number of species on the compressibility of neural networks. Our results demonstrate significant compression rates with minimal performance loss. We also provide benchmarking results for different hardware platforms and evaluate the feasibility of deploying energy-autonomous devices.

Keywords: edge AI, biodiversity monitoring, energy-autonomous, energy benchmarking.

7.1 Introduction

Among today's global environmental crises, the ongoing loss of biodiversity stands out as especially severe: it ensures access to vital resources [1] and contributes to various environmental services such as climate regulation, control of pollution and soil erosion, as well as pollination of crops, while also holding intrinsic value for cultural identity [2]. Currently, biodiversity is declining at unprecedented rates, highlighting the need for conservation efforts [3].

In this context, biodiversity monitoring provides essential information for tracking environmental changes and plays an integral role in assessing population trajectories of different species [4]. Birds are particularly well suited for monitoring due to their frequent and distinctive vocalizations [5], their role as indicators of ecosystem health [6], and their popular appeal [7].

Avian monitoring has been done mainly through point counts [8], where the goal is to record all birds seen or heard within a given time period, with the observer being stationary [9]. However, point counts are highly susceptible to external circumstances, such as weather conditions, dependent on human expertise [10], and their scalability is limited by logistic and financial constraints [11].

In recent years, Autonomous Recording Units (ARUs) have emerged as a cost-effective alternative to point counts, allowing long-term sound collection (Passive Acoustic Monitoring (PAM)) with minimal disturbance, broader spatial and temporal coverage, and permanent recordings for re-analysis [12]. However, analyzing these large datasets is challenging [13]: manual methods require reducing the number of recordings or species (e.g. [14]), while automatic approaches remain difficult. Deep Neural Networks (DNNs) show promise but face computational constraints ([15, 16]). *BirdNET* [11], capable of identifying thousands of species, is an example of a successful DNN-based solution and provides our method with a baseline for data collection and pre-processing. However, this approach is computationally expensive, requires internet access, and often exceeds the needs of localized surveys.

As an alternative, we propose species identification in real-time on an embedded, energy self-sustaining solution, shifting from retrospective analysis of ARU data to in-field processing, thereby reducing computational overhead while improving both energy and cost efficiency. The system is to be realized with edge Artificial Intelligence (AI) using a Microcontroller Unit (MCU), which introduces resource constraints such as limited memory, low processing capacity, and lack of parallelism [17]. To operate effectively under these constraints, deployment on edge devices like MCUs requires compact models, achieved either through lightweight network design or compression, to accommodate hardware constraints while preserving performance.

To assess the feasibility of avian monitoring on the edge and to examine target class influence on compressibility, we trained and compressed models for various numbers of avian target classes, benchmarked their energy consumption and latency on an *ARM Cortex-M4*, an *ARM Cortex-M7*, and a *Raspberry Pi 4*, and provided an estimate for the required battery capacity for real-life deployment. In the following, we describe our methodology, present and discuss the results, and conclude with an outlook on future work.

7.2 Methodology

An overview of our methodology is provided in Figure 7.1. The dataset was primarily compiled from *Xeno-Canto*, an open database of user-submitted bird recordings, resulting in a large but heterogeneous collection in both quality and duration. 500 species were selected based on the availability of sufficient samples, with preference first given to German, then European and finally global species. German species and data were prioritized to match the intended deployment region and to ensure data representativeness. For each species, 250 recordings were randomly chosen. In addition, the *ESC-50* [18] dataset was used to form a single non-avian class by merging 49 environmental sound categories (excluding bird calls). The data samples were pre-processed using the following steps:

1. Discarding audio samples shorter than 2 seconds, based on the average length of a bird vocalization of 1.94 seconds [19].
2. Removing silent sections, defined as amplitudes below 20 % of the maximum peak.

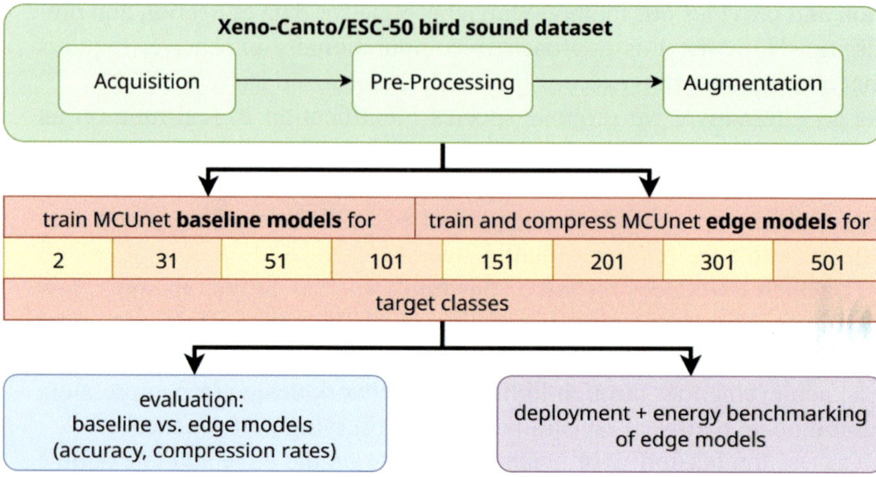

Figure 7.1 Methodology overview: workflow for dataset preparation, MCUNet model training, compression, and edge benchmarking

3. Sequentially splitting recordings into 2-second chunks with a maximum of 30 chunks per recording while discarding chunks without peaks (at least 7.5 % louder than surrounding points).
4. Normalizing each chunk so that its maximum absolute amplitude equals 1 to ensure consistency in amplitude throughout the dataset.
5. Converting the normalized chunks into mel-spectrograms, using a sample rate of 48 kHz, 64 mel bands, a Fast Fourier Transform (FFT) window size of 512 and a hop length of 384 [11]. The frequency was constrained to 150 Hz and 7.5 kHz.

This produced an easily attainable yet heterogeneous dataset, containing samples of varying quality with both avian and non-avian background noises. While not optimal for training, it realistically represents the acoustic challenges encountered in edge-deployed avian monitoring. On average, this resulted in 2452 chunks per bird species with a standard deviation of 874. The dataset was partitioned into training, validation, and test sets without data leakage.

To increase the diversity of our training data and to enhance the generalizability of our models, we applied the data augmentation pipeline outlined by [11] to our data. Four different augmentation methods were applied, as illustrated in Figure 7.2:

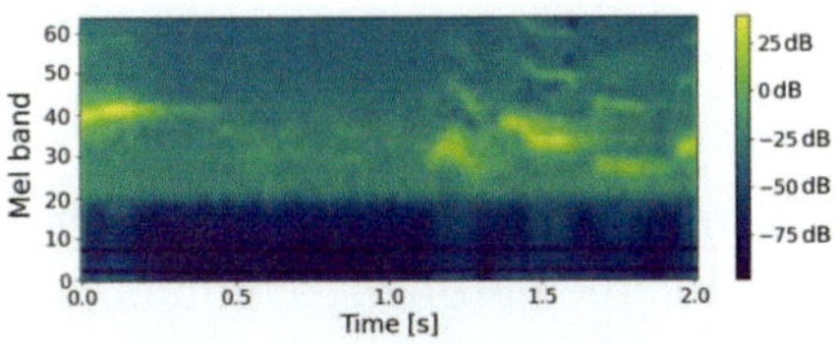

(a) Original input mel-spectrogram

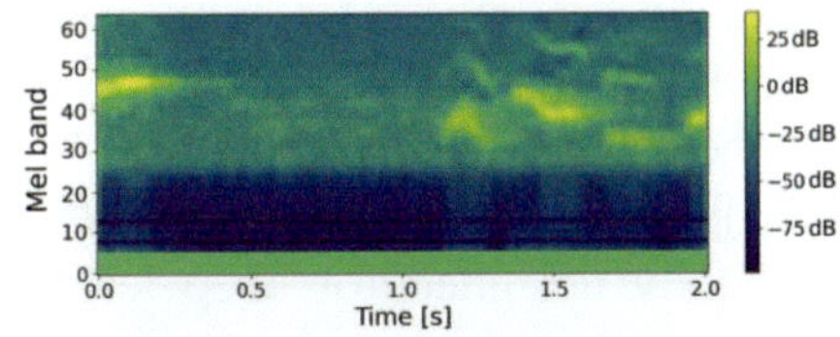

(b) Vertically shifted mel-spectrogram

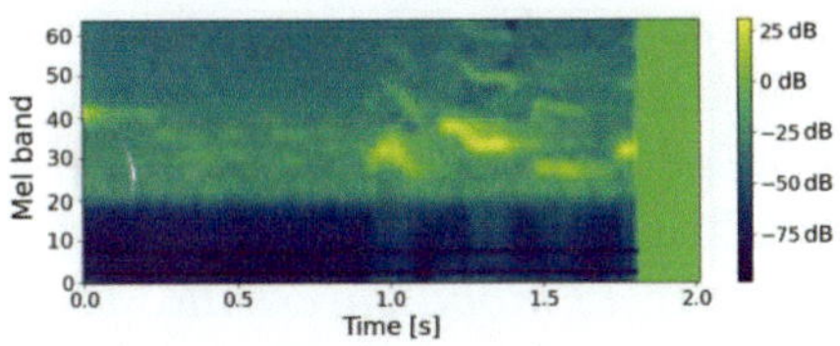

(c) Horizontally shifted mel-spectrogram

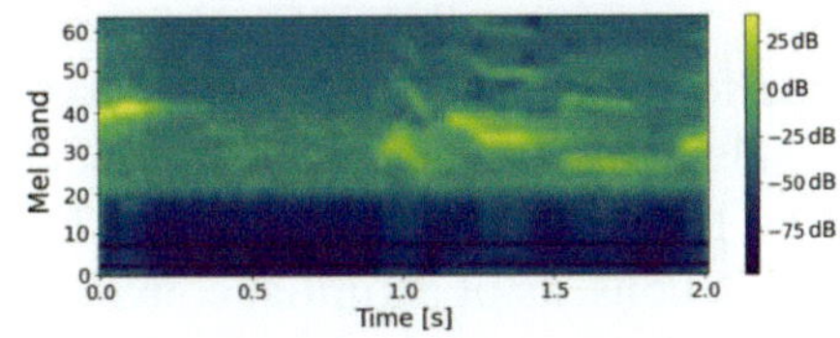

(d) Time-warped mel-spectrogram

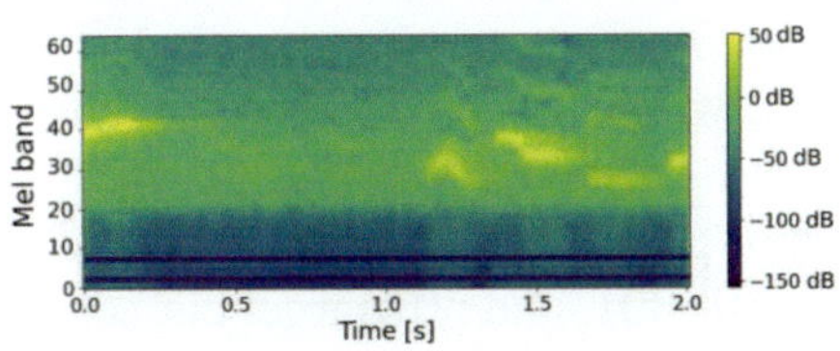

(e) Mel-spectrogram with added noise

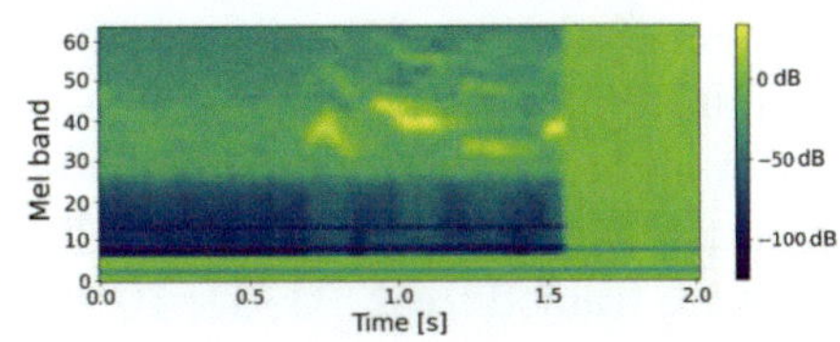

(f) Mel-spectrogram with all augmentations

Figure 7.2 Mel-spectrograms with different data augmentation methods applied

- **Random vertical shifts (frequency roll):** the mel-spectrogram was shifted up or down by a random factor between -5 % and 5 %, with the vacated area filled with zeros.
- **Random horizontal shifts (time roll):** the mel-spectrogram was shifted left or right by a random factor between -25 % and 25 %, with zeros filling the empty region.
- **Time warping:** the mel-spectrogram was deformed in time direction using the *SpecAugment* algorithm [20].
- **Addition of noise:** randomly selected noise chunks, previously discarded during preprocessing and verified to contain no bird calls, were added at a random intensity between 20 % and 80 %.

These augmentation methods all represent acoustic variations between training and test data like the changes in the vocal output of birds depending on environmental factors, high levels of ambient noise, and lack of training sample diversity [11]. Each augmentation was applied with a 50 % probability per chunk, in random order, with a maximum of three augmentations per chunk.

For the experiments, the *mcunet-in4* model from the *MCUNet* framework [21] was selected and adapted for bird sound classification. *MCUNet* is specifically designed for deep learning on microcontrollers, combining efficient neural architecture search (*TinyNAS*) with a memory-optimized inference engine (*TinyEngine*) to accommodate hardware constraints. Despite the existence of smaller *MCUNet* models, *mcunet-in4* was chosen for its better performance and to ensure support for higher numbers of target classes. Nevertheless, it still allows deployment on edge devices, which was also aided by further compression of the models. Its architecture, illustrated in Figure 7.3, consists of an initial convolutional layer, 17 *MobileInvertedResidualBlocks* [22], and a final linear layer. To accommodate mel-spectrogram inputs, the first layer was modified to accept a single input channel, while the output layer was adjusted to match the number of target classes (31, 51, 101, etc.), including a non-avian class. Pre-trained weights from ImageNet were loaded for all layers except the first and last.

In total, one uncompressed baseline model and 50 compressed edge models were trained for 2, 31, 51, 101, 151, 201, 301, and 501 target classes. For the model with only two target classes, the objective was to identify one bird species against 29 others, as well as non-bird data, i.e., it was trained with two classes, one consisting of data for the common blackbird (*turdus merula*), and the other one consisting of data of the 29 other most common

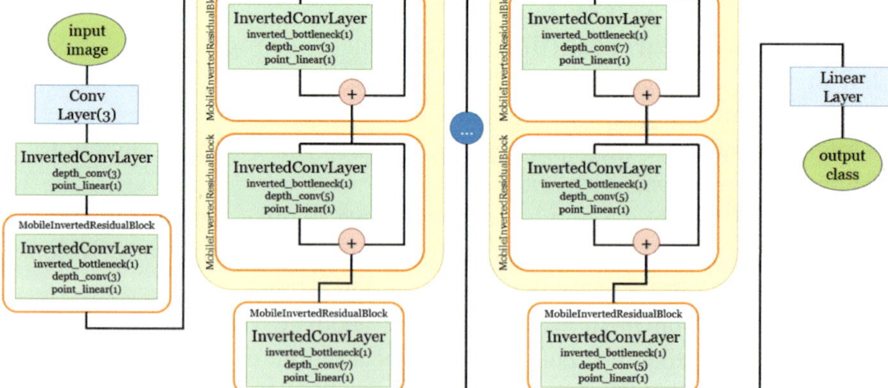

Figure 7.3 Structure and components of *MCUNet*.

bird species in Germany, as well as the environment data. From 31 target classes onward, the models were trained to identify 30 (or 50, 100, ...) bird species, as well as one non-event class.

The baseline models were trained with a set number of 30 training epochs. The training was conducted with a batch size of 32, using the Stochastic Gradient Descent (SGD) optimizer with a learning rate of 0.001 and a momentum of 0.9. Cross-entropy loss served as the loss function. The edge models were trained and compressed using an internal tool from *Fraunhofer IIS*. While the same general training configuration was utilized as for the baseline models, an interleaved pruning process with quantization at the end of the training process was employed. The tool implements the neural network compression approach from [23], performing multiple training and compression trials to maximize accuracy and minimize Read-Only Memory (ROM), Random-Access Memory (RAM), and Floating Point Operations (FLOPs) requirements. For each edge model, 50 trials were run, producing 50 compressed edge models, some of which are Pareto optimal across these objectives. A model is considered Pareto optimal if no other model performs better in one objective without performing worse in at least one other.

For the evaluation of the results, the performance of the edge models was first compared to the corresponding baseline models. A representative compressed model was selected from the 50 trials conducted for each target class number. To rank the trial t_x, the trade-off between accuracy (Eq. (7.1)) and the combined metrics of ROM, RAM, and FLOPs (Eq. (7.2)) was emphasized, as showcased in the ranking function r in Eq. (7.3).

$$\mathrm{acc}\left(t_x\right) = \frac{\mathrm{ACC}\left(t_x\right)}{\max\left\{\mathrm{ACC}\left(t_i\right) \mid i \in [0, 49]\right\}} \tag{7.1}$$

$$\mathrm{mem}\left(t_x\right) = \frac{1 - \frac{\mathrm{RAM}(t_x)}{\max\{RAM(t_i)\}} + 1 - \frac{\mathrm{ROM}(t_x)}{\max\{ROM(t_i)\}} + 1 - \frac{\mathrm{FLOPS}(t_x)}{\max\{\mathrm{FLOPS}(t_i)\}}}{3}, i \in [0, 49] \tag{7.2}$$

$$r\left(t_x\right) = \mathrm{mem}\left(t_x\right) + \mathrm{acc}\left(t_x\right) \tag{7.3}$$

To evaluate compressibility, we defined ROM, RAM, and FLOPs compression rates *cr*, shown in Eq. (7.4) for FLOPs, with the values for ROM and RAM computed analogously.

$$cr_{FLOPs}\left(FLOPs_{baseline}, FLOPs_{edge}\right) = 1 - \frac{FLOPs_{edge}}{FLOPs_{baseline}} \tag{7.4}$$

The overall compression rate of a model was defined as the mean of its FLOPs, ROM, and RAM compression rates, while the average overall compression rate was computed as the mean of these values across all Pareto-optimal trials for the target classes.

The *dnnruntime* framework [24] was used to convert the models to C code and create a deployable binary file. This binary file was then flashed onto *ARM Cortex-M4* and *ARM Cortex-M7* processors on a *SparkFun MicroMod ATP* carrier board to measure the latency and energy consumption of the models on the two microcontrollers. Additionally, we benchmarked the models on a *Raspberry Pi 4B* using the *onnxruntime* framework [25]. For an estimation of the feasibility of energy-autonomous deployment, we make the following assumptions:

1. The device is equipped with a battery which should be able to power the device for at least 48 hours without charging.
2. In addition, the device is equipped with a solar panel that should be able to fully charge the battery in 24 hours.
3. The device is in sleep mode per default and wakes up every 10 seconds. If the device recognizes sound from the microphone, inference is performed as long as sound is detected. Otherwise, the device returns to sleep for the next 10 seconds. We assume that the inference step is performed 10 % of the time.

Based on the power required during inference and idle, we can infer the required battery size of the device for running for 48 hours. The required size A of the solar cell can then be estimated by the average sun-radiation power density S_{rad} in Germany and by the required charging output P_{charge} as shown in Eq. (7.5). We assume a solar panel efficiency η_{solar} of 20 % and a charging efficiency η_{bat} of 90 %.

$$A = \frac{P_{charge}}{\eta_{solar} \cdot \eta_{solar} \cdot S_{rad}} \tag{7.5}$$

7.3 Results

To assess the general performance of the models, one baseline and one representative edge model per target class number were selected according to the rank defined in Eq. (7.3). Their validation accuracies are shown in Figure 7.4.

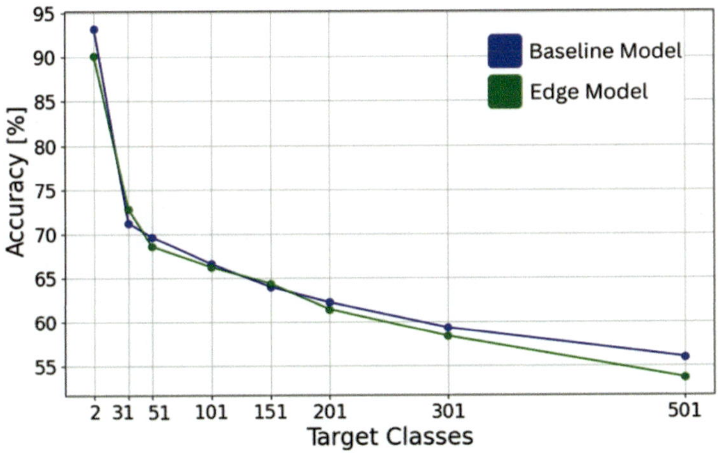

Figure 7.4 Validation accuracies for one baseline and one edge model per number of target classes.

Overall, validation accuracy declines as the number of target classes increases. While the models achieve high accuracy values for lower target class numbers, performance is more moderate with more target classes. Notably, there is almost no accuracy loss due to compression, as the accuracies of the baseline and edge models remain within a very similar range. To assess target class influence on compressibility, the average compression rate was computed across different target class numbers and is shown in Figure 7.5.

The results indicate a slight decline in compressibility with increasing class numbers. From 201 classes onward, however, this trend reverses, with compressibility improving for larger class counts. This result is unexpected, as a larger number of target classes would hypothetically require more complex architectures with higher memory and FLOPs demands, thereby reducing compressibility. While this trend is observed up to a certain point, it appears to reverse for larger class counts. Since the training and compression procedures are essentially a black box, a definitive explanation is difficult. Nonetheless, several factors may contribute: with more classes, models may exploit feature sharing more effectively, capturing overlapping features with fewer parameters [26]. Moreover, the inclusion of additional classes may encourage the learning of more generalized and compact representations, ultimately reducing resource requirements [27]. However, the observed decrease and subsequent increase in compressibility are subtle, with compression rates

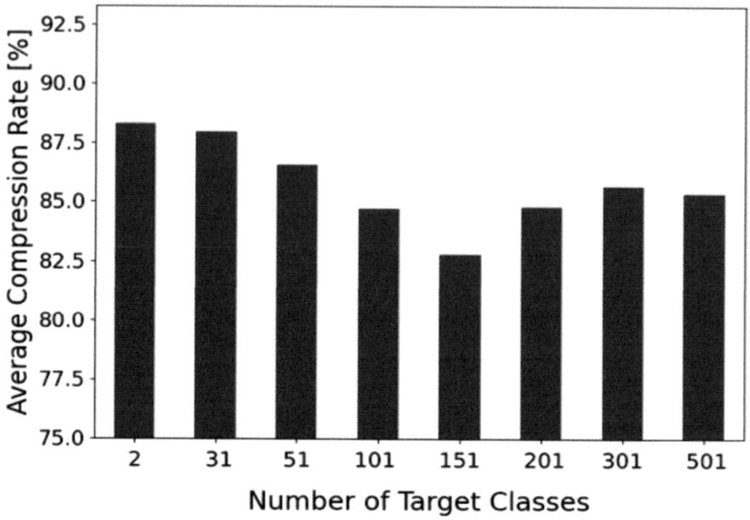

Figure 7.5 Average overall compression rate for all Pareto optimal trials per number of target classes regarding the reduction in RAM, ROM and FLOPs

ranging only between approximately 82 % and 88 % and thus may not reflect a clear or consistent trend.

To evaluate the feasibility of deploying the compressed models on an MCU, energy consumption and latency were measured for one model per number of target classes, selected according to the ranking in Eq. (7.3). The results are shown in Figure 7.6.

Overall, both latency and energy consumption increase with a growing number of target classes, though the improved compressibility of models with more than 151 classes is partially reflected in lower values for these metrics. Because both energy consumption and latency are largely determined by the number of FLOPs performed during inference, they are only indirectly related to compressibility. Since model selection accounted for FLOPs, ROM, and RAM, cases arise where a model with more FLOPs than its successor was chosen due to lower memory requirements. This explains, for example, why the 31-class model consumes more energy than the 51-class model. Finally, the benchmarking results indicate that the compressed models achieve energy and latency values suitable for real-world deployment on the *ARM Cortex-M7* and *Raspberry Pi 4*. In contrast, on the more resource-constrained *ARM Cortex-M4*, latency consistently exceeded the audio chunk length, making real-world deployment infeasible.

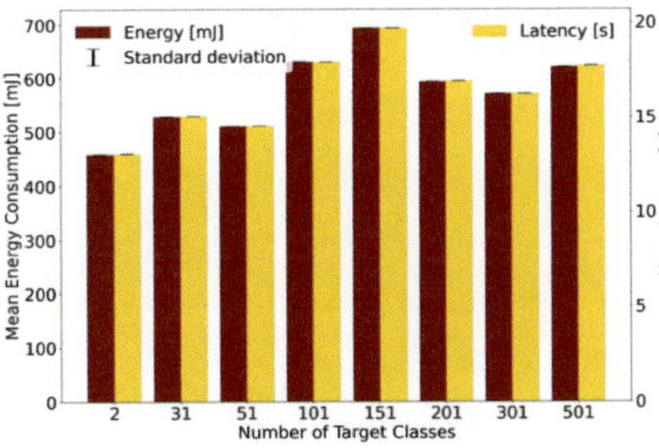

(a) *ARM Cortex M4*

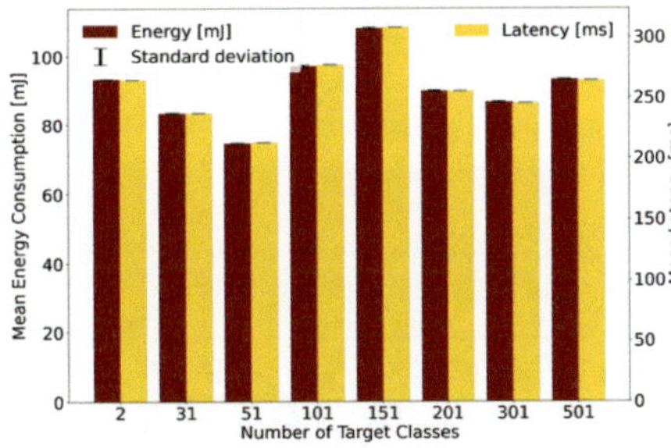

(b) *ARM Cortex M7*

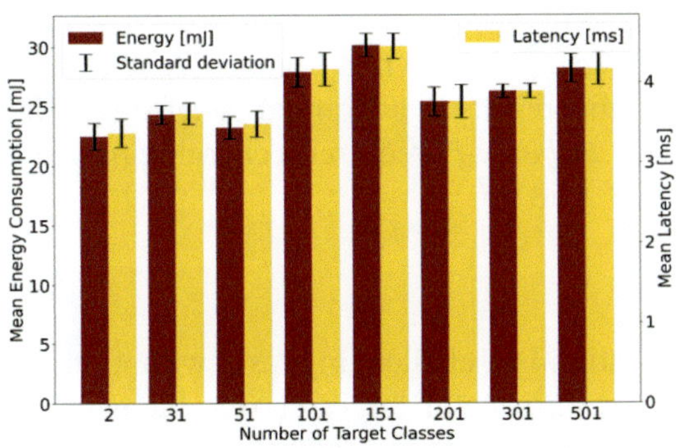

(c) *Raspberry Pi 4*

Figure 7.6 Average energy consumption and latency of one inference step of the best ranked model for each number of target classes

For the evaluation of energy-autonomous devices, we selected the model with 31 classes as an example. We measured an energy consumption of 83 mJ, a latency of 237 ms for the inference, and 55 mJ and 170 ms for the spectrogram generation on the *ARM Cortex M7*. This results in an average power of 339 mW. During sleep, we measured a power consumption of 116 mW, resulting in an average power consumption of 138.3 mW during the day. Overall, this leads to a required battery capacity of 6.6 Wh.

For the *Raspberry Pi 4*, we measured 24.3 mJ and 3.6 ms for the inference and 483 mJ and 80.9 ms for the mel-spectrogram generation, leading to an average power of 6.0 W. During idle, we measured a power consumption of 2.93 W, resulting in an average power of 3.24 W. In total, this would result in a required battery capacity of 155.5 Wh.

Based on these values, the required size of the solar panel can be calculated as described in Eq. (7.5). During December, the sun has the lowest

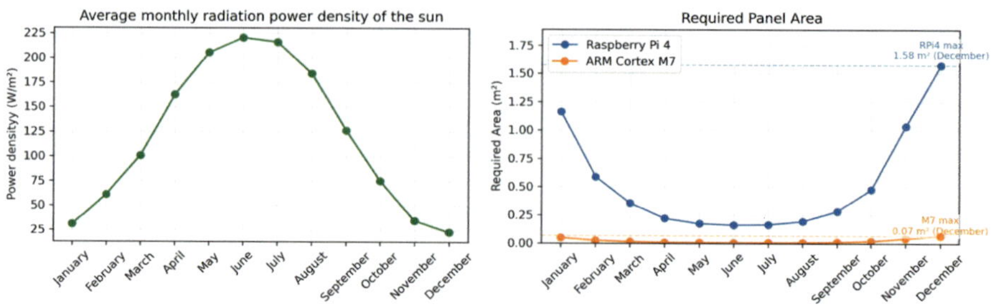

Figure 7.7 Average power density of the sun's radiation in Germany [28] (left) and the resulting area of the solar panel for each month (right).

power density of 22.8 Wm^{-2} as shown in Figure 7.7. With a required charging power of 275 mW, this results in a required panel area of 0.07 m^2 for the *ARM Cortex M7*. The *Raspberry Pi* requires a charging power of 6.48 W and therefore a panel size of 1.58 m^2.

7.4 Conclusion

Avian species identification is a challenging task, with model accuracy generally decreasing as the number of target classes increases. This is partly due to the heterogeneity of the dataset and the use of a single, relatively simple model architecture across all class numbers, which reflects realistic conditions for edge deployment and was necessary to facilitate comparability of compressibility across different target class numbers.

Our results demonstrate that high compression rates are achievable with minimal loss of accuracy across different numbers of target classes. Although compressibility initially decreased with increasing class numbers and later increased beyond 151 classes, the overall variation is minor and does not necessarily suggest a clear trend. Instead, it reflects the complex interplay between task complexity, model architecture, and learned representations. The evaluation of energy consumption and latency shows that real-world deployment is feasible on the *Raspberry Pi 4* and on the *ARM Cortex-M7*, but not on the more constrained *ARM Cortex-M4*, emphasizing the importance of selecting appropriate hardware for edge applications.

Overall, we showed that neural network compression is a practical and effective strategy for edge-based avian monitoring, even for large numbers of target classes. Finally, our results indicate that avian monitoring is feasible on energy-autonomous edge devices which could play a crucial role in wildlife monitoring and biodiversity conservation.

Future work could include curating a scientific dataset, exploring different species arrangements in the training data, comparing alternative compression frameworks, and investigating end-to-end audio models to reduce pre-processing overhead. Furthermore, real-life deployment will require additional functionalities, such as counting, data storage, and energy management, potentially combining edge AI with automated data collection technologies.

Acknowledgement

This work is part of the GreenICT@FMD project and is funded by the German Federal Ministry for Research, Technology and Space (BMFTR) (grant number 16ME0491K).

References

[1] V. Singh, S. Shukla, and A. Singh, "The principal factors responsible for biodiversity loss," *Open Journal of Plant Science*, vol. 6, no. 1, pp. 11–14, 2021. https://www.agriscigroup.us/articles/OJPS-6-126.php

[2] M. S. Habibullah, B. H. Din, S.-H. Tan, and H. Zahid, "Impact of climate change on biodiversity loss: global evidence," *Environmental Science and Pollution Research*, vol. 29, no. 1, pp. 1073–1086, 2022. https://doi.org/10.1007/s11356-021-15702-8

[3] R. E. Almond, M. Grooten, and T. Peterson, *Living Planet Report 2020—Bending the Curve of Biodiversity Loss*. World Wildlife Fund, 2020. https://pure.iiasa.ac.at/id/eprint/16870/1/ENGLISH-FULL.pdf

[4] D. Schmeller, K. Henle, A. Loyau, A. Besnard, and P.-Y. Henry, "Bird monitoring in Europe—A first overview of practices, motivations and aims," *Nature Conservation*, vol. 2, pp. 41–57, 2012. https://doi.org/10.3897/natureconservation.2.3644

[5] J. Shonfield and E. M. Bayne, "Autonomous recording units in avian ecological research: current use and future applications," *Avian Conservation & Ecology*, vol. 12, no. 1, 2017. https://doi.org/10.5751/ACE-00974-120114

[6] S. Mekonen, "Birds as biodiversity and environmental indicator," *Journal of Natural Sciences Research*, vol. 7, no. 21, 2017. https://www.iiste.org/Journals/index.php/JNSR/article/view/39931/41049

[7] H. Şekercioğlu, "Promoting community-based bird monitoring in the tropics: conservation, research, environmental education, capacity-building, and local incomes," *Biological Conservation*, vol. 151, no. 1, pp. 69–73, 2012. https://doi.org/10.1016/j.biocon.2011.10.024

[8] V. Cavarzere, G. P. Moraes, J. J. Roper, L. F. Silveira, and R. J. Donatelli, "Recommendations for monitoring avian populations with point counts: a case study in southeastern Brazil," *Papéis Avulsos de Zoologia*, vol. 53, pp. 439–449, 2013. https://doi.org/10.1590/S0031-104920130032 00001

[9] M. A. Etterson, G. J. Niemi, and N. P. Danz, "Estimating the effects of detection heterogeneity and overdispersion on trends estimated from avian point counts," *Ecological Applications*, vol. 19, no. 8, pp. 2049–2066, 2009. https://doi.org/10.1890/08-1317.1

[10] J. P. Brewster and T. R. Simons, "Testing the importance of auditory detections in avian point counts," *Journal of Field Ornithology*, vol. 80, no. 2, pp. 178–182, 2009. https://doi.org/10.1111/j.1557-9263.2009.0 0220.x

[11] S. Kahl, C. M. Wood, M. Eibl, and H. Klinck, "BirdNET: A deep learning solution for avian diversity monitoring," *Ecological Informatics*, vol. 61, p. 101236, 2021. https://doi.org/10.1016/j.ecoinf.2021.101236

[12] C. Pérez-Granados and J. Traba, "Estimating bird density using passive acoustic monitoring: a review of methods and suggestions for further research," *Ibis*, vol. 163, no. 3, pp. 765–783, 2021, https://doi.org/10.1 111/ibi.12944

[13] I. Molina-Mora, V. Ruíz-Gutiérrez, M. Vega-Hidalgo, and L. Sandoval, "The utility of passive acoustic monitoring for using birds as indicators of sustainable agricultural management practices," *Frontiers in Bird Science*, vol. 3, p. 1386759, 2024. https://doi.org/10.3389/fbirs.20 24.1386759

[14] B. J. Furnas, "Rapid and varied responses of songbirds to climate change in California coniferous forests," *Biological Conservation*, vol. 241, p. 108347, 2020. https://doi.org/10.1016/j.biocon.2019.108347

[15] I. Potamitis, S. Ntalampiras, O. Jahn, and K. Riede, "Automatic bird sound detection in long real-field recordings: applications and tools," *Applied Acoustics*, vol. 80, pp. 1–9, 2014. https://doi.org/10.1016/j.apac oust.2014.01.001

[16] E. Znidersic, M. Towsey, W. K. Roy, S. E. Darling, A. Truskinger, P. Roe, and D. M. Watson, "Using visualization and machine learning methods to monitor low-detectability species—The least bittern as a

case study," *Ecological Informatics*, vol. 55, p. 101014, 2020. https://doi.org/10.1016/j.ecoinf.2019.101014

[17] B. Sudharsan, J. G. Breslin, and M. I. Ali, "ML-MCU: A framework to train ML classifiers on MCU-based IoT edge devices," *IEEE Internet of Things Journal*, vol. 9, no. 16, pp. 15007–15017, 2021. https://doi.org/10.1109/JIOT.2021.3098166

[18] K. J. Piczak, "ESC: Dataset for environmental sound classification," in *Proceedings of the 23rd ACM International Conference on Multimedia*, 2015, pp. 1015–1018. https://doi.org/10.1145/2733373.2806390

[19] S. Kahl, "Identifying birds by sound: Large-scale acoustic event recognition for avian activity monitoring," Ph.D. dissertation, Chemnitz Univ. of Technology, 2019. https://nbn-resolving.org/urn:nbn:de:bsz:ch1-qucosa2-369869

[20] D. S. Park, W. Chan, Y. Zhang, C.-C. Chiu, B. Zoph, E. D. Cubuk, and Q. V. Le, "SpecAugment: A simple data augmentation method for automatic speech recognition," *arXiv preprint* arXiv:1904.08779, 2019. https://doi.org/10.48550/arXiv.1904.08779

[21] J. Lin, W.-M. Chen, Y. Lin, C. Gan, S. Han, *et al.*, "MCUNet: Tiny deep learning on IoT devices," *Advances in Neural Information Processing Systems*, vol. 33, pp. 11711–11722, 2020. https://proceedings.neurips.cc/paper_files/paper/2020/file/86c5167835 0f656dcc7f490a43946ee5-Paper.pdf

[22] M. Sandler, A. Howard, M. Zhu, A. Zhmoginov, and L.-C. Chen, "MobileNetV2: Inverted residuals and linear bottlenecks," in *Proc. IEEE Conf. Computer Vision and Pattern Recognition (CVPR)*, 2018, pp. 4510–4520. https://openaccess.thecvf.com/content_cvpr_2018/html/Sandler_MobileNetV2_Inverted_Residuals_CVPR_2018_paper.html

[23] M. Deutel, G. Kontes, C. Mutschler, and J. Teich, "Combining multi-objective Bayesian optimization with reinforcement learning for TinyML," *ACM Transactions on Evolutionary Learning*, vol. 5, no. 3, pp. 1–21, 2025. https://doi.org/10.1145/3715012

[24] M. Deutel, P. Woller, C. Mutschler, and J. Teich, "Energy-efficient deployment of deep learning applications on Cortex-M based microcontrollers using deep compression," in *MBMV 2023: 26th Workshop*, VDE, 2023, pp. 1–12. https://ieeexplore.ieee.org/document/10173060

[25] ONNX Runtime Developers, "ONNX runtime," 2021. https://onnxruntime.ai/

[26] G. Liu, H. Zeng, and D. K. Gifford, "Visualizing complex feature interactions and feature sharing in genomic deep neural networks," *BMC*

Bioinformatics, vol. 20, pp. 1–14, 2019. https://doi.org/10.1186/s12859-019-2957-4

[27] F. Zhu, X.-Y. Zhang, R.-Q. Wang, and C.-L. Liu, "Learning by seeing more classes," *IEEE Transactions on Pattern Analysis and Machine Intelligence*, vol. 45, no. 6, pp. 7477–7493, 2022. https://doi.org/10.1109/TPAMI.2022.3225117

[28] Deutscher Wetterdienst, "Global radiation in Germany 1991 - 2020," Available: https://www.dwd.de/EN/ourservices/solarenergy/maps_globalradiation_mvs.html.

8

When a model is not Enough: A Complementary AI Pipeline for Ultra-Safe PCBA Defect Detection

Alberto Faro, Francesco Cancelliere, Robin Faro, and Raffaele Mineo

Deepsensing s.r.l., Italy

Abstract

In safety-critical domains such as automotive and avionics, automated optical inspection (AOI) systems must meet extremely strict reliability thresholds, typically fewer than 10 false negatives per million inspected units, with high statistical confidence. This paper introduces a multi-stage AOI pipeline designed to meet such requirements under real-world imperfections, including imaging noise and process variability. The architecture uses a cascaded structure, where each stage is optimized to balance high recall with progressively improved precision. Through mathematical analysis and large-scale simulations, we show that single-stage AOI systems, even with recall artificially forced to 100%, fail to statistically guarantee zero defect escapes on large batches. This is due to variability in manufacturing conditions and model behaviour, which makes extremely high thresholds impractical without generating unacceptably high false positive rates. In contrast, our multi-stage system achieves the target of fewer than 10 defect escapes per million units with 90% statistical confidence, while maintaining acceptable production yield. The approach has been validated through simulation of a physical prototype with synchronized image acquisition and edge-based real-time processing. This architecture is scalable and applicable to increasingly

DOI: 10.1201/9788743815273-8

stringent industrial settings, offering a practical pathway to combining safety and efficiency in AI-powered visual inspection.

Keywords: edge AI, image recognition, PCBA AOI, Statistical Stability in Industrial Processes, Statistical Control on Large-Scale Production.

8.1 Introduction

Safety-critical industries such as automotive and avionics impose stringent quality requirements on electronic assemblies. In these domains, the cost of a missed defect is not merely financial: it can translate into operational failure, large-scale recalls and ultimately risks to human life. As a result, production systems are expected to achieve extremely low defect escape rates, commonly phrased as fewer than 10 false negatives per million inspected units ($\leq$10 ppm) with high statistical confidence. This requirement is widely recognized in the literature. For instance, *Wu et al.* discuss the challenges of training classifiers in highly imbalanced settings for rare-event detection [1], while *Guo et al.* explore cascaded architectures for anomaly detection without statistical guarantees [2].

When inspection targets printed circuit board assemblies (PCBA), this means that out of millions of boards shipped as "good", virtually none may contain latent defects. Traditional deep-learning-based Automated Optical Inspection (AOI) systems, even when they report high overall accuracy, struggle to meet these order-of-magnitude guarantees at scale.

This tension is rooted in a well-known precision-recall trade-off. Pushing recall toward unity (so that no defective unit is missed) generally requires lowering decision thresholds, which inflates false positives (good boards erroneously flagged as defective). In small laboratory datasets, the extra review load is tolerable; on a high-throughput line, however, every additional false positive triggers manual re-inspection, production slowdowns and work-in-progress (WIP) accumulation. The consequences are immediately visible in two key operational levers: capacity planning and *takt* time.

The **process capability index (*Cpk*)** measures how well a process produces outputs that fit within specification limits relative to its natural variability:

$$\mathrm{C}pk = \mathbf{min}[(\mathbf{USL} - -\mu)/\mathbf{3}\sigma, (\mu - \mathbf{LSL})/\mathbf{3}\sigma] \qquad (8.1)$$

where μ and σ are the process mean and standard deviation, [LSL, USL] are the lower and upper specification limits. In the context of AOI-driven quality, *Cpk* captures more than mechanical tolerances: it reflects how stable and predictable the *inspection + rework* process is. When AOI precision is low (i.e. many false positives), the inspection stage injects variability into the production flow: good boards are diverted to re-inspection queues, buffers grow (work in progress increases), operators are reassigned from value-adding tasks to sorting and confirmation, cycle time elongates and variability rises. All of this widens the effective standard deviation σ of the end-to-end process and reduces ***Cpk***. A lower ***Cpk*** means the process delivers fewer units within "on-time, in-spec" boundaries, which in turn results in missed ***takt*** and capacity loss.

In quantitative terms, automotive manufacturers generally require ***Cpk*** $\geq$ 1.67 ($\sim$99.97% process capability, $\sim$30 ppm defects), whereas avionics and aerospace production typically demands ***Cpk*** $\geq$ 2.0-2.33 ($\geq$ 99.999% accuracy, $\leq$ 3.4 ppm defects). Achieving such capability levels requires AOI systems whose effective consistently exceeds 99.995% under process variability, a target that single deep networks rarely sustain under real production variability.

Takt time defines the cadence the line must maintain to satisfy customer demand as follows:

Takt time = Available production time / Customer demand (8.2)

In a stable flow, inspection adds a small, predictable overhead that can be planned into the cycle time. But when AOI yields frequent false alarms, the effective cycle time becomes stochastic: units are repeatedly stopped, routed and re-tested. Two effects follow:

- **Direct delay:** each false positive consumes additional inspection time. On a line producing 60 boards per minute, even a 2% false-positive rate creates dozens of interruptions per hour, pushing average cycle time beyond *takt*
- **Propagation delay:** re-inspection queues cause blocking and starvation upstream and downstream. The line controller reacts conservatively, throttling feed rates to prevent overflows, which further increases cycle-time variance

As an illustrative example let us consider a line processing one million boards per year with a true defect rate of 0.1% (1.000 defective boards). A single-model AOI tuned to R = 0.999 and P = 0.990 yields roughly one false negative but about 9.990 false positives, that is nearly ten thousand unnecessary stops. If each re-inspection adds 45 seconds, the plant accrues more than 125 hours of non-value-added time, not counting the ripple effects on buffers and scheduling. ***Cpk*** drops because the variance of completion times increases and the line systematically misses ***takt*** during peaks or tight delivery windows. Even when **re-inspection is performed offline**, the accumulated rework time translates into substantial non-value-added effort and increased work-in-progress. The resulting increase in completion-time variability degrades process capability (**Cpk**), causing the line to miss ***takt time*** during production peaks or tight delivery windows.

The upshot is clear: **precision drives *Cpk*** and ***takt time***, while **recall drives safety**. A single classifier rarely sustains both simultaneously at the parts-per-million level. In practice, even classifiers reaching 97-98% accuracy are insufficient when scaled to millions of units. The residual 2-3% error rate, acceptable in consumer electronics, becomes catastrophic in safety-critical manufacturing.

Recent work has explored multi-stage or multi-view AOI pipelines using CNNs [3] or hybrid methods combining detection and filtering [4]. However, these approaches typically optimise either precision or recall, but not both in a statistically robust way. They also lack formal reasoning frameworks that guarantee ppm-level safety under production variability.

The central industrial question addressed in this paper is therefore: Can we raise recall to near unity (no defective PCBA escaping) without triggering unsustainable growth in false positives, re-inspections and ***takt*** time?

Section 2 deals with the problem formalization (single-model limits). In particular, it formalizes the problem by quantifying the theoretical limits of single-model AOI in ultra-safe regimes. In particular, it shows that under ppm-level constraints a single stage cannot simultaneously achieve near-zero False Negatives (FN) and very low False Positives (FP) at production scale. This analysis, grounded in the **Bernoulli/Poisson envelope** and one-sided **Clopper-Pearson bounds** (often referred to as **CP bounds**), lays the foundation for the multi-stage design that follows.

Section 3 introduces the main features of the three-stage pipeline and operational control**.** It presents a three-stage complementary pipeline that decouples safety from throughput: Stage 1 (T) is tuned for high recall and broad coverage of suspicious regions (tolerating some FP); Stage 2 (K1) emphasizes high precision, filtering false alarms and recovering good boards otherwise sent to rework; Stage 3 (K2) performs consistency checks on both "good" and "bad" flows, removing residual rare errors and providing traceable justifications. This decomposition preserves recall early while restoring precision downstream, stabilizing ***Cpk*** and keeping ***takt time*** within contractual limits. The section also addresses how to control variability in a more complex system, via image registration, illumination checks, inter-board similarity (IBS) and predictive maintenance on the vision/conveyor chain, so that process drift does not degrade the expected ***FN*** and ***FP*** agreed with the customer.

Section 4 points out the validation protocol and certification under worst-case assumptions. A detailed description of the validation and certification protocol is given by combining **Monte Carlo** simulation of realistic defect distributions with a **rare-event** reasoning framework inspired by, yet more elaborate than, the sequential filter approach used at **CERN for the Higgs boson discovery** [5]. Whereas CERN's triggers maximize precision at the expense of recall, our method balances both extremes: it minimizes defect escape (recall ≈ 1) while maintaining production-flow stability (precision ≈ 0.98), keeping ***Cpk*** high even under statistical variability.

Let **DPPM** denotes the number of defective units per one million produced units, this section also specifies what can be certified. We report monthly and cumulative point-estimate DPPM for operational monitoring together with one-sided 95% Clopper-Pearson DPPM for certification. We further note that the monitoring and fallback logic, including FP trend analysis, Inter-Board Similarity (IBS), illumination and focus drift detection, safe profiles; golden set reaches and predictive maintenance, helps ensure that the control system operates against worst-case conditions that may still arise in a controlled environment, thereby keeping the process within the agreed false negatives and false positives limits.

Finally, Section 5 previews industrial integration in ***VisioEdgeAI***, a robotic inspection platform where the three-stage logic operates over virtual flows on a single conveyor. Defective candidates are physically removed by a robot arm for laboratory confirmation, while "good" boards continue unimpeded. This architecture preserves high recall, restores high precision, stabilizes ***Cpk*** and protects ***takt time***, aligning AI-powered AOI with the uncompromising reliability thresholds of automotive and avionics production.

Related Work and Novelty of Our Approach

Several studies have proposed improvements to AOI systems using convolutional neural networks (CNNs), transformers and hybrid visual models [6], with a strong focus on enhancing classification accuracy. Other works have explored cascaded CNN pipelines [7] or Bayesian post-classification filters [8] to reduce false positives. However, these approaches rarely address process-level KPIs such as *takt* time or capability indices (***Cpk***) and generally offer no statistical guarantees regarding ppm-level defect escapes under real-world production variability.

In contrast, the approach proposed in this paper differs fundamentally. We introduce a complementary, multi-stage inspection pipeline, not merely for boosting accuracy, but for formally guaranteeing less than 10 escaped defects per million ($\leq$ 10 ppm) with $\geq$ 90% confidence. Our design explicitly balances sensitivity and selectivity while preserving ***Cpk*** $\geq$ 1.67-2.33, integrating statistical reasoning, explainability and real-time deploy ability on edge AI platforms. To our knowledge, this is the first work to rigorously analyse and simulate these trade-offs under realistic AOI constraints.

8.2 Theoretical Limits of Single-Model AOI

In high-volume digital manufacturing (millions of PCBAs/year), even tiny error rates produce large absolute counts of misclassified units. We adopt the standard metrics:

- **Precision:** fraction of flagged boards that are truly defective
- **Recall:** fraction of truly defective boards that are found
- **True Positives (TP):** defective boards correctly flagged
- **False Positives (FP):** good boards incorrectly flagged (waste)
- **False Negatives (FN):** defective boards missed (dangerous) where:

where:

$$FN = (\mathbf{1} - -\mathbf{Recall})\mathbf{Ndefective}, FP = (\mathbf{1} - -\mathbf{Precison})\mathbf{N_{good}} \tag{8.3}$$

Because typically Ngood $>>$ **Ndefective** even minute deviations from perfect recall or precision amplify into thousands of errors.

8.2.1 Hypothetical Extreme Case (Proof by Contradiction)

This proof considers a hypothetical extreme case to effectively convey the point in an engineering context. Assume a single-model AOI achieves near-perfect Recall = 0.999 and Precision = 0.999. On a production line with 10^6 boards per year and a 0.1% defect rate:

- ***FN*** = (1 - 0.999) $\times$ 1’000 = 1 missed defect
- ***FP*** = (1 - 0.999) $\times$ 999.000 = 999 false alarms

Even under this near-ideal scenario, ≈ 1.000 total misclassifications occur per million boards. This contradiction shows that statistical amplification renders single-model perfection unattainable at scale.

8.2.2 Threshold Dependence and Trade-off

The precision-recall curve highlights an inherent trade-off. Lowering the classification threshold increases recall (fewer $\boldsymbol{FN}$) but reduces precision (more FP); raising it has the opposite effect. Figure 8.1 illustrates that no fixed threshold can simultaneously optimize both. This trade-off is not merely theoretical: in AOI systems, lowering thresholds results in excessive re-inspections, while raising them risks letting critical defects pass undetected. Such tension makes static, single-model AOI unsuitable for high-assurance manufacturing contexts.

8.2.3 ROC and Asymptotic Limit

The Receiver Operating Characteristic (ROC) curve further emphasizes this limitation. As the decision threshold is relaxed, true positive rate or recall ($\boldsymbol{TPR}$) increases at the cost of the false positive rate ($\boldsymbol{FPR}$). In the ROC curve shown in Figure 8.2, the log-scaled x-axis highlights that pushing recall toward 1 yields orders-of-magnitude increases in $\boldsymbol{FPR}$, illustrating

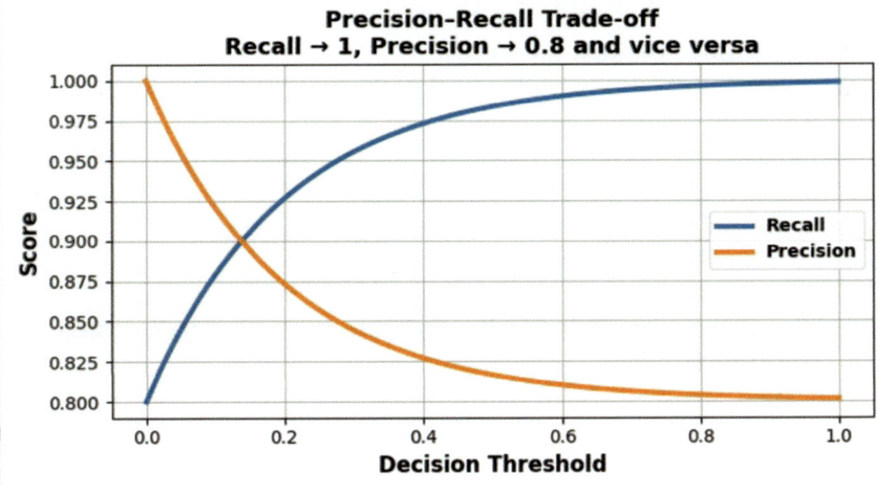

Figure 8.1 Precision and Recall Vs Decision Threshold

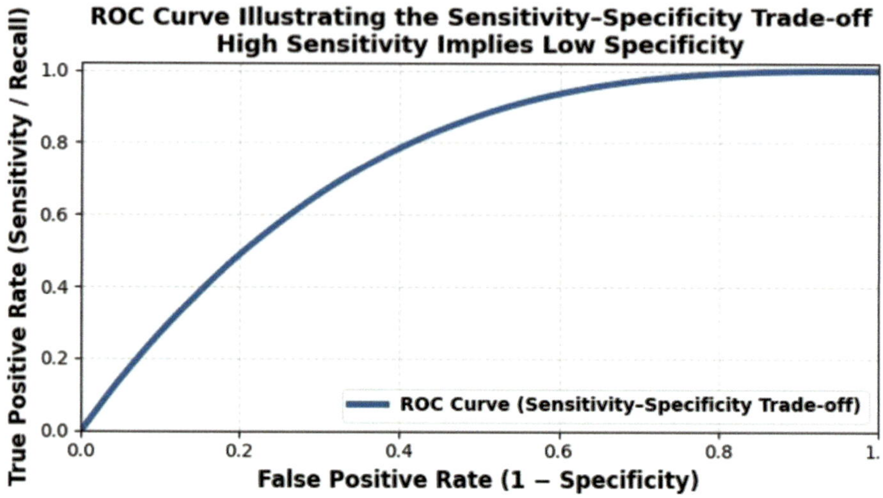

Figure 8.2 ROC curve (log-scaled ***FPR***).

the asymptotic barrier: attempting to saturate specificity (also referred to as selectivity) and sensitivity leads to a collapse in throughput rather than improved operational safety.

8.2.4 Statistical Impact and the Binomial Limit

8.2.4.1 Bernoulli/Poisson envelope

Even if recall is pushed arbitrarily close to 1, any non-zero per-defective escape probability implies a non-zero chance of at least one escape. Under a Bernoulli model (independent trials) [10], the probability of observing zero escapes decreases rapidly as the number of defectives tested grows; on large runs you will typically observe $x \geq 1$ escapes. Hence, "zero-escape" claims cannot be certified with finite evidence.

8.2.4.2 Worst-case confidence bound (Clopper-Pearson, exact; per-unit DPPM)

For certification we use distribution-free one-sided Clopper-Pearson bounds. If escapes are observed over N_total shipped/tested units, let $\boldsymbol{rU}$ be the 95% upper bound on the delivered escape rate, report:

$$\text{DPPM}_{95\%} = \boldsymbol{rU}\, 10^6 \tag{8.4}$$

Table 8.1 Clopper-Pearson bounds

Observed escapes	95% worst-case escapes (count)	DPPM95%
0	~3 .00	~ 3.00
1	~ 4.74	~ 4.74
2	~ 6.30	~ 6.30
3	~ 7.75	~ 7.75

Two practical cases (per-unit view):

- Zero events (x = 0) "rule of three": DPPM95% = $\mathbf{3} * 10^6$ / Ntotal , i.e. 3 **DPPM** when Ntotal = 10^6
- At least one event (x > 0) bound rises above the "3 DPPM" floor

For large Ntotal, the 95% worst-case counts (then scaled to DPPM at Ntotal =10^6) are reported in Table 8.1. Such values closely match the exact Clopper-Pearson upper bound for large Ntotal. For 95% confidence, multiply the counts (and DPPM) by ~1.5 (i.e. 3 -> 4.6).

Implications for certification *Bernoulli/Poisson* view explains why zero escapes are implausible at scale; the *Clopper-Pearson* bound provides the formal worst-case DPPM to report. As soon as x ≥1, the 95% bound exceeds the ~ 3 DPPM floor of the zero-event case.

8.2.5 Avionic Safety Constraint (3 ppm Limit)

In avionics and safety-critical electronics, the allowable number of escaped defects is typically below three per million units (3 ppm). Let p denote the per-defective residual escape probability, i.e., the probability that a truly defective unit is misclassified as acceptable. For N_defective = 1.000, the expected residual number E of residual escapes must satisfy:

$$E[FN\text{residual}] = N_{\text{defective}} \cdot p \leq 3 \Rightarrow p \leq 0.003 \qquad (8.5)$$

We may relate this bound to the classifier performance, by expressing:

$$\mathbf{p} = (\mathbf{1} - \mathbf{Precision})\epsilon \leq 0.003 \qquad (8.6)$$

where ϵ denotes the defect prevalence introduced above. Assuming ϵ = 0.01, the above constraint yelds a required **Precision ≥ 0.97.** Therefore, if Precision drops below 0.97, **even Recall = 1 is not enough** to meet safety standards. Moreover, boosting recall to 1 typically inflates ***FP*** to unsustainable levels. Figure 8.3 (Avionic Acceptance Zone) plots this safety threshold: only high-precision systems (> 0.97) can meet avionic requirements even

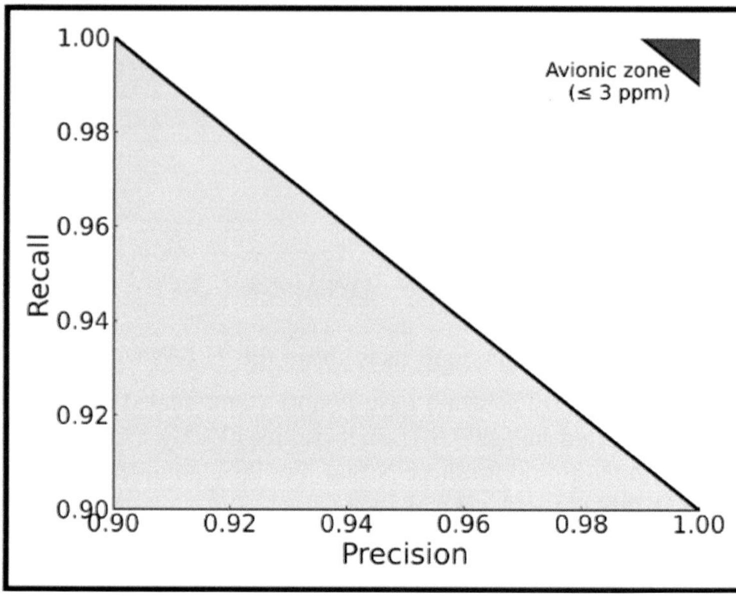

Figure 8.3 Avionic Acceptance Zone.

under perfect recall. This confirms that single-model AOI fails to deliver both safety and efficiency, especially in stringent sectors.

8.2.6 Empirical AOI Performance and Practical Limits

Real-world AOI systems, as reported in literature [3, 4], cluster around:

- Precision = 0.93-0.99
- Recall = 0.88-0.97

Recent surveys on these subjects, e.g., [9] show that even well-tuned single-stage AOIs cannot meet both perfect sensitivity and precision. Therefore, current AOI systems operate far from safety-optimal zones, validating the need for reflective multistage architectures like the one proposed in §3. This mainly depends on illumination, optics, surface complexity, and defect type.

8.2.7 Key Points

This section has shown that:

- Statistical leakage prevents hard guarantees of zero-defect escape

- Recall and precision are intrinsically in conflict
- For high-volume, safety-critical applications, single classifiers fail to meet both targets
- Achieving Recall ≈ 1 inflates false positives, blocking the line
- Conversely, tightening precision causes defect escapes, violating safety

Hence, a **modular, synergistic architecture with staged inspection logic** becomes necessary. Section 3 introduces such a design: a **three-stage AI pipeline** that balances sensitivity and selectivity across inspection layers.

8.3 Multi-stage Architecture and Statistical Stability in Industrial Processes

A robust way to detect rare defects at scale is to **stage** decisions: push **recall** high at the front gate (to protect safety), then **recover precision** downstream (to protect throughput). Unlike a one-way filter, the chain is **reflective**: later stages can correct early over-flags and recheck borderline "good" items.

8.3.1 AOI Architecture (T -> K1 -> K2)

In brief, the multi-stage AOI comprises three stages:

1. **T (front gate):** a high-recall filter that flags anything suspicious
2. **K1 (reject refinement):** re-analyses flagged items to recover good units and reduce false positives
3. **K2 (final gate):** re-checks the "good" stream to catch residual escapes (false negatives)

The flows among T, K1 and K2 are as follows:

- **From T** (front gate)
    - KO_T (predicted defective = ***TPT*** + ***FPT*** -> K1
    - OK_T (predicted good = ***TNT*** + ***FNT*** -> K2
- **At K1** (refines rejects from T)
    - OK_K1 (now predicted good = ***TNK1*** + ***FNK1*** -> K2
    - KO_K1 (still predicted defective = ***TPK1*** + ***FPK1*** -> scrap/repair (exits the system)
- **At K2** (final gate on the accepted stream)
    - KO_K2 (predicted defective = ***TPK2*** + ***FPK2*** -> scrap/repair
    - OK_K2 (predicted good = ***TNK2*** + ***FNK2*** -> ship to customer

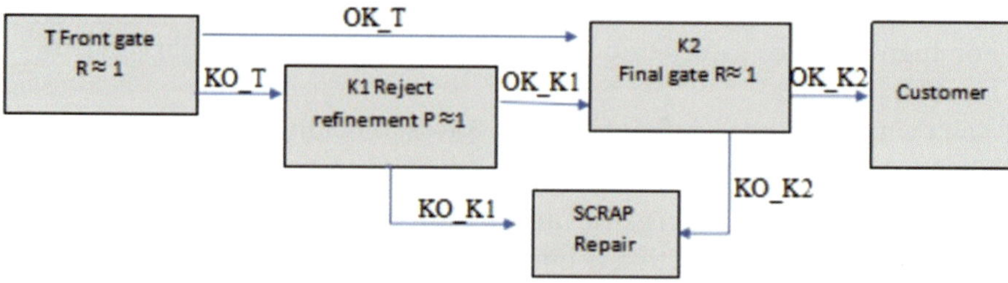

Figure 8.4 Block diagram of the three-stage AOI pipeline.

Table 8.2 Results (point estimates

Scenario	FP (good scrapped)	FN (escapes)	DPPM (= FN at $N = 10^{\circ}$)
T only	556	0	0
T +K1	50	100	100
T +K1 + K2	52(= 50 + 2)	1	1

Figure 8.4 shows the AOI pipeline pointing out that escapes are the ***FNK2*** contained in OK_K2, K1 recovers good units from KO_T stream (cuts ***FP***), while K2 catches residual defects that passed through T (reduces ***FN***).

8.3.2 Point-estimate simulation (10^6 boards; prevalence 0.5%)

Because point estimates reflect real on-line behaviour, they may be used to reveal the superiority of the three-stage AOI over T-only and alternative configurations. This is illustrated by the example below.

Assumptions per stage

- T: Recall = **1.00**, Precision = **0.90**
- K1: Recall = **0.98**, Precision = **0.99**
- K2: Recall = **0.99**, Precision = **0.98**
- Population: N = 10^6, prevalence = 0.5%,

where prevalence is defined as the number D of defective boards divided by the total production volume, => D = 5.000 and good boards G = 995.000

Computation sketch:

- T: ***TPT*** = 5.000; ***FNT*** = 0; ***FPT*** $\approx$ 556
- K1 (on KO_T): ***TPK1*** = 4.900; ***FNK1*** = 100; ***FPK1*** $\approx$ 50
- K2 (on OK_T + OK_K1): defectives-in = 100 $\Rightarrow$ ***FNK2*** = 1; ***FPK2*** $\approx$ 2

Result Interpretation

Table 8.2 is a deterministic operating estimate given nominal (***Recall, Precision***). For reporting/certification, it is suitable to use one-sided Clopper-Pearson bounds (see §2.4.2 and [11]):

- **T only** with x = 0 escapes cannot claim "0 DPPM"; the 95% floor is ∼ **3** DPPM at N = 10^6
- **T+K1** with x = 100 escapes implies a 95% upper bound > 100 DPPM (∼116 DPPM via Poisson/CP)
- **T+K1+K2** with x = 1 implies ≈ 4.74 DPPM95%

Table 8.2 shows that the multi-stage chain significantly reduces the false-reject burden. in our 1M/0.5% simulation ***FP*** drops by ∼10× versus T-only (556 -> 52 per million), while escapes fall to ∼1 DPPM by point estimate (T+K1+K2), instead of 100 DPPM with T+K1. Therefore, multi-stage AOI makes the operating risk tiny (∼1 DPPM by point estimate) and the certifiable risk acceptably low (∼4.7 DPPM). A single stage cannot substantiate a zero-escape claim (its 95% floor is ∼3 DPPM even if x = 0).

8.3.3 Keeping FN and FP under control (few, frequent actions)

Controlling ***FP*** and a few stable **process variables** is essential to keep the line statistically stable and to prevent hidden increases in ***FN***. Routine monitoring, paired with simple, pre-agreed actions, keeps day-to-day performance aligned with the one-sided 95% **Clopper-Pearson** bounds and prevents drift. Suggested actions (derived from the above):

- **Report two numbers (monthly + cumulative): Point DPPM** (what happened) and **CP-bounded DPPM95%** (what you can certify) is important for evaluating the status of the production line as will be discussed in the next section
- **Watch the FP trend:** simple per-shift FP chart with a stop-and-check rule (run a small golden set before changing thresholds)
- **Clear threshold split:** give **recall** to **T** (lower its threshold if FN risk rises) and **precision** to **K1/K2** (they filter the extra FP)
- **Weekly recall probe:** inject a few known-defect boards; if recall drops, lower threshold of T slightly and keep K2 strict until stable
- **Deterministic repeatability checks:** track **inter-board similarity (IBS)** and re-scan one unchanged board; if IBS falls or repeatability breaks, switch to a safe profile, re-run the golden board and correct illumination/focus/registration before resuming

These few controls keep the section actionable, tie directly to the formal bounds in §2 and avoid over-engineering.

8.4 Multi-stage AOI System and Statistical Control on Large-Scale Production

To meet ultra-low escape rates (automotive, avionics), we deploy a three-stage AOI that separates concerns: a high-recall front gate, a high-precision refinement on rejects and a final check on the "good" stream to catch residual escapes. All claims are reported with one-sided Clopper-Pearson bounds (see §2.4).

8.4.1 Annotation and classification-only strategy (no object detection)

In our implementation each component is pre-indexed from CAD/BOM and cropped into a fixed patch (one component per patch). This removes object detection and turns the task into pure classification ("conforming/non-conforming"). Benefits: higher accuracy (the model focuses on conformity), full traceability (ID/position known) and stability (fixed ROIs).

8.4.2 Three-stage pipeline and threshold policy

In details, the AOI used in our prototype *VisioEdgeAI* are as follows:

AOI-1 - Tiny-autoencoder Filter (High Recall)

A Tiny-autoencoder trained on golden boards detects any deviation from normality. Its threshold is adjusted to ensure **recall $\approx$ 1.0**, meaning that no defective component is missed, even at the cost of many false positives.

AOI-2 - KMeans Refiner (High Precision)

Only the flagged components are passed to an unsupervised method such as KMeans, which clusters them and isolates rare, subtle defect types. This stage acts as a **second filter**, drastically reducing the false positive rate by operating on a semantically aligned, low-dimensional space.

AOI-3 - Final Classifier (False Negative Recovery)

Despite the high recall of AOI-1, **residual false negatives** may still occur due to statistical effects or rare defect patterns. The third stage acts as a **fall back detector**, specifically optimized for **FN recovery** via a lightweight classifier trained on known defect prototypes. This final step ensures that even statistically rare errors are caught with high probability. Threshold policy is to allocate recall headroom to T and precision headroom to K1 (they filter the extra FP). Stress P increases at K1 whereas K2 reinforces recall on critical cases, improving robustness to statistic variation.

8.4.3 Analytical comparison with certification hooks (single vs. multi-stage)

Given the practical scope of our study, this section explains the engineering meaning of the three KPIs used in our analysis, i.e. Point, Bernoulli and Clopper-Pearson, so that operational performance and certification claims are interpreted consistently.

- Point (operational estimate): FP/FN expected on N units from the nominal (R, P) at each stage (i.e. "what happened" in production)
- Bernoulli (likelihood at scale): probability of at least one escape given per-defective escape PFN = 1 - R and the number of defectives i.e. "how likely an escape is" under current setting. At production scale, the probability of exceeding a tolerable number of escapes increases as the probability that a single defect escapes increases.
- Clopper-Pearson (certification bound): one-sided 95% upper bound on the delivered escape rate from the observed escapes x on N units; reported as DPPM95% = rU 10^6 i.e. "what you can safely claim"

The following example (same setting unless noted) may clarify how they are computed in practice. Assume N $=$ 10^6 boards, prevalence $=$ 0.5% defectives D $=$ 5.000, good G $=$ 995.000.

1) Point (operational) - T only

Take RT = 0.98 and PT = 0.90

- $FN = (1 - RT) * D = (1 - 0.98) * 5000 = 100$ DPPM
- $TP = RT$ D $= 0.98 * 5000 = 4900$
- $FP = TP\ (1 - PT)$ / D ≈ 544

2) Bernoulli (engineering likelihood of $\geq$1 escape)

Per defective escape PFN = 1 - R, with n defectives reaching the gate Probability of zero escapes: $(1 - PFN)^n$; hence $P(\geq 1) = 1 - (1 - PFN)^n$

if RT = 0,999 => PFN = 0,001, n = 5000 then $P(\geq 1) \approx$ 99,33%

if RT = 0,98 => PFN = 0,02, n = 5000 then $P(\geq 1) \approx$ 100 % i.e., virtually certain at this scale

3) Clopper-Pearson (certification, 95% upper bound)

Report DPPM 95%= ***rU*** 10^6, where ***rU*** is the CP 95% one-sided upper bound on the escape rate given observed escapes x over N. For N = 10^6

- x = 0 ⇒ ∼ 3.00 DPPM (zero-event "rule of three")
- x = 1 ⇒ ∼ 4.74 DPPM
- x = 2 ⇒ ∼ 116 DPPM (CP one-sided 95%)

These examples clearly demonstrate that an AOI using T-only could be enough for efficient certified production only if R is close to 1.

However, another example is suitable for illustrating that this is not completely true neither under this extreme condition. Indeed, the following Table 8.3, obtained using the same previour formulas, certifies that three stage AOI achieves similar ***FN*** but at a lower ***FP***. In this experiment we assume. N= 10^6 boards; prevalence 0.5% => 5.000 defectives, good G = 995.000 ,

Nominal stage metrics:

- T: ***R*** = 1, ***P*** = 0,90
- K1: ***R*** = 0,98, ***P*** = 0,99
- K2: ***R*** = 0,99, ***P*** = 0,98

Before discussing the results, we first clarify the table's columns and the computation sketches (Point and Bernoulli) used in this experiment; the Clopper–Pearson computation sketch follows the description provided above.

- **Point** = operational estimate from (***R, P***)
- **Bernoulli** (engineering view; [10]): probability of observing at least one escape at the stage that determines delivery (K1 if no K2; K2 if present), computed with n defectives reaching that stage and per-defective escape probability ***PFN***. It shows how likely an escape is in practice under the assumed operating point
- **Clopper-Pearson** (certification view; [11]): one-sided 95% upper bound on delivered DPPM from the observed count x of escapes (per §2.4.2): with x = 0 the bound is the familiar ∼3 DPPM floor at 10^6; with x = 1 it becomes ≈ 4.74 DPPM; with x = 100 it is ≈ 116 DPPM

Table 8.3 Results (point, Bernoulli, Clopper-Pearson)

Scenario	FP (point)	FN (point)	Point DPPM	Bernoulli Pr [≥ 1 escape]	CP-bounded DPPM (95%)
T only	556	0	0	0%	≈ 3.00
T + K1	50	100	100	≈ 100%	≈ 116
T + K1+ K2	2	1	1	≈ 63%	≈ 4.74

Computation sketch (Point)

- T: ***TPT*** = 5.000 ***FNT*** = 0 ***FPT*** $\approx$ 556
- K1: ***KOT TPT*** = 4.900 ***FNK1*** = 100 ***FPK1*** $\approx$ 50
- K2: ***OKT + OKK1*** defectives-in = 100 ***FNK2*** = 1 ***FPK2*** $\approx$ 2

Computation sketch (Bernoulli)

- T: 0% (since ***RT*** = 1)
- K1: n = 5.000, ***RT*** = 0,02 ***PFN*** = 1 - 0,98 ^{5000} => ***PFN*** $\approx$ 100 %
- K2: n = 100, ***RT*** = 0,01 ***PFN*** = 1 - 0,99 ^{100} => ***PFN*** $\approx$ 63 %

With that in mind, the table confirms that a T-only system cannot occupy the upper-right (high R, high P) corner at scale: raising ***PT*** lowers ***FP***, but any ***RT*** < 1 generates ***FN***; no single threshold achieves both tiny ***FN*** and tiny ***FP***. Adding K1 (emphasizing precision) recovers most ***FP***; adding K2 (emphasizing recall) collapses residual ***FN*** with negligible ***FP*** increase. Therefore, a multi-stage design is necessary, both operationally (point estimates and formally Clopper-Pearson bounds). As outlined in §3, it is also clear that reporting these two numbers monthly and cumulatively may give clear indication about maintenance. Point DPPM clarifies "what happened" and CP-bounded DPPM (95%) points out "what you can certify".

The monthly estimate captures drift; the cumulative bound tightens with volume (approximatively $3 * 10^6$ / Ncum) in the zero-event case), thus aligning operational monitoring with certification requirements and avoiding overclaims after quiet months.

Fixed per-component crops make the decision about conformity only; this tightens feature distributions and improves both ***P*** and ***R*** versus detection-based pipelines. We then stress stages by design: K1 toward precision on the reject stream P increases, K2 toward recall on the accepted stream ***R*** increases. The result is a stable operating point with FP $\ll$ T-only (i.e. 556 -> $\sim$52 per million) and escapes $\sim$ 1 DPPM by point estimate, paired with defensible CP bounds per §2.4.

8.5 Concluding remarks

The approach detailed in this paper has been adopted in the final design of the robotized conveyor AOI called *VisioEdgeAI*, both in the choice of a three-stage processing pipeline while boards pass under the camera and in the systematic reduction of variability sources that could jeopardize the targets.

Three-stage AOI is on the line. As each PCBA traverses the imaging station, the system executes: T (high-recall front gate), K1 (precision-oriented refinement of rejects) and K2 (recall-oriented final check on the accepted stream). This triplex design replaces earlier two-step error-recognition schemes and proved necessary to achieve low escapes with low false rejects at production scale. Two-step AOI remains a valid option for consumer-grade electronics lots where the risk and volume profile are less stringent [12]. Variability control by design has been taken into account. To minimize context variability:

- Detection-free, classification-only processing: components are pre-indexed from CAD/BOM; fixed crops (one component per patch) remove localization noise and stabilize the feature space
- Pose/placement tolerance: exact mechanical centering of the PCBA is not required; pre-processing alignment registers each image to a stable reference before inference
- Illumination stability: per-shift and daily checks track inter-board brightness drift; thresholds switch to a safe profile if limits are exceeded, followed by recalibration

Compute platforms are another aspect under study to achieve good time performance. Real-time execution is feasible on embedded GPU modules (i.e. NVIDIA Jetson Orin/TX2-class); FPGA-based pipelines are under evaluation to further reduce latency by exploiting data-parallel primitives in the image pipeline.

Algorithmic targets and tuning is under study. K1 and K2 are being characterized to deliver baseline $R \geq 0.98$ and $P \geq 0.98$ at nominal settings, enabling controlled "stress" toward P increasing at K1 or R increasing at K2 without materially penalizing the other metric. Early runs on small lots showed zero observed escapes, consistent with the design. Further classification algorithms are also under study to improve performance and assure a certain degree of statistical independence among them [13].

The dataset used in these preliminary runs was obtained from a production board. From images of this board, we extracted per-component image patches and generated PCBAs with representative defect conditions (e.g., missing components, rotations, burn marks, and overstressed or aged components). Approximately one hundred PCBAs of the same type were provided by HTS, with whom we are collaborating on the development of the VisioEdgeAI prototype. Each board contains around 40 components (resistors, capacitors, inductors, and integrated circuits).

The training dataset comprises 500 PCBA images derived from the best-quality image of the original HTS board. Each defective image includes four defective components, covering a range of defect types such as rotated components, missing components, burned components, imperfect solder joints, and incorrect components (i.e., components mounted in the wrong locations). Testing was conducted using defective images not included in the training set, as well as HTS boards on which defects were intentionally introduced.

Defect modeling and data augmentation will be used to evaluate long batches suitable for false-negative (FN) certification, which will follow the one-sided Clopper–Pearson framework discussed in §2 (i.e., zero observed events still imply a finite upper bound).

The paper stressed how maintenance and certification integration is also one important aim. To achieve both operational stability and certification credibility, we aim at integrating systematic/predictive maintenance into the imaging-conveyor chain and report both Point DPPM and 95% CP-bounded DPPM within an IATF QMS. Component maintenance, very relevant in this context (i.e. [14], reduces drift in illumination, focus and transport dynamics) primary drivers of FP/FN variance in digital inspection, while certification framing, i.e. [15], aligns internal control with customer-facing, audit-grade claims.

On the algorithmic side, patch-based anomaly detectors (i.e. *PatchCore*; *PaDiM*) and self-supervised backbones (i.e. *DINO-style ViTs*) will be considered to provide high-recall, high-precision building blocks; for imbalanced supervised stages, Focal Loss can further mitigate false decisions. Taken together, these elements, triplex AOI, detection-free classification, engineered variability control and certification-grade reporting, compose a coherent system that meets the operational and formal requirements set out in this work. The resulting architecture is explicitly designed to decouple safety from throughput, allowing recall to be pushed toward unity without inducing unsustainable false-positive rates, while preserving process capability and takt-time stability at production scale.

These conclusions are further supported by recent few-shot SMD inspection benchmarks, such as the PCB-SAID dataset [16], which empirically documents how rare and fine-grained defect distributions expose the practical limits of single-model AOI systems. In this sense, PCB-SAID provides complementary experimental evidence that aligns with the statistical and process-level arguments developed in this paper, reinforcing the need for multi-stage, reliability-oriented inspection pipelines in safety-critical electronics manufacturing.

Acknowledgements

This research was conducted as part of the EdgeAI "Edge AI Technologies for Optimised Performance Embedded Processing" project, which has received funding from Chips JU under grant agreement No 101097300. The Chips JU receives support from the European Union's Horizon Europe research and innovation program and Austria, Belgium, France, Greece, Italy, Latvia, Netherlands and Norway.

References

[1] Berthold Horn, Robot vision. Cambridge, Mass.: Mit Press; New York, 1986.

[2] J. Wu, J. M. Rehg, and M. Mullin, "Learning a Rare Event Detection Cascade by Direct Feature Selection," Advances in Neural Information Processing Systems, vol. 16, 2025, Accessed: Dec. 14, 2025. https://papers.neurips.cc/paper/2353-learning-a-rare-event-detection-cascade-by-direct-feature-selection

[3] X. Guo, J. W. Gichoya, S. Purkayastha, and I. Banerjee, "CVAD: A generic medical anomaly detector based on Cascade VAE," arXiv.org, 2021. https://arxiv.org/abs/2110.15811

[4] Masoud Jalayer, Reza Jalayer, Amin Kaboli, C. Orsenigo, and C. Vercellis, "Automatic Visual Inspection of Rare Defects: A Framework based on GP-WGAN and Enhanced Faster R-CNN," arXiv (Cornell University), Jan. 2021, https://doi.org/10.1109/iaict52856.2021.9532584.

[5] G. Grosso et al., "Triggerless data acquisition pipeline for Machine Learning based statistical anomaly detection," arXiv.org, 2023. https://arxiv.org/abs/2311.02038

[6] K.-J. Wang, H. Fan-Jiang, and Y.-X. Lee, "A multiple-stage defect detection model by convolutional neural network," Computers & Industrial Engineering, vol. 168, p. 108096, Jun. 2022, https://doi.org/10.1016/j.cie.2022.108096.

[7] R. Zhao, R. Yan, Z. Chen, K. Mao, P. Wang, and R. X. Gao, "Deep learning and its applications to machine health monitoring," Mechanical Systems and Signal Processing, vol. 115, pp. 213–237, Jan. 2019, https://doi.org/10.1016/j.ymssp.2018.05.050.

[8] D. Luo, Y. Cai, Z. Yang, Z. Zhang, Y. Zhou, and X. Bai, "Survey on industrial defect detection with deep learning," Zhongguo kexue, vol.

52, no. 6, pp. 1002–1002, Jun. 2022, https://doi.org/10.1360/ssi-2021-0336.

[9] C. Cantone, A. Faro, "An Overview of the Automated Optical Inspection (AOI) Edge AI Inference System Solutions," in Advancing Edge Artificial Intelligence - System Contexts, River Publishers, 2024, pp. 153-176

[10] J.K. Blitzstein and J. Hwang, Introduction to Probability, Second Edition. CRC Press, 2019.

[11] M. Thulin, "The cost of using exact confidence intervals for a binomial proportion," Electronic Journal of Statistics, vol. 8, no. 1, pp. 817–840, 2014, https://doi.org/10.1214/14-ejs909.

[12] R. Faro, A. Strano, F. Cancelliere, "Discovering and classifying digital and wooden industries products' defects at the edge by a yolo/resnet-based approach and beyond," European Conference on EDGE AI Technologies and Applications (EEAI 2024), Cagliari, 2024.

[13] K. Roth, Latha Pemula, J. Zepeda, Bernhard Schölkopf, T. Brox, and P. V. Gehler, "Towards Total Recall in Industrial Anomaly Detection," 2022 IEEE/CVF Conference on Computer Vision and Pattern Recognition (CVPR), Jun. 2022, https://doi.org/10.1109/cvpr52688.2022.01392.

[14] A. K. S. Jardine, D. Lin, and D. Banjevic, "A review on machinery diagnostics and prognostics implementing condition-based maintenance," Mechanical Systems and Signal Processing, vol. 20, no. 7, pp. 1483–1510, Oct. 2006, https://doi.org/10.1016/j.ymssp.2005.09.012.

[15] AS9100 (9100:2016) - Quality Management Systems - Requirements for Aviation, Space and Defense Organizations (IAQG/SAE).

[16] R. Mineo, A. Sorrenti, R. Faro, G. Mineo, F. Cancelliere, A. Faro, "PCB-SAID: A Low-Cost Camera-Based Dataset for Few-Shot SMD Assembly Inspection", 2025 IEEE/CVF International Conference on Computer Vision (ICCV), pp. 1351-1357, Oct 2025.

9

Towards Automated Liability Determination for Autonomous Vehicles in Road Accidents

Rohit Bohara[1], Omkar Joglekar[1], Mirko Ross[1], and Rob van Kranenburg[2]

[1]asvin GmbH, Germany
[2]Martel Innovate, Switzerland

Abstract

The rapid deployment of autonomous and semi-autonomous vehicles introduces fundamental challenges in liability assessment, as existing legal and regulatory frameworks are primarily designed for human drivers and do not directly apply to autonomous decision-making systems. Traditional investigation methods are manual, slow, subjective, and insufficient to capture the complex interactions among vehicles, infrastructure, and evolving mobility ecosystems. This work proposes an automated liability assessment framework that integrates edge intelligence, machine learning technology and graph theory to address the gaps and objectively and transparently assign responsibility in self-driving vehicle accident scenarios. Sensor data from vehicles, weather and roadside units is processed locally on embedded platforms using lightweight AI models optimized for real-time inference and low power consumption. The framework constructs event identity graphs to represent causal relationships among accident entities, factors, cross-referenced with insurance codes, traffic regulations, and ethical policies. The proposed framework integrates mechanisms that inherently support transparency, fairness, and explainability throughout the decision-making process. By rethinking liability assessment for autonomous vehicles, this approach reduces investigation delays, enhances transparency, and supports scalable, secure, and ethically aligned decision-making in the era of self-driving vehicles.

DOI: 10.1201/9788743815273-9

Keywords: Autonomous vehicle, Liability assessment, Incident Recording, Event Identity Graph.

9.1 Introduction

Road traffic injuries continue to represent one of the most critical global public health and socio-economic challenge of the modern era. Despite technological advancements in vehicle safety and the implementation of road safety policies, the absolute number of fatalities resulting from road crashes has continued to rise worldwide. According to [1], approximately 1.35 million people died in road traffic accidents in 2016, making road crashes a more significant cause of mortality than HIV/AIDS, tuberculosis, or diarrhoeal diseases. In Europe, 25,150 fatalities and approximately 135,000 serious injuries were recorded on roads in 2018 [2]. Beyond the humanitarian dimension, the economic burden of road crashes within the EU is estimated at €280 billion annually, equivalent to roughly 2% of total GDP, representing a significant drain on societal and economic resources. In 2022, approximately 891,831 reported road crashes resulted in 20,634 fatalities and 1,14,189 injured people in the EU member state as illustrated in Figure 9.1 [3].

The persistent burden of road traffic injuries underscores the need for transformative approaches to mobility safety. One of the most promising developments in this regard is the emergence of autonomous and semi-autonomous vehicle (AV) technologies, which leverage advanced sensors, machine learning algorithms, and real-time decision-making systems to

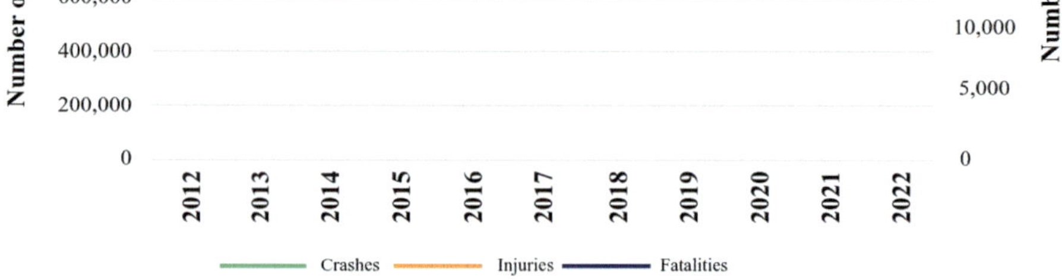

Figure 9.1 Number of road crashes, fatalities and injured people in the EU [3].

enhance driving performance and reduce human error. Human factors, such as distraction, fatigue, impaired judgment, reaction delay, alcohol, and drugs contribute to more than 90% traffic accidents [4–6], making them a primary target for intervention. AVs, by continuously monitoring the driving environment, predicting potential hazards, and executing precise control manoeuvres, have the potential to significantly mitigate collisions attributable to driver mistakes. Early studies and pilot deployments suggest that even partial automation can improve situational awareness, optimize vehicle spacing, and reduce collision severity, thereby lowering both fatalities and serious injuries [7–9].

Beyond improving road safety, AV technologies offer significant societal and economic benefits by transforming the way people and goods move. By optimizing traffic flow and enabling coordinated vehicle interactions, AVs can reduce congestion, shorten travel times, and increase overall productivity in urban and intercity transport networks. They also enhance mobility access for populations traditionally limited by age, disability, or the inability to obtain a driver's license, including the elderly, teenagers and individuals with certain medical conditions. By combining enhanced safety with improved accessibility and efficiency, AVs have the potential to create more inclusive, resilient, and productive transportation systems.

Despite their potential to improve safety and mobility, AVs introduce complex and unresolved challenges in liability and accountability assessment. Traditional legal and regulatory frameworks are designed for human drivers and do not directly apply to software-based decision-making. In accidents involving AVs, fault may arise from multiple sources, including vehicle manufacturers, software developers, fleet operators, infrastructure managers, or even end users, making causal attribution highly complex. Current approaches are manual, slow, subjective, and unable to capture the interactions among vehicles, infrastructure, and adaptive mobility systems. These challenges are compounded by privacy concerns and the proprietary nature of AV data, which can limit access to crucial evidence for liability determination.

The contribution of this work is a conceptual framework for automated liability assessment in accidents involving AVs. The framework integrates three strands of research that are rarely combined in this domain. First, it employs lightweight artificial intelligence models on embedded platforms to enable real-time, low-power processing of vehicle and roadside sensor data at the edge. Second, it employs graph theory to capture causal relationships of entities involved and connect them to insurance codes, traffic regulations, and ethical guidelines. Finally, the framework embeds fairness auditing to systematically evaluate and mitigate bias in liability outcomes, keeping transparency and explainability at the core. Together these elements form a structured, scalable, and ethically grounded approach to liability assessment that addresses both the technical limitations of traditional investigation methods for software-driven vehicles.

9.2 Background and Related Work

Autonomous vehicles represent a transformative advancement in modern transportation, combining sophisticated sensing, perception, and decision-making systems to operate with minimal or no human intervention. The Society of Automotive Engineers (SAE) classifies vehicle automation into six levels (0-5), starting from no automation (Level 0), driver assistance (Level 1), partial automation (Level 2), conditional automation (Level 3), high automation (Level 4) to full automation without human oversight (Level 5) [10].

Levels 0-2, associated with Advanced Driver Assistance Systems (ADAS), are categorized as driver support features in which the human driver retains full responsibility for monitoring the driving environment and maintaining vehicle control. In contrast, Levels 3–5, representing Automated Driving Systems (ADS), encompass automated driving features capable of performing the entire dynamic driving task under specific (Level 3–4) or all (Level 5) conditions. This classification framework underscores the technological evolution from assistive automation (using ADAS) to high and full automation (using ADS), reflecting a fundamental shift toward autonomous mobility [10, 11].

AV technologies rely on a combination of heterogeneous sensors, including light detection and ranging (LiDAR), cameras, ultrasonic sensors, Global Positioning System (GPS) etc, to perceive the vehicle's surrounding environment [12]. Artificial intelligence (AI) lies at the core of processing these data streams: sensor fusion techniques, powered by machine learning models, integrate multiple inputs to generate robust and accurate representations of the driving environment [13]. Perception and prediction systems, typically based on deep learning and computer vision algorithms, not only detect and classify objects such as vehicles, pedestrians, and traffic signals but also predict the behaviour and intent of surrounding agents. AI enables vehicles to anticipate the actions of other drivers, pedestrians, or cyclists, and supports motion planning algorithms that determine safe and efficient trajectories under diverse weather, lighting, and traffic conditions. AI empowers AVs to perceive their environment, predict events, plan actions, and control the vehicle. Vehicle-to-Everything (V2X) communication further enhances situational awareness by allowing vehicles to exchange information with other vehicles, roadside infrastructure, and cloud services. This connectivity supports coordinated manoeuvres, real-time traffic management, and early hazard detection, which are particularly critical in urban and high-density traffic environments.

Traditional approaches to road accident analysis rely primarily on post-incident investigation, including police reports, witness statements, and expert reconstruction of crash events [14, 15]. These standards say that all possibilities for clarifying the course of a traffic accident must be exploited, including use of digital evidence from vehicles, event data recorders, smartphones, etc. Also, when the police investigate an accident, they must reserve traces at the accident scene and secure evidence at the scene: witness data, spontaneous statements from involved parties, photographs of the scene, the positions of vehicles, etc [15]. Each report so submitted should include, at a minimum, the following information relating to the crash: location, date, time, identification of drivers, owners, pedestrians, passengers, motor vehicles, direction of travel each motor vehicle, a narrative description of the events and circumstances leading up to the time of the crash and immediately after the crash [14].

While these methods provide valuable insights, they are often time-consuming, subjective, and limited in capturing the complex interactions among vehicles, road infrastructure, environmental conditions, and human behaviour. Accident reconstruction frequently depends on manual interpretation of physical evidence, which may be incomplete or degraded, leading to delayed or inconsistent assessments. Moreover, conventional analyses are typically designed for scenarios involving human drivers, and are ill-suited for multi-agent, automated, and connected traffic environments.

Road traffic crash analysis literature can be broadly divided into pre-crash predictive models and post-crash severity models, both offering valuable insights for safety and liability assessment. Pre-crash models estimate the likelihood and potential severity of crashes using traffic, environmental, and driver-related factors. [16] showed that traffic congestion significantly influences crash severity, highlighting how human driver behaviour interacts with traffic conditions. It is demonstrated in [17] that interactions between vehicles affect severity outcomes through a copula-based model, emphasizing the interdependence of driver actions. [18] found that real-time weather conditions significantly impact freeway crash risk, and [19] successfully predicted motorcycle crash outcomes using multivariate Bayesian models. While these studies are effective for forecasting crash likelihood and risk exposure, they focus on human-driven scenarios and cannot fully account for autonomous system interventions, algorithmic decision-making, or control handovers, which are critical in AV environments. Thus, these pre-crash models cannot alone determine actual liability in post-crash scenarios involving autonomous or mixed-traffic vehicles.

Post-crash models provide evidence of actual crash dynamics, occupant injuries, and environmental impacts, essential for liability determination. [20] linked kinetic energy dissipation to injury severity, illustrating how crash physics predict harm. Vehicle and crash characteristics strongly influence injury outcomes in side-impact collisions [21], while [22] demonstrated that fixed roadside objects exacerbate injury severity. Correlation was established between the extent of vehicle damage and occupant injury in head-on crashes in [23]. While these models accurately capture outcomes in human-driven crashes, they do not account for AV-specific factors such as automated braking, emergency manoeuvres, or interaction with mixed human-autonomous traffic. Traditional post-crash severity models, such as [20] and [21], rely on detailed vehicle dynamics, occupant injury data, and environmental factors to reconstruct crashes and assess liability. In contrast, the model in [24] analyses statistical trends in crashes and AV disengagements, making it a macro-level post-crash analysis rather than a micro-level reconstruction of individual crash mechanics.

The transition to autonomous and semi-autonomous vehicles further complicates liability determination. In AV-related accidents, fault may arise from a combination of factors, including vehicle software, sensor performance, manufacturer design choices, operator intervention, or infrastructure deficiencies. Current regulatory and legal frameworks are largely unprepared to address these distributed sources of responsibility, creating ambiguity in fault attribution and insurance claims. In addition, the increasing volume of sensor and telematics data generated by AVs introduces both opportunities and challenges: while these datasets can provide high-resolution evidence of accident dynamics, they also raise privacy, security, and data integration issues. These limitations underscore the need for automated, data-driven frameworks that can systematically analyse accident events, incorporate causal reasoning, and provide transparent and equitable liability assessments in the context of autonomous mobility.

9.3 Event Identity Graph Framework

The paper proposes the Event Identity Graph Framework (EIGF) which provides an automated, transparent, and fairness-aware approach to liability assessment in autonomous vehicle accident scenarios. It integrates edge intelligence, machine learning, and causal graph modelling to process distributed sensor data securely and interpret complex interactions among vehicles, infrastructure, and environmental factors. The framework is designed to capture the multimodal and dynamic nature of AV ecosystems, where responsibility can no longer be attributed solely to human drivers but must be inferred from a network of interconnected agents and decision-making systems.

The EIGF operates through four primary steps: (i) event context data ingestion and pre-processing at edge; (ii) Event Identity Graph (EIG) construction using graph theory, which represents causal relationships among entities (vehicles, humans, objects, regulators, insurer, police etc.) and contextual factors (vehicle condition, telemetry, environment conditions, insurance codes, traffic rule) and (iii) liability assessment and report generation using graph theory and large language model (LLM) and (iv) fairness, transparency and ethicality assessment. The proposed EIGF models accident analysis and liability assessment as a structured flow of information from data acquisition to explainable decision outcomes. Figure 9.2 illustrates the overall architecture of the proposed framework, organized according to the classical **input–processing–output** paradigm. The **input layer** represents multimodal data sources, including sensor streams, contextual metadata, and regulatory texts. The **processing layer** captures causal reasoning and entity-relationship modelling within the event graph, while the **output layer** delivers structured liability assessments, interpretability reports, and fairness evaluations.

An Event Identity Graph is a directed graph, illustrated in Figure 9.3, representing events and the entities involved, functioning as an advanced, machine-readable equivalent of a traditional crash report. Unlike conventional reports that primarily describe incidents in narrative form, the EIG captures the full context of a crash, including the vehicles, drivers, sensors, environmental conditions, and any preceding or resulting events. The EIG not only facilitates the explanation of the crash by making explicit how different factors contributed to the incident but also provides a foundation for privacy-preserving, and ethically aligned systematic liability analysis, bridging the gap between technical performance and legal accountability in autonomous mobility. Moreover, its machine-interpretable format ensures interoperability

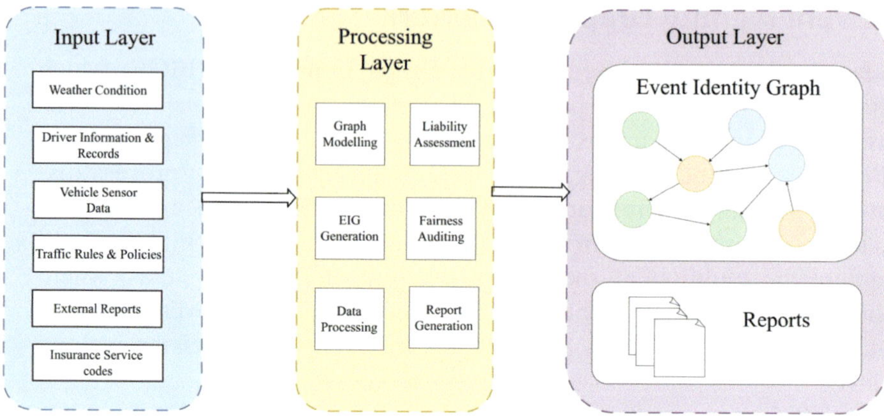

Figure 9.2 Event Identity Graph Framework Architecture.

with AI-based assessment tools, predictive analytics, and fairness auditing frameworks, making it an essential component in modern crash investigation and liability determination. The subsequent sub-sections elaborate on the fundamental processes and architectural elements that constitute the proposed framework.

9.3.1 Data Acquisition and Preprocessing

Accurate and reliable data acquisition forms the foundation of the EIGF, as liability assessment in AV accidents depends on the integrity and diversity of multimodal information. The input layer of the framework acquires and pre-process heterogeneous and distributed data streams originating from vehicles, infrastructure, and Roadside Units (RSUs) to create a unified representation of an event. The data includes onboard vehicle sensors data (e.g., LiDAR, camera, GPS), vehicle telemetry data (speed, braking force, steering angle, system state), human-related factors (driver profile, reaction time), traffic flow from RSUs. Supplementary data such as traffic signal states, environment, weather conditions, traffic laws, insurance codes, manufacturer guidelines and map-based infrastructure information are also integrated to provide a comprehensive situational view.

Each input is temporally stamped and semantically categorized to ensure accurate event reconstruction. The preprocessing pipeline includes data validation, temporal synchronization, across heterogeneous sensors, noise reduction and filtering for signal integrity, and feature extraction to derive semantically meaningful representations such as vehicle trajectories, relative

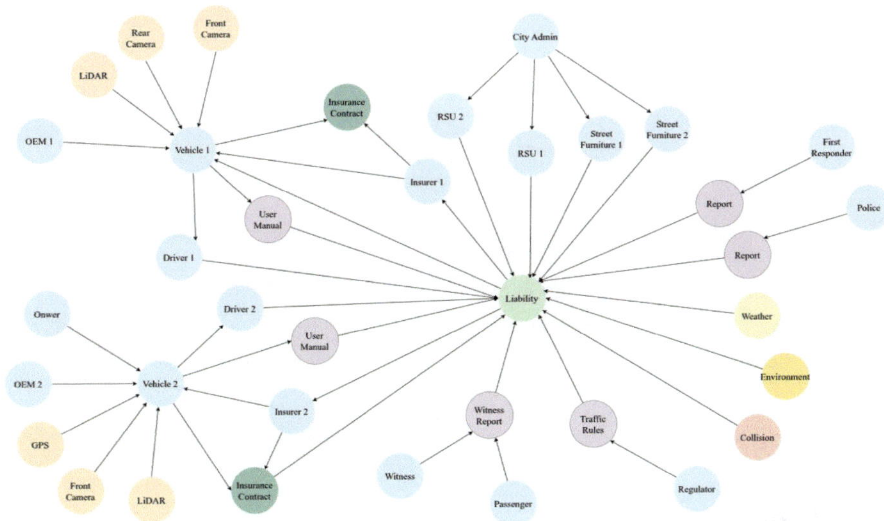

Figure 9.3 Entity Identity Graph.

distances and context tagging before being structured into a graph-compatible schema for downstream analysis. This multi-source approach ensures that both micro-level driving behaviours and macro-level environmental interactions are captured, enabling holistic and high-fidelity reconstruction of event with causal reasoning and supporting granular liability attribution.

9.3.2 Event Identity Graph Construction

An EIG serves as the core analytical representation within the proposed framework, translating complex accident scenarios into structured causal relationships. Each graph as shown in Figure 9.3, is composed of nodes representing entities such as vehicles, drivers, passenger, infrastructure components, environmental conditions, and regulators, and edges denoting the interactions and dependencies among them. These relationships capture both temporal (e.g., sequence of braking or acceleration events) and causal (e.g., vehicle A's manoeuvre causing vehicle B's reaction) connections, allowing for an interpretable reconstruction of the event chain. Machine readable JSON and XML formats of an EIG can be found at [25]. Data streams collected at the edge layer are abstracted into event descriptors and contextual attributes, which are then mapped to graph components through a combination of rule-based logic, temporal correlation, and causal discovery algorithms.

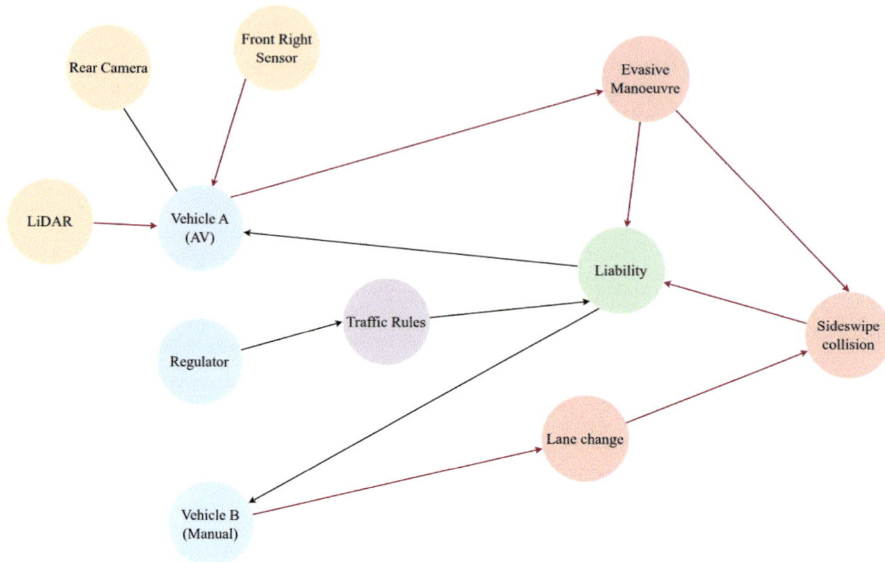

Figure 9.4 Entity Identity Graph Example Walkthrough.

Once constructed, the EIG becomes a dynamic knowledge graph capable of representing both micro-level interactions and macro-level contextual factors that influence accident outcomes. By encoding cause-effect relationships, the EIG provides a foundation for explainable reasoning, enabling the system to trace back the origin of each contributing factor and assess its relative significance. The graph structure also facilitates multi-source integration, linking sensor data with regulatory databases and insurance codes for comprehensive liability assessment. This approach ensures that the resulting interpretations are not only data-driven but also context-aware and legally grounded, bridging the technical and normative dimensions of AV accountability.

Let us explore this further with help of a simple example scenarios where a manually driven vehicle (Vehicle B) performs an unsignalled lane change into the path of an AV (Vehicle A). The AV detects the intrusion, initiates an evasive manoeuvre, and a minor sideswipe occurs. This would result in an event identity graph shown in Figure 9.4. The resulting EIG captures a minimal causal chain: Lane change (Vehicle B) $\rightarrow$ detection by Front Right Sensor and LiDAR (Vehicle A) $\rightarrow$ evasive manoeuvre (Vehicle A) $\rightarrow$ collision, with Vehicle B's rule-violating manoeuvre as the primary causal factor, and Vehicle A's evasive action as a mitigating response.

9.3.3 Liability Inference

The Liability Inference constitutes the reasoning core of the EIGF, transforming the structured causal information encoded in the EIG into transparent, legally grounded, and ethically defensible responsibility assessments. Each node and edge in the EIG is evaluated to determine the contribution of vehicles, pedestrians, infrastructure, and other entities to the sequence of events leading to an accident. Established principles of causal inference and graph-based influence propagation algorithms are employed to quantify influence, identify proximate, estimate causal impact and distal causes, and ensure that liability determinations are consistent with traffic regulations, and insurance policies. The EIGF also draws on principles from neuro-symbolic AI [28] and knowledge-graph reasoning [29], which demonstrate how structured causal representations can support explainable, rule-consistent inference in safety-critical domains.

To enhance interpretability and contextual understanding, the module incorporates an LLM-augmented reasoning layer. The LLM interprets graph-based relationships alongside unstructured textual data-such as regulation documents, motor vehicle laws, police reports, and witness statements, to generate human-readable explanations of liability assignments. It also cross-validates outcomes against traffic codes and regulatory guidelines, providing a semantic audit of decisions and highlighting potential inconsistencies or biases. Outputs include structured liability assessments, confidence scores, and traceable decision pathways, accompanied by natural-language reports for investigators, insurers, or regulatory authorities as depicted in Figure 9.2. By combining causal graph reasoning with LLM-augmented interpretive capabilities, EIGF delivers a scalable, transparent, and traceable methodology for automated liability assessment in autonomous vehicle ecosystems.

9.3.4 Fairness and Transparency, and Compliance Assessment

Ensuring fairness, transparency, and legal compliance is essential for any automated liability assessment system, particularly in the context of autonomous vehicles where decisions directly impact human safety, legal outcomes, and insurance claims. The proposed framework incorporates a dedicated auditing layer that evaluates both algorithmic bias and procedural fairness. It ensures that every decision or liability attribution is transparent, auditable, and ethically defensible.

Fairness is achieved by accompanying each inference or liability assignment by contextual metadata, such as the underlying data source, model confidence score, and reasoning chain derived from causal inference models. An EIG visually encodes these relationships, making it possible to trace how specific actions, sensor readings, or environmental factors contributed to the final liability outcome. Transparency is achieved through graph-based explainability and LLM-augmented natural-language reports, which provide human-interpretable rationales for each liability decision. Decision pathways, causal weights, and contributing factors are logged in traceable and auditable formats, enabling investigators, insurers, or regulatory authorities to verify the reasoning behind each outcome. Regulatory compliance is further reinforced by integrating traffic laws, insurance codes, and normative guidelines directly into the liability inference process.

9.4 Discussion

By representing incidents as structured causal graphs, the EIGF allows investigators and insurers to quickly identify contributing factors, assign responsibility, and generate interpretable reports. This structured approach reduces reliance on manual reconstruction and subjective judgment, thereby shortening investigation times and improving consistency in liability assessments.

Beyond operational efficiency, the EIGF enhances transparency and accountability in decision-making. Stakeholders, including vehicle manufacturers, regulatory agencies, and insurance companies, can trace the chain of events leading to a decision, fostering trust in automated systems.

From a technical perspective, the framework introduces several innovations. Edge intelligence allows real-time event detection on embedded platforms, while graph-based causal modelling captures complex interactions among vehicles, infrastructure, and environmental factors. The integration of LLM-augmented reasoning adds semantic understanding of unstructured data, generating interpretable explanations and validating outcomes against regulations. Collectively, these features provide a scalable, explainable, and robust mechanism for automated liability assessment.

9.4.1 Limitations and Challenges

Despite its conceptual strengths, the EIGF faces several limitations. Its effectiveness depends on high-quality, synchronized, and comprehensive data from vehicles, infrastructure, and environmental sensors. Gaps in sensor coverage, data loss, or inaccurate inputs could compromise graph construction and liability inference.

Another challenge lies in algorithmic misattribution. While causal inference and LLM reasoning provide structured analysis, errors in model predictions or incomplete knowledge could lead to incorrect liability assignments. Human oversight may still be required to validate and correct outcomes in complex or ambiguous cases.

One significant challenge in developing and evaluating liability assessment frameworks is the scarcity of publicly available, high-fidelity datasets on autonomous vehicle collisions. Because such accidents are relatively rare and often subject to proprietary, regulatory, or privacy constraints, researchers lack large-scale, multimodal datasets that capture the full sensor, telemetry, contextual, and legal data needed to validate causal and liability models. For instance, the California Department of Motor Vehicles maintains an Autonomous Vehicle Collision Reports database in which AV testing entities must report any collision involving property damage, bodily injury, or death within 10 days [26]. As of October 10, 2025, the DMV has received 875 Autonomous Vehicle Collision Reports, with older reports archived and available upon request.

Similarly, the National Highway Traffic Safety Administration (NHTSA) has issued a Standing General Order [27] requiring manufacturers and operators of vehicles equipped with ADS or Level 2 ADAS to report certain crashes involving these vehicles. This initiative aims to provide timely and transparent notification of real-world crashes associated with ADS and Level 2 ADAS technologies, enabling NHTSA to respond to crashes that raise safety concerns through further investigation and enforcement. While both DMV and NHTSA are valuable initiatives, the dataset remains limited in scope, coverage, and granularity, especially concerning raw sensor logs or internal system states. Without extensive annotated datasets, concept frameworks such as the Event Identity Graph Framework will face difficulty in rigorous empirical validation and benchmarking, potentially slowing progress toward real-world deployment.

The adoption of such systems also raises ethical, legal, and societal challenges. Trust in automated liability decisions may vary across stakeholders, and regulatory acceptance will depend on demonstrable accuracy, fairness, and transparency. Public perception and the willingness of insurers, regulators, and the legal system to rely on AI-driven assessments are critical factors.

9.4.2 Future Directions

Future research will focus on developing a functional prototype of the EIGF framework to demonstrate its practical feasibility. For edge computing platforms NVIDIA Jetson Nano and Raspberry Pi will be employed to host lightweight AI models for real-time event detection and local inference. Graph databases such as Neo4j will be used to model accident events and relationships among entities, supporting efficient traversal, causal reasoning, and graph analytics.

Additionally, LLM-based models such as LegalBERT or GBERT will be integrated to extract and interpret regulatory, traffic, and insurance-related textual information, enabling the framework to link unstructured legal and policy data to structured graph representations. Since such LLMs exceed the computational capabilities of edge devices, the LLM-augmented reasoning layer described earlier will be executed on a cloud or backend service. This allows the edge to remain lightweight and real-time while the cloud handles the heavier semantic reasoning tasks.

Ensuring fairness and transparency will continue to be a central objective. Toolkits such as AI Fairness 360 will be utilized to audit liability assessments, detect potential biases, and enforce fairness across sensitive attributes such as driver demographics, vehicle types, or geographic regions. Hybrid human–AI workflows will be developed to combine automated causal reasoning with expert oversight, enhancing reliability and trust.

9.5 Conclusion

This paper has proposed Event Identity Graph Framework for automated liability assessment in autonomous vehicle accident scenarios. The framework integrates causal graph modelling, edge intelligence concepts, and LLM-augmented reasoning to provide a structured, interpretable, and scalable approach for analysing complex interactions among vehicles, infrastructure, and environmental factors. It emphasizes the integration of traffic regulations, insurance policies, and safety guidelines, while incorporating fairness auditing and explainability mechanisms to ensure that liability assessments are socially and legally defensible. Future work will explore implementing the framework for multi-agent traffic networks, integrating regulatory, insurance, and urban planning considerations, and incorporating semantic analysis of legal and policy texts using models such as LegalBERT or GBERT.

Acknowledgements

This work has been supported by the EdgeAI-Trust "Decentralized Edge Intelligence: Advancing Trust, Safety, and Sustainability in Europe" project which has received funding from Chips Joint Undertaking (Chips JU) under grant agreement No 101139892. The Project website, https://www.edgeai-trust.eu/ provides more information.

References

[1] World Health Organization, "Global Status Report on Road Safety 2018," 2018 Geneva, Switzerland.
[2] European Commission, "EU Road Safety Policy Framework 2021–2030 – Next Steps Towards Vision Zero," 2019, Brussels, Belgium.
[3] H. Atasayar, M. Fleischer, M. Donabauer "Annual statistical report on road safety in the EU 2024," Feb 2024.
[4] A. Smiley and K. Brookhuis, "Alcohol, Drugs and Traffic Safety. Road Users and Traffic Safety," 1987.
[5] National Motor Vehicle Crash Causation Survey. National Highway Traffic Safety Administration, U.S. Department of Transportation.
[6] Bureau of Infrastructure, Transport and Regional Economics "Fatal Road crashes in Australia in the 1990s and 2000s: crash types and major factors," BITRE Canberra ACT.
[7] Mark Mario Morando, Long T. Truong, Hai L. Vu, "Investigating safety impacts of autonomous vehicles using traffic micro-simulation," Australasian Transport Research Forum 2017, Auckland, New Zealand
[8] P. S. Oruganti, E. Deosthale and C. L. Jimenez, "Assessing safe autonomous vehicle behavior via large scale traffic simulation," 2023 IEEE Intelligent Vehicles Symposium (IV), Anchorage, AK, USA, 2023.
[9] N. Novat, E. Kidando, B. Kutela, and A. E. Kitali, "A comparative study of collision types between automated and conventional vehicles using Bayesian probabilistic inferences," Journal of Safety Research, Feb. 2023.
[10] SAE International Recommended Practice, "Taxonomy and Definitions for Terms Related to Driving Automation Systems for On-Road Motor Vehicles," SAE Standard J3016_202104, Revised April 2021

[11] UNECE, GRVA-WS06-03 "Global Technical Regulation on Automated Driving System (ADS)," 6th GRVA Workshop on Automated Driving System (ADS), Geneva, Switzerland 2025.

[12] M. Martínez-Díaz and F. Soriguera, "Autonomous vehicles: theoretical and practical challenges," Transportation Research Procedia, 2018.

[13] A. E. Sallab, M. Abdou, E. Perot, and S. Yogamani, "Deep Reinforcement Learning framework for Autonomous Driving," ei, vol. 29, no. 19, pp. 70–76, Jan. 2017.

[14] National Highway Traffic Safety Administration, "Highway Safety Program Guideline No. 18: Motor Vehicle Crash Investigation and Incident Reporting" Washington, DC, 2017.

[15] Deutscher Verkehrssicherheitsrat (DVR), Standards zur Verkehrsunfallaufnahme, Vorstandsbeschluss vom 28.04.2025, May 2025, Berlin

[16] M. A. Quddus, C. Wang, and S. G. Ison, "Road Traffic Congestion and Crash Severity: Econometric Analysis Using Ordered Response Models," J. Transp. Eng., May 2010.

[17] T. A. Rana, S. Sikder, and A. R. Pinjari, "Copula-Based Method for Addressing Endogeneity in Models of Severity of Traffic Crash Injuries: Application to Two-Vehicle Crashes," Transportation Research Record, Jan. 2010.

[18] Q. Zeng, W. Hao, J. Lee, and F. Chen, "Investigating the Impacts of Real-Time Weather Conditions on Freeway Crash Severity: A Bayesian Spatial Analysis," IJERPH, Apr. 2020.

[19] W. Cheng, G. S. Gill, T. Sakrani, M. Dasu, and J. Zhou, "Predicting motorcycle crash injury severity using weather data and alternative Bayesian multivariate crash frequency models," Nov. 2017

[20] A. Sobhani, W. Young, D. Logan, and S. Bahrololoom, "A kinetic energy model of two-vehicle crash injury severity," Accident Analysis & Prevention, May 2011.

[21] C. M. Farmer, E. R. Braver, and E. L. Mitter, "Two-vehicle side impact crashes: The relationship of vehicle and crash characteristics to injury severity," Accident Analysis & Prevention, May 1997.

[22] J. M. Holdridge, V. N. Shankar, and G. F. Ulfarsson, "The crash severity impacts of fixed roadside objects," Journal of Safety Research, Jan. 2005.

[23] C. Conroy et al., "The influence of vehicle damage on injury severity of drivers in head-on motor vehicle crashes," Accident Analysis & Prevention, July 2008.

[24] A. Sinha, V. Vu, S. Chand, K. Wijayaratna, and V. Dixit, "A Crash Injury Model Involving Autonomous Vehicle: Investigating of Crash and Disengagement Reports," Sustainability, July 2021.
[25] R. Bohara, M. Ross, and O. Joglekar, "Event Identity Graph Framework - Supplementary information," https://github.com/asvin-io/eigf2025.
[26] California Department of Motor Vehicles, "Autonomous Vehicle Collision Reports," DMV.
[27] National Highway Traffic Safety Administration, "Standing General Order on Crash Reporting," Washington, DC.
[28] A. d'Avila Garcez, M. Gori, L. C. Lamb, L. Serafini, M. Spranger, and S. N. Tran, "Neural-Symbolic Computing: An Effective Methodology for Principled Reasoning and Learning," May 2019.
[29] M. Nickel, K. Murphy, V. Tresp and E. Gabrilovich, "A Review of Relational Machine Learning for Knowledge Graphs," Jan 2016.

10

Edge-Optimized Modular Architecture for Real-Time Vehicle Re-Identification

Tomass Zutis[1], Dimitrios Georgiadis[2], Tassos Kanelos[3], Janis Judvaitis[1], Pēteris Račinskis[1], Konstantina Karathanasopoulou[2], George Dimitrakopoulos[2], Janis Arents[1], and Modris Greitans[1]

[1]Institute of Electronics and Computer Science (EDI), Latvia
[2]Harokopio University of Athens, Greece
[3]G.N.T. Information Systems S.A., Greece

Abstract

This work addresses the challenge of real-time vehicle re-identification (ReID) on resource-constrained edge devices. Our research aims to design and deploy a modular, edge-optimized system that integrates object detection and ReID for intelligent transportation applications. The proposed architecture combines a lightweight detection module with a ReID embedding generator, enabling accurate multi-camera vehicle tracking under strict computational limits. We evaluate the system on NVIDIA Jetson platforms, applying quantization, pruning, and TensorRT optimization to achieve low-latency inference while maintaining accuracy. Additionally, we explore scheduling strategies for day and night operations to optimize energy consumption and performance. The impact of 360-degree fisheye camera distortion on detection and ReID accuracy is analyzed. Experimental results demonstrate that the system achieves real-time performance on edge hardware without sacrificing reliability, making it suitable for large-scale deployment in smart city environments. This study highlights the feasibility of deploying deep learning computer vision pipelines on edge AI platforms for robust, privacy-preserving vehicle analytics.

Keywords: edge AI, privacy preservation, image recognition, object detection, object re-identification, 360-degree fisheye camera.

DOI: 10.1201/9788743815273-10

10.1 Introduction and Background

If the same vehicle drives past a person two times, during different parts of the day and in different locations, how often would a person be able to re-identify this vehicle? If such a task is not trivial for the human eye and memory, it is even less likely that it could somehow be a trivial, out-of-the-box computerized solution. Vision-based object re-identification is a problem of growing interest in security, traffic monitoring, and environment monitoring applications. Real-time footage analysis from network-connected cameras that contain imagery of vehicles in transit is a topic that the research community has taken the greatest interest in regarding vision-based re-identification problems [1, 2].

In [3] T.Zutis et al., who are also co-authors of this article, presented a multi-step object Re-identification pipeline - a prototype (proof-of-concept) with specifications comparable to those needed for deployment on edge devices. This Vehicle Re-Identification pipeline can be a valuable tool for identifying vehicles and tracking them in real-life scenarios without using license plate information and compromising personal information. A fully connected pipeline was presented that consisted of steps to detect objects in video streams, crop them from the corresponding frames, assign IDs, track their position through the field-of-view (FOV), and, once the vehicle had left the FOV, save it into a vector database. The vector database could later be queried for the vehicle from cameras in other locations. During development, this pipeline was split into two parts: vehicle detection and re-identification (or feature extraction, saving, and querying) itself. The first step in the larger pipeline was object detection. For this, the authors used an out-of-the-box YOLO v8 [4] model. For tracking, the *ByteTrack* [5] package was chosen to assign IDs and track them through consecutive frames of the same camera FOV. For the re-identification part, however, a precise and effective feature extraction model had to be trained and tailored. The development of this model and the training results are described in the cited article. The model was tested both with publicly and non-publicly available datasets and network camera video gathered at the Institute of Electronics and Computer Science of Latvia.

The most recent work, however, focused on delivering this pipeline for a true edge computing architecture. The concept and design of the system have undergone many iterations of improvements in speed, implementation, deployment, versatility, and compatibility. True to the original concept of splitting the pipeline into vehicle detection and re-identification during development, the pipeline has been modularised and consists of separate systems for object detection, feature extraction, and vector database operations. The development of the object detection, feature extraction, and partly also database operator by separate development teams fulfils many other system requirements and makes each component reusable and functional in different contexts. The integration of the object detection system and the feature extraction module is also one of the key development steps that will be described in this article. The modular architecture has required research into integration and data flows. These data flows are enabled by a pub/sub messaging system based on the MQTT stack.

Even though the object detection system is designed also as a standalone obstacle and road conditions perception software, in this article, it fits into a role that seeks to replace the vanilla YOLO v8 solution that was used previously. The system focuses on embedded AI platforms through compression and quantization techniques (ONNX), while using custom inference engines (ONNX Runtime or TensorRT) for inference efficiency and resource minimization. Additionally, it integrates motion-gated frame admission (MOG2, hysteresis), ROIs (Regions of Interest), image tiling and tile scheduling for adaptive load management and low latency. Post-processing after object detection and tracking requires logical reasoning such as zone violation.

Another key aspect of improvement is the deployment of this pipeline on the Nvidia Jetson Orin [6] edge computing device. This proves the applicability of the system in real-world circumstances and enables measuring the performance and computing requirements of our systems. The models and accompanying software have been optimized for the Nvidia Jetson Orin.

An additional direction of experimentation in this work, though still in its earliest stages, has been the use of fisheye cameras for object detection and vehicle re-identification. Such cameras offer a drastically wider field of view compared to conventional surveillance optics, potentially allowing a single unit to cover larger intersections or parking areas. However, the severe geometric distortion introduced by fisheye lenses poses challenges for detection, tracking, and feature extraction, as the vehicle appearance may be warped differently depending on its position in the FOV. Early investigations have been exploratory rather than conclusive, and the research performed so far aims to offer practical engeneering solutions to analysis of distorted vehicle input.

In the following chapters, we aim to describe this proof-of-concept solution on edge devices, the evaluation that has been done to substantiate our claims of success and the results that the authors find consequential for the advancement of these technologies.

In the last chapter - Discussion and Future Work we present the envisioned architecture. Its main aim is to describe the departure from the proof-of-concept version that functions on a single Jetson device to one including a meta edge server and removal of the vector database from the deep-edge. This chapter can be read in paralel to the rest of the article as it gives more context for why the edge optimisation is ultimately necessary.

10.2 Approach

10.2.1 Overall modular architecture

10.2.1.1 Object detection system

The primary models for the object detection system are the YOLOv8's line models provided by Ultralytics which are exported to ONNX (FP16 is preferred) and executed in pure inference engines.

The system is initiated through frame acquisition determined by hardware limitations, influencing the quality and quantity of frames, that pass through the pipeline. It utilizes the FFmpeg video decoder that can feed raw BGR frames into the pipeline.

Next, a motion-gating (frame-level prefilter) technique is incorporated with a background subtractor (MOG2-downscaled) to generate the binary mask. This represents the relative area per frame and performs a morphological cleanup, followed by a simplistic hysteresis approach to avoid brief dropouts.

Initially, the frames are cropped via predefined regions, capturing the keypoints inside the image topology, maximizing the effective resolution for potential activity and simultaneously reducing the tiling load balancing, with fewer necessary tiles per image. Each tile is formatted to accommodate the inference model's inputs, with image tiling accounting for overlapping, thus correctly covering detection in a tile's edges. When ready, the tiles are fed one-by-one to generators and are then batched for concurrent inference.

Frames are also parsed through generators to be called only when necessary, reducing memory overload. This micro-batching reports the inference results from the GPU, which is where the ONNX Runtime with CUDA providers or a pure TensorRT engine are employed. During inference, inputs and outputs are bound to CUDA buffers and in both cases, the model is "warmed-up" for each batch shape, stabilizing latency and building of the engines. Prebinding outputs results in reusing memory that has already been allocated. Once the results have been obtained, an initial mutliclass NMS is performed on each tile and while this may lower operational performance, it reduces the size of the batched tensor detections. Then, all detections are rescaled into the original input's format and are captured on top of their corresponding frame. The inference results (pre-NMS) are a single tensor (raw inference) and after NMS these become end-to-end four outputs including the bounding boxes, scores and class confidence scores for every detection.

Inference results are decomposed into meaningful information with post-processing mapping tile boxes onto the original frames. These are enhanced and validated using a global Non-Max Suppression (NMS), mixing batched-NMs and single-class NMS. Between engine inference and post-processing, minimal CPU traffic is generated with small tensors or metadata. Tracking is also enabled via the *ByteTracker* model to identify vehicles through frames, which is integrated in a custom way to enable seamless cooperation with the compressed detection model. Lastly, the system crops the finalized outputs, keeping only the detected objects, to maximize transmission efficiency between systems.

10.2.1.2 Re-identification system

The main component of the re-identification system is the re-identification model. The architecture of this model is applicable to re-identification of all types of objects; however, it has been specifically trained to recognize and extract features of vehicles. The model, its training, and the results have been described in the previously mentioned paper [3]. Here, we describe the model regarding its deployment on the edge, the model's and the surrounding software's optimization.

The feature extraction model (originally built in *Pytorch*) was first converted to run on ONNX runtime inference engine. This has also been the first step in optimizing the model, slightly decreasing its size. This way, we also standardized the model for deployment across different runtime environments (e.g., Jetson, CPU/GPU, cloud). Then, considering the goal of edge deployment on a Jetson device, a further conversion of the model to a TensorRT engine was performed. TensorRT [7] is an Nvidia GPU native engine format that further reduces latency and memory footprint. In fact, when converting the model to a TensoRT engine, some optimizations are performed automatically, like layer fusion and kernel auto-tuning.

Beyond model-level optimizations, consecutive load management strategies have been built into the algorithms surrounding the re-identification logic and feature extraction model. This reduces redundant computation across the detection, feature extraction, and database layers.

1. At the feature extraction stage, a zone-based filtering mechanism is applied: FOV's are divided into configurable sub-regions and embeddings are only generated when a tracked object enters a new zone. This prevents unnecessary feature extraction for vehicles that remain static or confined to a single region of interest. This also lets us focus on saving the features of vehicles in different poses/locations, improving the ReID precision.
2. On the detection side, a binary ROI mask is used to restrict the effective input area of the model, allowing the system to ignore irrelevant regions such as sidewalks or sky and thereby reduce the number of unnecessary detections.
3. Finally, database operations employ lightweight caching and periodic cleanup: repeated queries for the same vehicle ID within short timescales are resolved locally, while expired entries are automatically purged to maintain storage efficiency and improve ReID precision.

Together, these mechanisms balance resource usage across the pipeline and support real-time performance under limited computational resources.

10.2.1.3 System integration, data flows etc.

This proof-of-concept indicates that the system integration and data flow are, in most cases, beyond the state of the art (SoTA) and not readily found in the available literature, since most research concerning this matter is still very cloud-centric and relies on simple benchmark testing to signal ReID capability.

The first step in deploying the system onto an edge device was preparing the code for NVIDIA Jetson ORIN. The chosen strategy for this was the separation of the system into 3 different modules with 2 additional external services needed to run the pipeline. The 3 different modules of the pipeline: the object detection system, the feature extraction/Re-Identification module and the database operations module were developed by different entities; hence they had to be run in different environments and with different requirements.

The chosen path that has worked best for the implementation of these different modules on the NVIDIA Jetson has been containerization. Each module was transferred to a Docker container by crafting a Docker image that is suited both for the software requirements and the Jetson architecture, including the limited and specific software distributions available. In this prototype version both the MQTT broker and the Opensearch database have also been deployed as docker containers in the same network as the 3 modules.

The Dockerization process itself was non-trivial, as the Jetson architecture (based on *JetPack* L4T) only supports specific CUDA, cuDNN, and TensorRT versions. This required building the containers on top of NVIDIA-provided base images (e.g., nvcr.io/nvidia/tensorrt:23.10-py3 for the feature extraction model) to ensure compatibility with the hardware. Furthermore, since the detection, feature extraction, and database operation modules were developed independently with heterogeneous dependencies, each had to be isolated in its own container to avoid version conflicts. GPU access also needed to be explicitly configured using the NVIDIA container runtime, as mismatches between *JetPack* libraries and container environments often led to runtime errors. Finally, resource limitations of the Jetson platform necessitated careful management, particularly because the database and inference engines competed for CPU and memory.

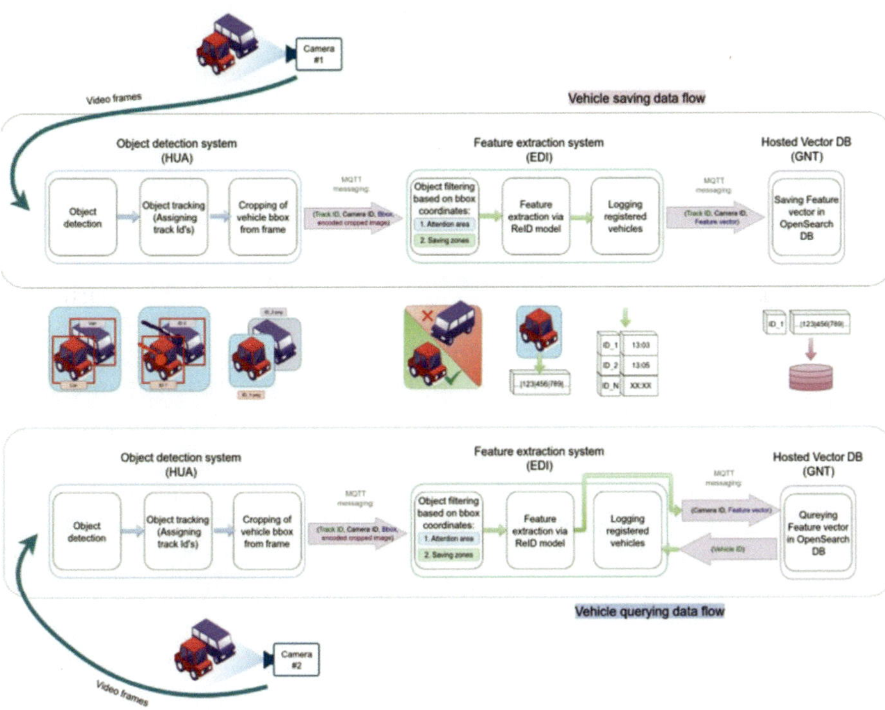

Figure 10.1 Depiction of the logical dataflow in the modularised re-identification pipeline.

After the separation of the pipeline into different modules, a data flow solution was devised (see Figure 10.1). The communication between containers is done via MQTT. The idea behind the data flow is as follows:

1. The object detection system detects different object classes on the roads and intersections. These object classes can be various, including People, Vehicles, and different obstacles. Some of these detections will be valuable for other systems unrelated to ours.
2. For this pipeline, the object detection system will then proceed to select the vehicle detections exclusively. These detections will be forwarded to the feature extraction module. Forwarding a detection means sending an MQTT message consisting of tracking ID, camera ID, bounding box (bbox) coordinates, and *Numpy* image array of the cropped vehicle. MQTT messages between the different modules are presented for comparison in Figure 10.2.
3. Upon reception into the feature extraction module, the vehicles will be filtered by the zone-based mechanism. The mechanism will take the bbox coordinates from the detection outputs into consideration to establish in which zone the current detection is located and if it has changed its zone from the previous time it was detected. If the zone has indeed been changed for the detected object with the same track ID, then it will proceed forward to the feature extraction model. If the vehicle with the same track ID is detected in the same zone as before, it will be discarded. More on this logic can be found in the previously published article.
4. In the next step, the cropped image of the detection is passed through the feature extraction model and converted into a feature vector.
5. Subsequently, the feature extraction model will construct an MQTT message that will be sent upstream to the database operations module. Even though this will be heavily changed upon departure from the proof-of-concept version. The message will consist of the track ID, camera ID and the feature vector.
6. Upon receiving the message, the database operations module first checks whether this track from the same camera has already been cached locally. If so, it avoids redundant queries and directly updates the database with the new vector.
7. If the track is new, the module queries the vector database (in this case, *OpenSearch*, configured with vector fields and k-NN search). The query uses cosine similarity to compare the incoming feature vector against stored vehicle embeddings.

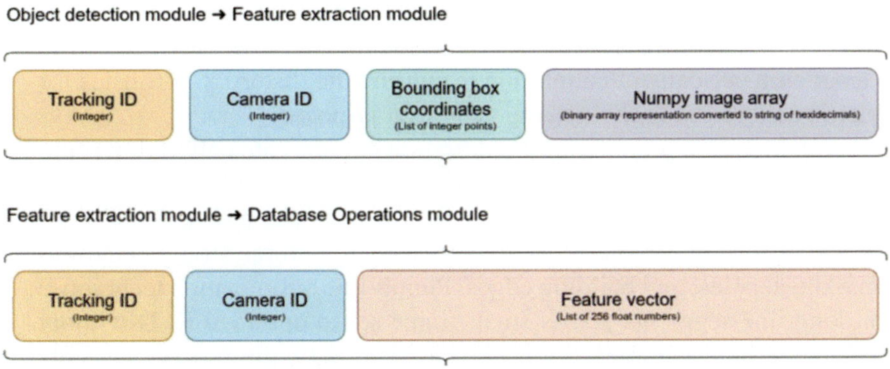

Figure 10.2 MQTT messages being sent from one module to another.

8. Depending on the result of the similarity search:
   a. If a sufficiently similar vehicle is found, the feature vector is added to that vehicle's existing entry (reinforcing the embedding).
   b. If no match is found, a new ID (composed of the camera ID + track ID) is generated and inserted into the database.
9. The database operations container also runs periodic cleanup. A time-based deletion process removes vectors older than a configured threshold (e.g., 60 seconds in one test setup)

The networking between modules has been another challenge: the prototype communication via MQTT required configuring a shared *Docker* network that also included the *Opensearch* database and broker.

10.2.1.4 Switching to Fisheye camera usage

To expand the real-world applicability of the pipeline, the design has shifted to considering the possible inclusion of fisheye cameras for vehicle detection. The motivation for this shift stems from the growing deployment of wide-angle surveillance cameras in intersections and parking environments, where a single fisheye lens can cover multiple lanes or regions of interest.

10.2.2 Fisheye camera usage in object detection

The initial step in preprocessing fisheye camera frames is to calibrate the camera lens. Calibration acquires camera intrinsics (K) and distortion coefficient (D) for the specific camera utilized. Calibration is essential for determining a metric mapping between image pixels and the real-world scene. For preliminary experimentation, the object detection pipeline was fed the Fish-Eye8K [8] dataset, which has been evaluated with YOLOv8. However, since it does not ship per-camera calibration, capturing the distortion intrinsics for true metric calibration is challenging and often ill-posed.

Existing literature proposes self-calibration or surrogate calibration [9] to fit parameters using scene constraints. Typically, these methods initialize a principal point near the image centre to perform grid-search on a global FOV to estimate distortion. Refinements are necessary to enforce straight edges to lane markings, poles, and building edges. Plumb-line optimization techniques exploit long line segments across small frame set to optimize K, D without requiring a calibration target. For each candidate FOV, the process involves de-warping a few tangent views and validating line straightness, with the FOV that minimizes curvature being selected. Although these approaches exist and can work without a "checkerboard", their accuracy depends on how much geometric signal is contained within the dataset, leading to noisier results than target-based calibration.

A computationally efficient and calibration-free alternative is distorting the initial frames to match the model's rectilinear profile. Conceptually, this constitutes a domain shift problem, from fisheye imagery to rectilinear. Precise K, D aren't required as we can approximate undistortion, leveraging barrel correction to straighten edges near borders while mild center cropping is used to remove the most warped peripheral regions. In fisheye imagery, the strongest distortion regions occur near the periphery, whereas the central region closely approximates a pinhole projection. Accordingly, a "de-fish" warp functionality compresses outer regions and expands inner ones, remapping pixels so that radial lines appear straighter. When the projection type is unknown, radial or polynomial distortion models can serve as estimation tools. Radial undistortion applies the inverse of such models, compensating for radial deviation by introducing a mapping that restores line straightness. This method assumes a generic k that flattens curvature enough to determine a pinhole image.

While de-fishing inherently stretches central pixels and compresses the edges which will result in resolution loss near the periphery and undefined regions at the corners it remains a real-time deployment mechanism with minimal computational overhead. It provides a practical replacement when neither calibration nor retraining is feasible, acting as a fast heuristic to recover baseline detection accuracy. For future extensions of the object detection pipeline, a geometry-based calibration procedure will be incorporated to obtain accurate K, D and achieve true metric undistortion.

10.2.3 Fisheye camera usage in feature extraction

For vehicle feature extraction, experiments were conducted to evaluate the performance of the feature extraction model under fisheye camera conditions. To simulate this scenario, the existing AICity [10] test dataset was modified by applying synthetic fisheye distortion to each frame, mimicking the radial deformation characteristics of such optics. The modified dataset also adjusted the ground truth annotations, enabling a direct comparison of model precision between standard and distorted inputs.

While no dedicated fisheye-specific training or correction layers were applied at this stage, running the pipeline on this experimental footage establishes a baseline for future work with geometric adaptation and fisheye lens effects.

10.3 Evaluation

10.3.1 Object detection system

The object detection system must not be evaluated only on the detection performance of the well-established YOLO models but should address the accuracy and effectiveness holistically. The KPIs recommended in this subsection align directly to the structure of the pipeline. On the model's side, the fundamental mAP/Precision/Recall and F1 are computed on the finalized, full-frame outputs after the post-processing mechanism is completed, hence right after the global-NMS. This provides a clear measurement of detection quality, when utilizing ONNX or TensorRT backends. Such metrics alongside Frames-per-Second are standard in literature as per [11], where a streaming evaluation protocol is introduced to assess latency-aware detection and report the FPS vs accuracy comparison. Similarily, approaches can be found in [12] and [13], which have a more focused end-to-end benchmarking scheme, integrating NMS performance and on edge devices such as Jetson-enabled GPUs. For this work's pipeline NMS is incorporated for evaluation, specifically duplicate rate across tiles which are removed by NMS (suppression ratio). Additionally, misses near tile boundaries directly validate per-tile NMS and final-frame global NMS strategy with tile overlap. Background motion gating is validated by accounting for frames saved (background-filter lift) and recall under motion gating as per [14], thus ensuring the pipeline skips frames without missing vehicles. Contextually aligned, tracking can be validated through the traditional MOTA (Multi-Object Tracking Accuracy) and the modern HOTA (Higher Order Tracking Accuracy) [15] are attained to reflect how well the *ByteTrack* stiches final detection into stable tracks.

Such a pipeline is required to be applicable for resource-constrained platforms. Measurements, mostly involve the throughput (FPS) and end-to-end latency with the p50/p95/p99 percentiles to yield the system's response times and to capture real-tile performance. Also, a pipeline stage breakdown shows time expenditure based on each component and allows for fair comparison between the inference engines. Batch efficiency, indicated as the ratio of tiles inside the buffer per the maximum buffer size and suppression ratio for the global NMS quantify processing concurrency and deduplication. Lastly, GPU utilization and peak RAM memory allocation can be combined with CPU utilization and outlier counts or dropped frames to connect performance back to the hardware limitations and data movements. These are tailored for tuning image tiling, batch sizes and gating parameters to hit the target FPS and latency budget without sacrificing detection and tracking quality.

10.3.2 Feature extraction

The following subsections describe the ways we have evaluated the optimisation of our solution. We looked at the inference speed per image for the feature extraction model optimization and the precision of re-identification on distorted fisheye projection imagery together with a comparison of the embedding similarity in the feature space for normal and distorted images.

10.3.2.1 Inference speed per image

The feature extraction model will be embedded into a Jetson + Docker + TensorRT setup. This setup is what allows us to deploy a real-time solution on the edge. Feature extraction models have been successfully converted to ONNX and further optimized to run with TensorRT.

The evaluation compares the original PyTorch implementation of the re-identification model, the ONNX and TensorRT conversions. First the model was exported to the ONNX format for hardware-agnostic inference combined with several automatic graph-level optimizations (constant folding, operator fusion, and elimination of redundant nodes). Following this step, the ONNX model was compiled using NVIDIA TensorRT. TensorRT applies additional layer and precision optimizations, such as kernel auto-tuning, dynamic tensor memory management, to achieve substantial runtime acceleration on the Jetson platform.

The evaluation of the three model representations: PyTorch, ONNX, and TensorRT, was performed using the same AICity test dataset and batch size, with two metrics.

The first metric is inference time measured as the average inference time per image (in milliseconds). Inference time is crucial to real-time deployments. When processing inputs from a live-stream video of detected vehicles, processing one image should take as little time as possible. If inference time is too long, the feature extraction risks becoming a bottleneck in the pipeline and disrupting real-time re-identification. It is also noteworthy that there is no set limit to how many vehicles the model would have to process in a second, as traffic is irregular, and some moments can see more cars on the road than at others. The second metric is memory consumption, recorded as the average GPU memory usage (in gigabytes) during the inference test. Having low memory consumption for feature extraction is crucial because the computation will be done on an edge device. The feature extraction module is also planned to be the most resource consuming process in the entire pipeline.

For the same feature extraction model, these metrics can vary when deployed on different devices; hence, it is important to test them on the Nvidia Jetson ORIN device. These metrics provide a crucial understanding of the model's performance on a resource-limited computational device.

10.3.2.2 Re-identification on Fisheye projection images

The evaluation of Fisheye distorted image impact on the extracted vehicle features consisted of two main analyses. First, the pipeline's re-identification Rank-1 accuracy [16] was measured on the distorted dataset, showing how the existing model, trained on (mostly but not exclusively) perspective projection camera images, generalizes to fisheye conditions. Second, feature vector cosine similarity [17] was examined in the embedding space, comparing cosine distances between features extracted from the same vehicles before and after distortion. This allowed for a quantitative estimation of how the distortion affects the learned feature representations.

Re-running the tests of the previous article, where the model was first presented, with distorted images is an obvious choice due to the direct comparability between the two types of images. If the Re-identification test results were to fall it could be directly attributed to the image distortion.

Measuring the vector distance in the embedding space is a slightly more in-depth analysis of the distortion effects. If images of the same vehicles were further apart in the embedding space after fisheye distortion was applied, we could directly indicate that the model's learned embedding function is sensitive to geometric deformation, causing vehicles that should be recognized as identical to occupy disjoint regions of the feature space. Conversely, a small or negligible change in intra-class distances would suggest that the feature extractor preserves its discriminative capability despite the altered image geometry. This embedding-based comparison thus provides a quantitative complement to the precision and recall measurements, offering deeper insight into how fisheye distortion affects the internal feature representations used for vehicle re-identification.

10.3.2.3 System integration

The fully containerized system, consisting of the object detection, feature extraction, and database operations modules, is to be deployed and executed on the NVIDIA Jetson Orin edge device. Successful operation of these modules will confirm the feasibility of running the complete pipeline as each module depends on at least one other.

To evaluate the reliability of the data flow between modules, message transmission metrics were recorded. Specifically, the number of detection messages sent from the object detection module was compared against the number of messages received by the feature extraction module. This measurement served to confirm that the MQTT communication setup was stable and lossless under continuous operation.

A second comparison was made between the number of detections received by the feature extraction module and the number of feature vectors it produced and sent onward to the database operation module. This ratio reflects the effectiveness of the load-reduction mechanisms within the feature extraction module, such as motion gating and zone-based filtering, which intentionally suppress redundant detections to optimize processing throughput.

10.4 Results

10.4.1 Object detection performance

Experimentation of the object detection system was executed through real-time, publicly available camera sources, set on top of highways. For reference the current results have all been gathered for a 1920x1080 resolution video in rectilinear format extracted from these sources, capturing 2 minutes and 3 seconds. For this evaluation ONNX runtime and TensorRT engine were separately used. We consider that the GPU and RAM utilization start from 0 for ease of demonstration purposes.

Table 10.1 Object detection system speed and resource consumption overview of ONNX Runtime and TensorRT

Metric	ONNX Runtime	TensorRT
Total Execution Time (s)	**294.8**	344.1
Peak Memory Usage (MB)	211.07	**210.92**
GPU Utilization (%)	29.2	**7.96**
Avg. Inference time (ms)	**70.52**	122.70
Mean FPS	**5.49**	4.7

Both systems were executed with a batch size of 16 tiles. Preprocessing involved motion-gating, initial ROI cropping and transformation into tensors. Image tiling is performed with a grid of (2,4) tiles. NMS is performed per tile before depicting the finalized detection back to the original image and then a global NMS ensures no duplicates are remaining. Tracking is also enabled.

In Table 10.1 ONNX runtime which uses the CUDA execution provider, appears faster but more memory-intense due to the more brute-force and less-optimized execution pattern, which keeps the GPU busier and less resource efficient. It achieves higher FPS, due to lighter setup overhead and more aggressive kernel dispatching. Hence, ONNX runtime reflects higher kernel activity and shorter inter-kernel gaps despite less optimization. Conversely, TensorRT performs layer fusion and kernel optimization during engine building, leading to longer setup times, but saves execution time during warmup.

Analytically the p50/p95/p99 per operation and mean time are depicted in Table 10.2. Precision handling influences both systems in how they operate.

Table 10.2 Object detection performance comparison in seconds between ONNX Runtime and TensorRT

Metric	TensorRT	ONNX Runtime
Setup Process (mean)	**1.25**	1.49
Setup Model (mean)	5.46	**3.37**
Setup Logic (mean)	**4.7**	6.1
Setup MQTT (mean)	0.203	**0.202**
Warmup Session (mean)	**5.58**	9.51
ROI Cropping (mean)	**0.202**	0.301
Motion-Gating (mean)	**0.85**	0.86
Post Process (mean)	**1.025**	1.094
Frame Time p50	0.201	**0.168**
Frame Time p95	0.310	**0.279**
Frame Time p99	0.332	**0.291**

ONNX Runtime is set up for FP32 (full precision). TensorRT engine is also built for FP32, thus limiting acceleration benefits for smaller precision. while keeping all the overhead required. Additionally, total inference time includes synchronization points, forcing all asynchronous streams to be completed, making the measured time much longer. By default, ONNX runtime hides this by pipelining operations on multiple streams.

It is important to contextualize the overall performance of the pipeline in terms of end-to-end FPS, due to this metric showcasing the cumulative cost of all separate processing stages rather than the raw model inference, explicitly. The reported measurements, thus, reflect the complete system, including the motion-gating mechanism, model warm-up, optional image tiling, ROI handling, and also post-processing steps such as frame cropping, sub-mask generation and downstream communication or in-memory buffering. In its current state, the pipeline underperforms compared to state of the art deployments, which handle regular camera feeds. Isolated from the rest of the system, the detection model achieves an effective latency of approximately 60 ms per batch ($\approx$3.75 ms per frame for a batch size of 16), but inference on high-resolution fisheye imagery increases to roughly 100 ms per batch ($\approx$6.25 ms per frame). By comparison optimized TensorRT deployments of YOLOv8 on embedded AI platforms have reported mean inference latencies of approximately 3.2 ms per frame under comparable conditions. While this highlights a current performance gap, ongoing optimization efforts across preprocessing, memory transfers and post-processing are steadily reducing latency, with successive iterations returning measurable improvements towards state of the art performance.

10.4.2 ReID Feature extraction performance

10.4.2.1 Inference speed per image results

The results are summarized in Figure 10.3, showing that, specifically for the feature extraction perfromed by the ReID model, the TensorRT implementation achieves the lowest latency and the smallest memory footprint among the three frameworks, confirming its suitability for real-time edge deployment of our usecase.

The average inference speed on Jetson ORIN per image fell from around 40 milliseconds (ms) for the *PyTorch* model to approx. 35 ms for the optimized ONNX model. Implementation of the model in the TensorRT framework resulted in a decrease of a further 20 ms. The 15 ms per image is explained by the deep optimization capabilities of TensorRT, including

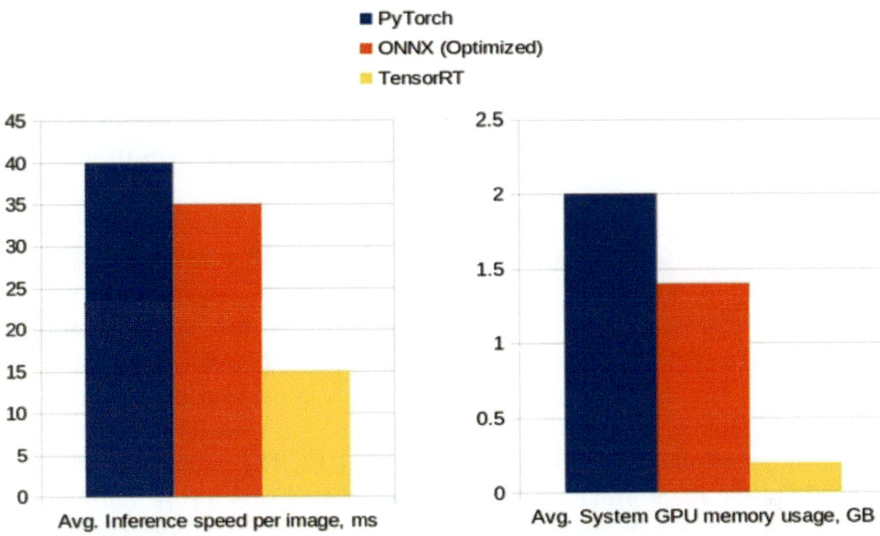

Figure 10.3 Comparison of average inference speed and average GPU memory usage between the three different iterations of the re-identification model implementation in different frameworks: Pytorch, ONNX and TensorRT.

kernel fusion, layer reordering, and dynamic tensor memory management. These optimizations allow the engine to exploit the Jetson's GPU and tensor cores more effectively than generic inference runtimes.

In addition to latency improvements, a notable reduction in average GPU memory usage was observed across the three versions. The *PyTorch* implementation consistently required the largest memory allocation (~2GB) due to its dynamic computation graph, while ONNX reduced memory overhead (~1,4GB) through static graph optimization. The NVIDIA native TensorRT engine achieved the lowest average GPU memory footprint (~0.2GB), indicating efficient memory reuse and reduced buffer fragmentation during inference.

Overall, these results confirm that deploying the model through TensorRT significantly enhances both inference speed and resource efficiency, enabling the proposed re-identification system to operate within the real-time constraints on the edge.

It is also worthy of mentioning that the results gained in this chapter do not nescessarily correspond to the preference that the ONNX Runtime garnered in the chapter for Object detection results. It is evident that each of the models (and their surrounding software systems) may better perform with a different engine and runtime than the other. These differences may be attributed to the different models used, the various software packages enabling the systems and various surrounding code implementations like batching, pre- and post- processing, filtering or motion gating, sizes of input data and others.

10.4.2.2 Re-identification on Fisheye projection images results

To evaluate the potential effect of fisheye distortion on vehicle re-identification performance, the previously used AICity test scenario was reprocessed with a synthetic fisheye lens transformation applied to all frames. The same model was then evaluated on both the original and the distorted datasets under identical conditions.

The accuracy results are summarized in Table 10.3. The overall accuracy difference between the normal and fisheye-transformed versions is minimal, suggesting that the current model maintains a largely stable performance despite geometric distortion.

The minor difference in re-identification accuracy, together with the nearly identical average cosine similarity in the embedding space, indicates that the model's feature representations are relatively robust to moderate fish-eye distortion. Given the small scale of variation, these results are considered preliminary and within expected uncertainty.

10.4.2.3 System integration results

To verify the reliability of the deployed modular system and the effectiveness of its internal data flow, message transmission and reception statistics were collected during testing with the AICity dataset. The three key metrics observed were the number of detection messages published by the object detection module, the number of messages received by the feature extraction module, and the number of vehicle detections that were finally processed and forwarded to the database module.

The results are summarized in Table 10.4. The one-to-one correspondence between published and received messages confirms the stability and lossless

Table 10.3 Effect of fisheye distortion on vehicle feature extraction

Metric	**Normal video**	**Fisheye video**
Re-ID CMC Rank-1 Accuracy (%)	72.90	73.24
Average Cosine Similarity (across IDs)	0.6526	0.6317

Table 10.4 MQTT communication and filtering statistics during test on AICity dataset videos

Metric	Count
Detection module messages published	5771
Feature extraction module messages received	5771
Feature extraction module detections processed and forwarded	473

operation of the MQTT-based communication setup. Furthermore, the significantly lower number of forwarded detections demonstrates the intended behaviour of the zone-based and motion-gating filtering mechanisms within the feature extraction module to reduce processing load on the edge device.

These results validate that the system integration is operational and that the intra-pipeline communication is reliable. The filtering mechanisms effectively reduce the computational load, allowing the feature extraction model to focus on the most relevant vehicle observations for re-identification.

10.5 Discussion and Future Work

As described in [2], scaling a network camera perception system across a wider area is possible. The prototype implementation described in the previous chapters served as a proof of concept for validating the pipeline under real-world constraints. This setup has been deployed on a single Jetson device with a MQTT-based communication layer. This configuration successfully demonstrated the technical feasibility and performance of the ReID system.

Additionally, detecting and monitoring traffic via computer vision and deep learning methods require moving away from a single data collection and management site, as stated in [18]. Both the processing power of a single machine and the capacity of network paths are bottlenecks in smart city scenarios and a multi-tier edge computing based architecture is proposed. This architecture extends our proof-of-concept version to a distributed, multi-layered infrastructure with secure communication between multiple Road-Side Perception Units (RSPUs) and a meta-edge server.

In the envisioned architecture, the modular design established so far is preserved, but communication and data management responsibilities are expanded across two levels: a deep-edge layer, comprising the Jetson-based RSPUs, and a meta-edge layer, hosting data aggregation, indexing, and visualization services. This separation allows for efficient message handling, cross-device data fusion, and secure long-term storage, while maintaining low latency for inference tasks executed at the edge.

The following subsections describe in detail the communication mechanisms, data security provisions, and operational scheduling that enhance the envisioned system architecture.

10.5.1 Explanding the architecture

While the current proof-of-concept architecture featured a local MQTT broker and *OpenSearch* database deployment on the same Jetson device, this architecture will be improved in the deployments going forward with parts of the architecture having already been tested out.

Since the *OpenSearch* database can quickly grow during real-world deployment, it might not be possible to have it on the individual Jetson edge device. The Jetson edge devices will be joined by the meta-edge server in the architecture. On board the Jetson, we will have an MQTT broker and it will be coupled with an InfluxDB [19]. At the meta-edge server, we will also have a stack comprising Kafka and OpenSearch. Although there might be a small gain in using InfluxDB for the ReID case, it will be used by other regions of interest. The dataflow will be enabled by an MQTT broker on the Jetson that's connected to a Kafka Proxy (on the same Jetson), streaming data to the *OpenSearch* on the meta-edge and further to Grafana.

A dedicated module forwards MQTT messages published on the corresponding topic to a *Kafka* broker that is hosted on a server at higher edge layer (meta-edge) and aggregates messages from multiple Jetson devices. Another module at the meta-edge forwards messages published on a dedicated Kafka topic to a corresponding index of the database operations module (*OpenSearch* repository).

10.5.2 Dual Data Fusion mechanism for supporting communications

Communication within each module on board the Jetson and communication between multiple Jetson devices is made possible via a **dual data fusion mechanism**.

This mechanism is based on the use of the pub/sub messaging pattern that allows for loosely coupled and scalable interaction between modules, efficient and robust exchange of information [20, 21], thus facilitating integration and interoperability. In this context, a distributed messaging system is employed on a dual level: (1) at the level of each RSPU Jetson device (deep-edge layer) enabling communication between modules and microservices hosted on board the device and (2) at the level of a central server (meta-edge layer), enabling communication between multiple RSPU Jetson devices through the server. On each level, the messaging system is responsible for aggregating and fusing data from modules that act as data producers and re-distributing it to all necessary modules that act as data consumers. At the deep-edge layer, the messaging system is implemented through the use of an MQTT message broker, which is more lightweight in terms of computational resource demands, while at the meta-edge layer, it is implemented through the use of an Apache Kafka broker that requires increased resources, but offers enhanced reliability and scalability features.

The data fusion mechanism is complemented with the following modules:

1. On board the Jetson devices, a **proxy service** is deployed that is responsible for subscribing to selected MQTT topics of the deep-edge message broker and relaying the received information to the meta-edge by publishing it to corresponding topics of the Kafka message broker.
2. At the meta-edge server, a **data repository** based on the *OpenSearch* stack is deployed, where information published to the *Kafka* message broker is persistently stored. This is achieved using a dedicated **ingestion service** that subscribes to selected *Kafka* topics and registers the incoming published data to corresponding indices of the OpenSearch data repository. The data remains on this repository for any subsequent access, including the use of vector search queries, natively supported by the API exposed by *OpenSearch*.

The data fusion mechanism includes a **security layer** implemented on both architecture levels (i.e., deep-edge and meta-edge). At the deep-edge level, the security layer refers to the protection of communications between the MQTT pub/sub messaging system and MQTT producer and consumer clients within each RSPU device. In such a configuration, even though both MQTT broker and clients are hosted on the same RSPU device, the clients could still be exposed to local threats, such as privilege escalation, malware or insider threats, while the communication could be susceptible to Man-in-the-Middle (MitM) attacks. In addition, future needs of the data fusion mechanism may demand the connection of the MQTT broker to clients that are deployed on other hosts. The provided solution addresses all these issues and is based on X.509 certificates that are used for authenticating MQTT clients and enabling TLS encryption in communications and is complemented by custom RBAC configurations that can provide fine-grained authorization of clients to access MQTT topics. At the meta-edge level, a similar solution is provided, i.e., X.509 certificates, mTLS authentication and encryption, a centralised PKI and RBAC mechanisms are used to protect communications with the Kafka-based pub/sub messaging system. In this case, there are multiple producer clients at the deep-edge level that propagate data from the deep-edge level to the meta-edge level, where the Kafka broker is hosted. Each such producer client is embedded within the aforementioned **proxy service** that acts as a central gateway on each RSPU for communications with the meta-edge. This design of a single point-of-contact further reinforces cyber-security protection as it reduces the attack surface to a single service on board each RSPU. Finally, it should be noted that the entire deployment is limited to the edge layer and only extends to a meta-edge system. All the host computational infrastructure is self-managed and/or on-premises, thus contributing to a further increase of secure and reliable edge analytics by design. The absence of a cloud layer or infrastructure managed by a third party provides an additional level of security, as **(a)** data control is exclusively maintained and not delegated to a third party, **(b)** there is a reduced risk of unauthorized access and data breaches because the involved resources, networks and data can be physically or logically isolated from external sources and **(c)** the entire deployment is less exposed to external access, leading to a reduction of the potential attack surface.

10.5.3 Scheduling plan for deployment

The Jetson devices are deployed as part of a networked infrastructure of multiple Road-Side Perception Units (RSPUs) that are responsible for a series of functions apart from the ones that explicitly support the re-identification use case described herein. For example, RSPUs are also used to collect data from deployed environmental sensors and to process these data to perform Air Quality Index (AQI) Forecasting. In this use case, RSPUs are also used for local ML model training based on locally aggregated data and are connected through a server at the meta-edge layer, as part of a Federated Learning framework. Special provisions have been made to allow for complementarity between the vehicle re-identification use case and the AQI Forecasting use case. In particular, a challenge that was considered was that the local ML model training for the AQI Forecasting use case has a significant computational footprint, demanding increased resources for a period of a few hours per day in order to process the data collected within the day and produce an updated ML model. A concurrent operation of the ML training and the inference for vehicle re-identification would not be possible, as the latter is also considerably demanding in terms of consumed computational resources.

This conflict was solved by scheduling the ML training process to be activated during nighttime, when the vehicle re-identification use case is inactive due to lack of visibility from the deployed cameras. This results in an efficient and complementary operation for both use cases and demonstrates the wide spectrum of application fields that the RSPU can handle.

Acknowledgements

This work was supported by Chips Joint Undertaking EdgeAI project. The project EdgeAI "Edge AI Technologies for Optimised Performance Embedded Processing" is supported by the Chips Joint Undertaking and its members including top-up funding by Austria, Belgium, France, Greece, Italy, Latvia, Netherlands, and Norway under grant agreement No 101097300.

References

[1] X. Li and Z. Zhou, "Object Re-Identification Based on Deep Learning," *IntechOpen eBooks*, Jul. 2019, https://doi.org/10.5772/intechopen.86564.

[2] J. Barthélemy, N. Verstaevel, H. Forehead, and P. Perez, "Edge-Computing Video Analytics for Real-Time Traffic Monitoring in a Smart City," *Sensors*, vol. 19, no. 9, p. 2048, May 2019, https://doi.org/10.3390/s19092048.

[3] T. Zutis *et al.*, "Multi-Step Object Re-Identification on Edge Devices: A Pipeline for Vehicle Re-Identification", *Charting the Intelligence Frontiers – Edge AI Systems Nexus*, 2025, https://doi.org/10.13052/rp-9788743808831. https://cloud.riverpublishers.com/pdf/ebook/RP_E9788743808831.pdf

[4] Glenn Jocher and Ayush Chaurasia and Jing Qiu, 2023, Ultralytics YOLOv8, 8.0.0, https://github.com/ultralytics/ultralytics.

[5] Y. Zhang *et al.*, "ByteTrack: Multi-Object Tracking by Associating Every Detection Box," *arXiv:2110.06864 [cs]*, Apr. 2022, https://arxiv.org/abs/2110.06864

[6] L. Karumbunathan, "NVIDIA Jetson AGX Orin Series A Giant Leap Forward for Robotics and Edge AI Applications Technical Brief," *NVIDIA Jetson AGX Orin Series Technical Brief*, vol. 1, no. 2, 2022, https://www.nvidia.cn/content/dam/en-zz/Solutions/gtcf21/jetson-orin/nvidia-jetson-agx-orin-technical-brief.pdf

[7] Abbas Aqeel Kareem, Dalal Abdulmohsin Hammood, and Ruaa Ali Khamees, "Optimizing Siamese neural network with TensorRT on NVIDIA jetson nano," *AIP conference proceedings*, Jan. 2023, https://doi.org/10.1063/5.0154881.

[8] M. Gochoo *et al.*, "FishEye8K: A Benchmark and Dataset for Fisheye Camera Object Detection." https://openaccess.thecvf.com/content/CVPR2023W/AICity/papers/Gochoo_FishEye8K_A_Benchmark_and_Dataset_for_Fisheye_Camera_Object_Detection_CVPRW_2023_paper.pdf

[9] K. Liao *et al.*, "Deep Learning for Camera Calibration and Beyond: A Survey." https://arxiv.org/pdf/2303.10559

[10] Z. Tang *et al.*, "CityFlow: A City-Scale Benchmark for Multi-Target Multi-Camera Vehicle Tracking and Re-Identification." Accessed: Oct. 17, 2025. https://openaccess.thecvf.com/content_CVPR_2019/papers/Tang_CityFlow_A_City-Scale_Benchmark_for_Multi-Target_Multi-Camera_Vehicle_Tracking_and_CVPR_2019_paper.pdf

[11] J. Yang, S. Liu, Z. Li, X. Li, and J. Sun, "Real-time Object Detection for Streaming Perception." Accessed: Oct. 17, 2025. https://openaccess.thecvf.com/content/CVPR2022/papers/Yang_Real-Time_Object_Detection_for_Streaming_Perception_CVPR_2022_paper.pdf

[12] Y. Zhao *et al.*, "DETRs Beat YOLOs on Real-time Object Detection." https://openaccess.thecvf.com/content/CVPR2024/papers/Zhao_DETRs_Beat_YOLOs_on_Real-time_Object_Detection_CVPR_2024_paper.pdf

[13] P. Ganesh, Y. Chen, Y. Yang, D. Chen, and M. Winslett, "YOLO-ReT: Towards High Accuracy Real-time Object Detection on Edge GPUs." Accessed: Oct. 17, 2025. https://openaccess.thecvf.com/content/WACV2022/papers/Ganesh_YOLO-ReT_Towards_High_Accuracy_Real-Time_Object_Detection_on_Edge_GPUs_WACV_2022_paper.pdf

[14] Z. Fu, Y. Chen, H. Yong, R. Jiang, L. Zhang, and X.-S. Hua, "Foreground Gating and Background Refining Network for Surveillance Object Detection," *IEEE transactions on image processing*, vol. 28, no. 12, pp. 6077–6090, Jun. 2019, https://doi.org/10.1109/tip.2019.2922095.

[15] J. Luiten *et al.*, "HOTA: A Higher Order Metric for Evaluating Multi-object Tracking," *International Journal of Computer Vision*, vol. 129, no. 2, pp. 548–578, Oct. 2020, https://doi.org/10.1007/s11263-020-01375-2.

[16] T. Xiao, "Evaluation Metrics — Open-ReID documentation," *Github.io*, 2017. https://cysu.github.io/open-reid/notes/evaluation_metrics.html.

[17] "Measuring similarity from embeddings," *Google for Developers*, 2025. https://developers.google.com/machine-learning/clustering/dnn-clustering/supervised-similarity.

[18] G. Liu *et al.*, "Smart Traffic Monitoring System Using Computer Vision and Edge Computing," *IEEE Transactions on Intelligent Transportation Systems*, vol. 23, no. 8, pp. 1–12, 2021, https://doi.org/10.1109/tits.2021.3109481.

[19] M. Schneider *et al.*, "Open Traffic Data for Mobility-as-a-Service Applications – Architecture and Challenges," *River Publishers eBooks*, pp. 375–385, Sep. 2022, https://doi.org/10.1201/9781003337232-31.

[20] Kansakar, Anila. "Integrating Message Queuing Telemetry Transport (Mqtt) With Kafka Connect For Processing Iot Data." Diss. Pulchowk Campus, 2019. https://elibrary.tucl.edu.np/JQ99OgQIizUxyjI9nB0on9OyLkqsGIf4/api/core/bitstreams/6c7b6130-0691-44bd-bc86-51156784d20c/content

[21] K. N. Haque, "Decentralized pub/sub architecture for real-time remote patient monitoring," *Urn.fi*, 2024, https://oulurepo.oulu.fi/handle/10024/51125.

11

Edge Deployment of Multi-Task Vision Models for Smart City Infrastructures

Carmelo Scribano[1,3], Mohammad Mahdi[2], Filippo Muzzini[1], Nedyalko Prisadnikov[2], Yuqian Fu[2], Micaela Verucchi[1], Ignacio Sanudo Olmedo[1], Danda Pani Paudel[2], and Luc Van Gool[2]

[1]HiPeRT, University of Modena and Reggio Emilia, Italy
[2]INSAIT, Sofia University "St. Kliment Ohridski", Bulgaria
[3]Institute of Informatics and Telematics, National Research Council, Italy

Abstract

The ability to deploy complex vision pipelines at the edge is crucial for next-generation smart city infrastructures. Running inference locally avoids transmitting raw images, thereby reducing bandwidth usage, preserving privacy, and improving system robustness through a distributed paradigm. Achieving this, however, requires models that are both powerful and efficient. In this context, the multi-task paradigm emerges as a key enabler, supporting concurrent prediction across diverse tasks such as object detection, panoptic segmentation, and depth estimation. We introduce a novel pipeline built around a multi-task model explicitly designed to balance expressive power with inference efficiency under resource-constrained conditions. In parallel, we propose an optimization workflow that minimizes inference costs for edge deployment. Experimental results in a real-world setting demonstrate the effectiveness of our approach and establish a strong baseline for future smart city applications.

Keywords: smart city, edge inference, multi-task learning, model compression.

DOI: 10.1201/9788743815273-11

11.1 Introduction

Camera-based smart-city systems leverage computer vision, machine learning, and data anonymization techniques to monitor public areas in real time, detecting and recognizing vehicles and pedestrians. Processing camera streams locally mitigates network bottlenecks and enhances privacy preservation. However, this edge-side processing also introduces significant computational challenges, as modern perception pipelines rely on deep neural networks that are typically resource-intensive. Achieving low-latency inference is crucial to enable real-time interaction between the smart city infrastructure and connected vehicles, thereby extending vehicle perception capabilities with contextual environmental information.

11.1.1 Use Case Definition

The HAura device, previously introduced in [1], is a smart roadside unit designed for safety management and data analytics in urban and industrial environments. The system continuously processes image data from two cameras. The resulting metadata is transmitted to a central server that can implement various urban monitoring and management policies based on the extracted information. At the core of HAura lies the NVIDIA Jetson Orin Nano embedded platform. This platform is a popular choice for edge computer vision applications due to its integrated NVIDIA GPU, which delivers a favorable balance between performance, power efficiency, and programmability within a compact form factor.

11.1.2 Multi-Task Perception Model Deployment

This work focuses on the deployment and optimization of a multi-task perception pipeline on the HAura edge device. The perception model, based on a DINOv2 backbone, jointly performs semantic segmentation, instance segmentation, object detection, and depth estimation within a unified architecture (see Figure 11.1). This paradigm significantly reduces the computational overhead compared to the use of multiple single-task models, leading to a more efficient and scalable deployment on resource-constrained hardware. The primary contribution of this work lies in the integration, adaptation, and optimization of the perception stack for real-time execution on the NVIDIA Jetson Orin Nano platform. The goal is to achieve an end-to-end processing latency below 100ms per frame, including all post-processing stages, while maintaining task performance. The paper details the software

Figure 11.1 Sample outputs for the Multi-task perception pipeline deployed in a smart-city scenario. Right to Left: object detection, instance segmentation, semantic segmentation, and monocular depth estimation.

stack (Section 21.3), runtime configuration (Section 21.4), and performance evaluation methodology used to reach this target on a resource-constrained embedded platform (Section 21.5).

11.2 Related Work

Traffic and urban monitoring have been widely addressed in the literature. The needs, perspectives, and enabling technologies of an urban monitoring system are discussed in [2]. In [3] the authors propose a method for counting vehicles at an intersection using recorded or live video. In [4] a deep neural network is proposed to identify emergencies in the streets. Similarly, in [5] the model recognizes human abnormal activity in an urban area. In [6] computer vision is used to retrieve changes in the urban environment.

The cited approaches require huge computation or a centralized server. This scales poorly, as the number of monitoring areas in a city can be very large, eventually reaching computational and latency limits. A distributed approach, in which each intersection has its own embedded system, can overcome this problem. To achieve this situation is important to use smart cameras or sensors equipped with an embedded GPU, as in [1]. In this work, we show the trade-off between the accuracy and latencies on an embedded system for a model that addresses most of the tasks required in traffic and urban monitoring.

11.2.1 Vision Models for Urban Monitoring

In the considered scenario, multi-task models are the most promising solution [7]. They leverage the Vision Transformers (ViTs) [8, 9] that can extract rich features from images. One of the most popular models that use ViTs is Dino-v2 [10, 11]. Using Dino-v2 makes it possible to train a multitask model since it was used in different tasks such as Object Detection [12, 13] or Segmentation [14]. In this work, we show that the multitask models can be used on an embedded system for urban monitoring, and we investigate how to reduce the latencies of these models to meet the real-time requirements.

11.3 Model Description

The multi-task perception model analyzed in this work is derived from an extension of the architecture presented in [15]. This architecture combines the powerful Dino-V2 foundation transformer as a shared feature extractor with a shallow upscaling decoder and per-task projection layers to produce the task-specific outputs. The rationale behind this design is multifold: leveraging Dino-v2 as the shared deep feature encoder provides a strong feature representation that has been extensively shown to achieve state-of-the-art performance on several downstream tasks. The shared shallow decoder upscales the patch-level Dino-V2 embeddings to pixel-level, keeping the projection shared across the tasks. Finally, the per-task projection is used to map the shared pixel-space to produce the correct feature dimension required by each task (see Figure 11.2).

Specifically, the Dino-V2 encoder is based on the ViT architecture [16] with a patch size of 14×14, the authors provide four different architectural variations which are compared in Table 11.1. The model analyzed in this paper is based on the Large backbone, which was chosen for its superior performance. The analysis presented can easily be extended to different

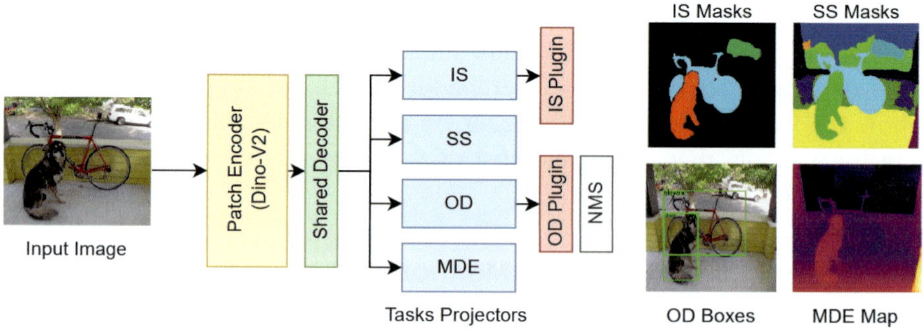

Figure 11.2 Schematized architecture of the considered Multi-modal model.

Table 11.1 DINOv2 model variants and core architecture specs

Variant	Architecture	Emb dim	# Parameters	# Attention heads	# Blocks
SMALL	ViT-S/14	384	21M	6	12
BASE	ViT-B/14	768	86M	12	12
LARGE	ViT-L/14	1024	300M	16	24
GIANT	ViT-L/14	1536	1,100M	24	40

variants to satisfy different latency-performance tradeoffs. Given an input image $I \in \mathbb{R}^{3 \times H \times W}$ each encoder block produces an intermediate output $z_b \in \mathbb{R}^{\frac{H}{p} \times \frac{W}{p} \times d}$ there p denotes the patch size and d denotes the embedding dimension.

The upscaling decoder takes as input the intermediate patch-level embeddings Dino-V2 ViT blocks, concatenated along the embedding dimension $z_c = [z_{b1}|z_{b_2}|z_{b3}|z_{b4}] \in \mathbb{R}^{\frac{H}{p} \times \frac{W}{p} \times 4d}$. First, it projects to the decoder embedding dimension e with a 1×1 convolution, then it gradually up-scales to the pixel-space with four layers of transposed convolution. This yields an $8\times$ upscaling of the patch space, which corresponds to $\frac{8}{p}$ of the original input resolution.

11.3.1 Multi-Task Design

The output of the upscaling decoder, described in the previous section, is used as input by the Task Projectors. The considered Task Projectors are: **Object detection (OD)**, **Instance Segmentation (IS)**, **Semantic Segmentation (SS)**, and **Monocular Depth estimation (MDE)**. All these tasks are trained simultaneously using labels from the COCO dataset [17], except MDE, which is pseudo-labeled on COCO images, leveraging state-of-the-art zero-shot depth estimation DepthAnything-V2 [18]. The design of the task-specific projectors is detailed hereafter.

Semantic Segmentation: The SS task is cast as per-pixel multi-class classification. The projection for this task is a single 3×3 convolution to project from the decoder embedding dimension e to the number of semantic classes C_S. The semantic class is trivially decoded with a per-pixel argmax operation.

Instance Segmentation: Conversely, IS uses the most complex encoding, proposed in [15]. The IS projection head produces an output $O_{IS} \in \mathbb{R}^{H_O \times W_O \times 4L}$, each location (i, j) regresses the coordinate of the mask centroids it belongs to, or a void centroid for unlabeled regions. Denoting as $O(u, v)$ the set of pixel locations belonging to the instance mask with centroid

(i, j), the regression target is formalized as:

$$O_{IS}(i,j) = \begin{cases} \text{concat}\left(\gamma(u), \gamma(v)\right) & \text{if} \quad (i,j) \in O(u,v) \\ \vec{0} \in \mathbb{R}^{4L} & \text{otherwise} \end{cases} \quad (21.1)$$

where the positional encoding $\gamma(p)$ derived from [19] is defined as:

$$\gamma(p) = \left(sin\left(2^l \pi p\right), cos\left(2^l \pi p\right)\right)_{l=0}^{L-1} \quad (22.2)$$

This encoding, while achieving strong performance on the task, poses significant challenges for deployment. Post-processing O_{IS} to obtain the decoded instance mask poses a substantial overhead on end-to-end execution latency. In the next section, we detail the implementation of an efficient CUDA-accelerated post-processing stage that can be built in the TensorRT inference engine, achieving substantial speedup over the baseline Pytorch implementation.

Object Detection: The object detection is based on anchor-free YoLo [20]. The input image is mapped to a $S \times S$ grid, at each grid location B candidate bounding boxes are regressed, each encoded as (c_x, c_y, w, h, p) with (c_x, c_y) denoting the normalized center point coordinates expressed in cell-relative coordinates, (w, h) box width and height normalized with respect to the image dimensions and s a confidence score. In addition, a single C_o class classification is regressed at each cell location. Therefore, the OD projection produces an output:

$$O_{OD} \in \mathbb{R}^{S \times S \times (5B+C)} \quad (22.3)$$

Decoding YOLO-style predictions requires mapping grid-relative box coordinates to image coordinates, followed by Non-Maximum Suppression (NMS) to remove overlaps. While TensorRT's INMSLayer efficiently handles NMS, it lacks the preceding coordinate transformation. To enable end-to-end inference without breaking the TensorRT execution graph, we implement a custom CUDA plugin that performs on-device box decoding and filtering, keeping all postprocessing within the optimized graph.

Monocular Depth Estimation: The depth estimation is cast as a raw per-pixel regression problem. In this case, no additional post-processing is required. Similar to SS, the MDE projection simply up-scales the decoder features to the output resolution, producing the single-channel depth map.

11.4 Deployment

Our target application involves distributed smart city monitoring, which imposes two key constraints: the model must run on embedded hardware and operate in real time. Achieving these requirements depends on an appropriate deployment configuration, including the backbone size, input resolution, batch size, and arithmetic precision (FP32, FP16, or INT8). Each of these parameters directly affects both accuracy and task performance. A critical step is defining a latency deadline: the maximum acceptable inference time per frame. In practice, processing results that arrive too late (e.g., one second after capture) become irrelevant, as the scene has already changed. The deadline should not exceed the camera's frame period; otherwise, the system remains idle between frames. For our use case, we adopt a 100ms deadline, which ensures timely scene updates without perceptible information loss. Driven by this observation, in the remainder of this section we detail the main technical solution experimented with to meet the latency constraint. Later, Section 21.5 presents experimental results used to identify the optimal deployment settings

11.4.1 Mixed-Precision Inference

Out of the box, TensorRT supports mixed-precision inference with FP32, FP16, and INT8 arithmetic, all natively accelerated on the NVIDIA Orin Nano via Ampere Tensor Cores. In addition, the TensorRT model compiler applies aggressive graph-level optimizations; in our case, self-attention layers are automatically fused and replaced with FlashAttention-V2 [21] at FP16 and INT8 precision, yielding more efficient memory access and higher throughput. While FP16 arithmetic can be enabled without additional steps, INT8 arithmetic requires an additional calibration stage to determine the scaling values that map floating-point activations and weights into the discrete 8-bit integer range.

Post Training Quantization: TensorRT's explicit quantization workflow represents INT8 computation using Quantize (Q) and Dequantize (DQ) operator pairs inserted directly into the network graph, explicitly defining the quantization boundaries for each tensor. During Post-Training Quantization (PTQ), calibration data is used to collect activation statistics and determine the scaling factors that map FP32 tensors into the INT8 domain, typically through entropy or percentile-based range estimation. Weight tensors are quantized offline, while activation quantization parameters are computed dynamically during calibration. For this work, we leverage the Post Training Quantization (PTQ) pipeline provided by Nvidia TensorRT-Model-Optimizer (ModelOpt); specifically, leveraging ModelOpt's implementation of the SmoothQuant calibration method [22] which redistributes activation ranges into the corresponding weights to mitigate outliers and improve quantization robustness. We employ per-channel quantization for weights and per-tensor quantization for activations. In Section 21.5, we compare the performance-speed tradeoff under different arithmetic.

11.4.2 Processors Plugins

Instance Segmentation: Since the entire model, from input to output, is subject to real-time constraints, we accelerated the processors using Nvidia CUDA. The encoded output of this task is defined in Eq. 1 each element $O_{IS}(i, j)$ stores a tuple representing an estimate of the coordinates of the centroid (i.e. the mask) associated with pixel (i, j). The proximity between this tuple and the actual centroid coordinates serves as a confidence score: the closer the value, the higher the likelihood that the corresponding point is a true centroid.

To compute these scores, we calculate the distance between each pixel and every potential centroid. This is performed by launching a CUDA kernel in which each thread is associated with a pixel of O_{IS} and a candidate centroid. Each thread computes the two-dimensional distance and stores the corresponding score derived from this distance. Since multiple pixels may contribute to the same centroid, their scores are accumulated. To minimize memory accesses, we exploit CUDA shared memory and the synchthreads() primitive to coordinate partial sums efficiently. Next, a second kernel is launched in which each candidate centroid is assigned to a thread. Each thread examines neighboring centroids and, if it holds the highest accumulated score, it designates itself as the centroid of a distinct mask. Finally, a third kernel is executed, where each thread corresponds to a pixel–mask pair. If a pixel is associated with a specific mask (recall that, as defined in Eq. 1, some pixels may correspond to a null mask), the thread writes a value of 1 at the corresponding position for that mask.

Since all these phases operate at the pixel level, they can be executed in parallel, resulting in significant speedup. Some operations require coordination between neighboring pixels to prevent race conditions, but the use of shared memory and the synchthreads() primitive effectively reduces synchronization overhead.

Object Detection: To post-process the object detection output defined in Eq. 3, a single CUDA kernel is employed. Each thread is assigned to a cell of size $S \times S$ and selects the optimal bounding box among the available candidates based on the corresponding confidence score. The thread then computes the bounding box coordinates using the parameters (c_x, c_y, w, h) of the selected box. Similarly, the object class is determined according to the class confidence score, which is also stored in the output.

The final result consists of three arrays: (i) the bounding box coordinates, (ii) the associated class for each box, and (iii) the corresponding class confidence values. The CUDA implementation significantly accelerates this computation, as each cell is processed independently, enabling full parallelization across threads.

11.5 Experiments

11.5.1 Experimental Setup

Performance Assessment: To comprehensively evaluate the effectiveness of our multi-task model, we assess the performance of each task-specific head using standard benchmarks commonly adopted in the literature: mean Average Precision at 0.5 IoU threshold (**mAP@50**) [23] for object detection, mean Intersection over Union (**mIoU**) [24] for semantic segmentation, Panoptic Quality (**PQ**) [25] for instance segmentation, and Root Mean Square Error (**RMSE**) [26] depth estimation. We report task metrics on the COCO validation split, using the pseudo-labels for the MDE task.

Benchmarking: The multi-task model is implemented in PyTorch, following the standard deployment pipeline of exporting the network to the ONNX format via JIT tracing. This export process preserves the Quantize/Dequantize (Q/DQ) operators introduced during Post-Training Quantization (PTQ), as well as any custom CUDA plugins, which are automatically recognized and integrated by the TensorRT builder with their corresponding device-level implementations. All latency and memory measurements are collected on an NVIDIA Jetson Orin Nano running JetPack 6.1, which includes TensorRT 10.3 and CUDA 12.x. Benchmark results are obtained under identical inference conditions across precision modes (FP32, FP16, and INT8) to ensure fair comparison of performance and efficiency. Latency measurements are obtained using the TensorRT trtexec utility with real-time scheduling to ensure deterministic timing:

```
$ trtexec –loadEngine=model.trt –useCudaGraph –noDataTransfers –useSpinWait
–iterations=100 –avgRuns=100 –exportTimes=measure.json
```

The reported latency corresponds to end-to-end inference time, averaged over multiple runs after warm-up. Memory footprint is assessed using the TensorRT Python inference API, implementing a custom CUDA memory allocator to track dynamic allocations and measure peak device memory consumption during inference. All benchmarks are performed under identical runtime conditions across precision modes (FP32, FP16, and INT8) to ensure fair and reproducible comparison.

11.5.2 Post-Processing Acceleration

First, we discuss the impact of the proposed implementation on the efficient decoding of the Instance Segmentation and Object Detection outputs. To this end, we benchmark and compare only the post-processing layer, comparing side-by-side the TensorRT and reference Pytorch implementations.

Instance Segmentation: Instance segmentation represents the most computationally demanding component of the multi-task pipeline, primarily due to the high cost of mask post-processing. We evaluate two implementations under two feature map resolutions: $192{\times}192$ (corresponding to an image resolution of $336{\times}336$) and $256{\times}256$ (corresponding to an input resolution of $448{\times}448$). By default, the proposed TensorRT plugin aggregates centroid candidates over a coarse grid of $32{\times}32$ buckets and explicitly decodes all 1024 candidate masks. In contrast, the baseline PyTorch implementation accumulates candidates on a finer $80{\times}80$ grid but decodes only a subset of selected masks. As summarized in Table 11.2, at an input resolution of $(336{\times}336)$, the plugin achieves $\sim 3\times$ speedup when using a coarser bucket grid $32{\times}32$ and a $\sim 2.5\times$ speedup when both implementations use the same grid configuration. While the plugin exhibits a higher memory footprint, caused by the CUDA buffer allocations, it substantially reduces inference latency, demonstrating the benefit of GPU-resident post-processing for instance segmentation.

Object Detection: We perform a similar evaluation for the post-processing stage of the object detection task (see Table 11.3). compares the PyTorch baseline with our custom TensorRT plugin implementation, including both cases with and without Non-Maximum Suppression (NMS). The TensorRT

Table 11.2 Benchmarking of Instance Segmentation Post-processor

Framework	Buckets	Feature res	Infer (ms)	Memory (MB)
Pytorch	80×80	192	134.39	30.72
		256	150.85	50.04
	32×32	192	100.70	29.82
		256	117.28	48.98
Plugin	32×32	192	34.89	162.81
		256	62.07	289.42

Table 11.3 Benchmarking of Object Detection Post-processor

Framework	NMS	Infer (ms)	Memory (MB)
Pytorch	No	4.014	0.029
	Yes	43.22	8.17
Plugin	No	0.017	0.02
	Yes	0.451	0.03

version leverages the optimized INMSLayer for NMS execution, which is fully integrated into the inference graph. As shown in Table 11.3, the plugin achieves a substantial latency reduction compared to the PyTorch implementation, yielding up to two orders of magnitude speedup in both configurations. When NMS is enabled, the TensorRT INMSLayer adds minimal overhead (0.451 ms vs. 0.017 ms), whereas the PyTorch implementation incurs a significant slowdown due to host-side execution. Memory usage remains nearly constant across settings, confirming that the proposed plugin and INMSLayer enable fully GPU-resident post-processing with negligible additional footprint.

11.5.3 Performance Assessment

We conducted different experiments varying: (a) The input resolution (b) The precision format (FP32, FP16, INT8) (c) post-processors implementation. We measured both the task metrics (mAP@50, mIoU, PQ, RMSE) and their runtime performance and memory footprints. The results, summarized in Table 11.4, show that lower precision formats (FP16 and INT8) introduce negligible degradation in the task metrics while offering substantial reductions in inference latency.

For the Object detection tasks (mAP@50 metric) and Instance Segmentation (PQ metric), we compare PyTorch-based post-processing (reported in braces) with custom CUDA-optimized runtime plugins. Interestingly, the mAP@50 consistently improves when using the efficient decoding implementation. Conversely, the PQ metric shows a slight degradation with

Table 11.4 Multi-task model performance assessment under different configurations of input resolution and arithmetic precision. map@50 and PQ are evaluated both using the proposed post-processors plugin and with the Pytorch reference implementation (value in brackets).

Res.	Precision	mAP@50	mIoU	PQ	RMSE	Infer (ms)	Mem (MB)
336	FP32	23.22 (17.28)	63.65	43.27 (46.62)	0.56	272.0 (377.8)	1585.7
	FP16	23.21 (17.35)	63.65	43.26 (46.63)	0.56	126.3 (232.7)	864.4
	INT8	22.58 (16.99)	63.60	42.94 (46.41)	0.56	112.0 (218.3)	556.0
448	FP32	35.54 (26.80)	64.35	44.06 (46.18)	0.47	544.0 (638.8)	1795.9
	FP16	35.58 (26.73)	64.35	44.06 (46.19)	0.47	225.8 (322.0)	1029.8
	INT8	35.53 (26.05)	64.10	43.86 (46.02)	0.47	200.0 (295.3)	725.8

the efficient post-processing, likely due to the reduced number of accumulation buckets (32×32 compared to 80×80), which limits the precision of instance-level mask aggregation.

11.5.4 End-To-End Results

The analyzed optimizations collectively nearly enable end-to-end perception pipeline execution under 100ms per frame at a resolution of 336×336, demonstrating promising results for fulfilling the real-time processing requirement for deployment on the HAura platform. In Figure 11.3 we

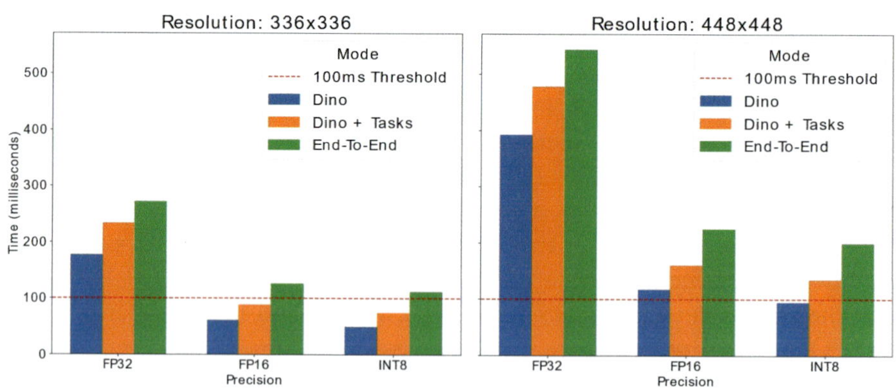

Figure 11.3 Latency breakdown of the perception pipeline for backbone only ("Dino"), full model ("Dino+Tasks"), and end-to-end execution.

further dissect the source of latency, comparing the execution of the backbone alone ("Dino"), the complete model of decoders and task projectors ("Dino+Tasks"), and the end-to-end execution including post-processing ("End-To-End"). In the most optimized INT8 configuration, post-processing time accounts for approximately 1/3 of the end-to-end execution time. Considering this, future developments will focus further on improving decoding efficiency, especially for the task of instance segmentation.

11.6 Conclusions

In this paper, we investigated the deployment of a multi-task deep neural network in an urban monitoring scenario. We first discussed how system-level constraints, such as real-time deadlines and the number of video streams to process, affect the overall design and performance. We then identified several tunable parameters that can be adjusted to meet timing requirements. Furthermore, we proposed an accelerated implementation of the post-processing modules used in multi-task models, which significantly improves end-to-end latency.

Our experimental evaluation demonstrated how the selected parameters influence overall performance, confirming that optimizing post-processing can yield substantial latency reductions. As future work, we plan to further enhance the post-processor implementation and investigate additional tuning parameters, such as batch size, to generalize our approach and meet a wider range of system requirements.

Acknowledgements

This research was partially funded by the dAIedge project (HORIZON-CL4-2022-HUMAN-02-02, Grant Agreement Number: 101120726) and the Ministry of Education and Science of Bulgaria (support for INSAIT, part of the Bulgarian National Roadmap for Research Infrastructure). C. Scribano work was partly funded by the Partenariato Esteso PE00000013 - "FAIR", funded by the European Commission under the NextGeneration EU program, PNRR - M4C2 Investimento 1.3.

References

[1] C. Scribano, I. Sanudo Olmedo, M. Verucchi, M. Bertogna e others, ≪ On-the-Edge Inference Enabled Vision System for Smart Cities, ≫

in SMART 2025, The Fourteenth International Conference on Smart Cities, Systems, Devices and Technologies, 2025.

[2] C. Scribano e F. Muzzini, ≪ Emergency vehicles in the Smart Cities: challenges and enabling technologies, ≫ in 2024 IEEE Symposium on Computers and Communications (ISCC), 2024.

[3] G. M. Lingani, D. B. Rawat e M. Garuba, ≪ Smart traffic management system using deep learning for smart city applications, ≫ in 2019 IEEE 9th annual computing and communication workshop and conference (CCWC), 2019.

[4] N. T. Ha, N. P. D. Tuan, T. H. Khanh, L. T. Du, T. C. Dinh, D. N. Sang, N. Van Son, N. L. D. Luan e N. T. Le, ≪ Leveraging Deep Learning Model for Emergency Situations Detection on Urban Road Using Images from CCTV Cameras, ≫ in 2022 International Conference on Engineering and Emerging Technologies (ICEET), 2022.

[5] R. Nouisser, S. K. Jarraya e M. Hammami, ≪ A Review of Vision-based Abnormal Human Activity Analysis for Elderly Emergency Detection, ≫ in 2023 International Conference on Innovations in Intelligent Systems and Applications (INISTA), 2023.

[6] N. Naik, S. D. Kominers, R. Raskar, E. L. Glaeser e C. A. Hidalgo, ≪ Computer vision uncovers predictors of physical urban change, ≫ Proceedings of the National Academy of Sciences, vol. 114, p. 7571–7576, 2017.

[7] K.-H. Thung e C.-Y. Wee, ≪ A brief review on multi-task learning, ≫ Multimedia Tools and Applications, vol. 77, p. 29705–29725, 2018.

[8] S. Khan, M. Naseer, M. Hayat, S. W. Zamir, F. S. Khan e M. Shah, ≪ Transformers in vision: A survey, ≫ ACM computing surveys (CSUR), vol. 54, p. 1–41, 2022.

[9] R. Ranftl, A. Bochkovskiy e V. Koltun, ≪ Vision transformers for dense prediction, ≫ in Proceedings of the IEEE/CVF international conference on computer vision, 2021.

[10] M. Caron, H. Touvron, I. Misra, H. Jégou, J. Mairal, P. Bojanowski e A. Joulin, ≪ Emerging properties in self-supervised vision transformers, ≫ in Proceedings of the IEEE/CVF international conference on computer vision, 2021.

[11] M. Oquab, T. Darcet, T. Moutakanni, H. V. Vo, M. Szafraniec, V. Khalidov, P. Fernandez, D. HAZIZA, F. Massa, A. El-Nouby, M. Assran, N. Ballas, W. Galuba, R. Howes, P.-Y. Huang, S.-W. Li, I. Misra, M. Rabbat, V. Sharma, G. Synnaeve, H. Xu, H. Jegou, J. Mairal, P. Labatut, A. Joulin e P. Bojanowski, ≪ DINOv2: Learning Robust Visual Features

without Supervision, ≫ Transactions on Machine Learning Research, 2024.

[12] S. Liu, Z. Zeng, T. Ren, F. Li, H. Zhang, J. Yang, Q. Jiang, C. Li, J. Yang, H. Su e others, ≪ Grounding dino: Marrying dino with grounded pre-training for open-set object detection, ≫ in European conference on computer vision, 2024.

[13] T. Ren, Q. Jiang, S. Liu, Z. Zeng, W. Liu, H. Gao, H. Huang, Z. Ma, X. Jiang, Y. Chen e others, ≪ Grounding dino 1.5: Advance the" edge" of open-set object detection, ≫ arXiv preprint arXiv:2405.10300, 2024.

[14] T. Ren, Y. Chen, Q. Jiang, Z. Zeng, Y. Xiong, W. Liu, Z. Ma, J. Shen, Y. Gao, X. Jiang e others, ≪ Dino-x: A unified vision model for open-world object detection and understanding, ≫ arXiv preprint arXiv:2411.14347, 2024.

[15] N. Prisadnikov, W. Van Gansbeke, D. P. Paudel e L. Van Gool, ≪ A simple and generalist approach for panoptic segmentation, ≫ arXiv preprint arXiv:2408.16504, 2024.

[16] A. Dosovitskiy, L. Beyer, A. Kolesnikov, D. Weissenborn, X. Zhai, T. Unterthiner, M. Dehghani, M. Minderer, G. Heigold, S. Gelly, J. Uszkoreit e N. Houlsby, ≪ An Image is Worth 16x16 Words: Transformers for Image Recognition at Scale, ≫ ICLR, 2021.

[17] T.-Y. Lin, M. Maire, S. Belongie, J. Hays, P. Perona, D. Ramanan, P. Dollár e C. L. Zitnick, ≪ Microsoft coco: Common objects in context, ≫ in European conference on computer vision, 2014.

[18] L. Yang, B. Kang, Z. Huang, Z. Zhao, X. Xu, J. Feng e H. Zhao, ≪ Depth anything v2, ≫ Advances in Neural Information Processing Systems, vol. 37, p. 21875–21911, 2024.

[19] A. Vaswani, N. Shazeer, N. Parmar, J. Uszkoreit, L. Jones, A. N. Gomez, Ł. Kaiser e I. Polosukhin, ≪ Attention is all you need, ≫ Advances in neural information processing systems, vol. 30, 2017.

[20] J. Redmon, S. Divvala, R. Girshick e A. Farhadi, ≪ You only look once: Unified, real-time object detection, ≫ in Proceedings of the IEEE conference on computer vision and pattern recognition, 2016.

[21] T. Dao, ≪ FlashAttention-2: Faster Attention with Better Parallelism and Work Partitioning, ≫ in International Conference on Learning Representations (ICLR), 2024.

[22] G. Xiao, J. Lin, M. Seznec, H. Wu, J. Demouth e S. Han, ≪ Smoothquant: Accurate and efficient post-training quantization for large language models, ≫ in International conference on machine learning, 2023.

[23] M. Everingham, L. Van Gool, C. K. I. Williams, J. Winn e A. Zisserman, ≪ The pascal visual object classes (voc) challenge, ≫ International journal of computer vision, vol. 88, p. 303–338, 2010.

[24] A. Garcia-Garcia, S. Orts-Escolano, S. Oprea, V. Villena-Martinez e J. Garcia-Rodriguez, ≪ A review on deep learning techniques applied to semantic segmentation, ≫ arXiv preprint arXiv:1704.06857, 2017.

[25] A. Kirillov, K. He, R. Girshick, C. Rother e P. Dollár, ≪ Panoptic segmentation, ≫ in Proceedings of the IEEE/CVF conference on computer vision and pattern recognition, 2019.

[26] D. Eigen, C. Puhrsch e R. Fergus, ≪ Depth map prediction from a single image using a multi-scale deep network, ≫ Advances in neural information processing systems, vol. 27, 2014.

12

Experiences in Deploying a Weapon Detector in a Smart City

Juan Daniel Muñoz[1], Hugo Albandea Merino[1], Jesus Ruiz-Santaquiteria[1], Oscar Deniz[1], and Micaela Verucchi[2]

[1]VISILAB, University of Castilla-La Mancha, Spain
[2]Hipert Srl., Italy

Abstract

This work presents the ongoing development of a handgun detection system for a smart city. This detector is expected to continuously analyse images taken by a surveillance camera installed at the entrance hall of a public building. The detector is deployed on a Jetson Orin Nano-based device with constrained computational resources. The development process began with an analysis of hardware limitations, which guided the design of lightweight yet effective deep learning models. Several processing pipelines were considered: a two-stage approach involving person detection followed by hand-region classification, and a direct handgun detection approach. Custom datasets were built and used to train models adapted to the device, while carefully avoiding overfitting. Performance was systematically evaluated using metrics such as mean Average Precision (mAP) and frames per second (FPS). The best trade-off between accuracy and inference speed was obtained with a YOLOv8s model trained exclusively for handgun detection, achieving 75.15% AP50 on the test set and sustaining 20 FPS. The detector was further integrated with MQTT for seamless communication with ThingsBoard, enabling the automatic transmission of detection events. Additional necessary work included

DOI: 10.1201/9788743815273-12

fully headless execution and real-time parameter adjustment through terminal commands. Current work focuses on refining detection performance and exploring alternative models to further improve efficiency and accuracy.

Keywords: weapon detection, edge AI, deep learning, real time, computer vision, MQTT.

12.1 Introduction and Background

Gun violence remains a major threat to public safety, especially in crowded urban areas where rapid intervention is critical [1]. Detecting firearms in real time has thus become a key objective of intelligent surveillance systems. Traditional methods rely on controlled screening environments (such as baggage inspection or millimetric wave scanners) where image acquisition is highly structured [2]. In contrast, open-scene detection introduces challenges such as varying illumination, occlusions, and limited computational capacity at the edge.

Recent advances in deep learning have significantly improved visible firearm detection in CCTV footage, enabling reliable recognition in unconstrained environments [3]. Mehta et al. [4] proposed a multi-purpose YOLOv3-based system capable of detecting both guns and fire in real time, processing video streams at 45 frames per second, and demonstrating high robustness across several datasets, achieving a maximum accuracy of 89.3%. Similarly, Bhatti et al. [5] compared multiple deep learning detectors, including VGG16, Faster R-CNN, and YOLOv4, and found YOLOv4 to deliver the best performance for handgun identification in surveillance videos, reaching an mAP of 91.72%.

Despite their accuracy, these appearance-based methods often produce false alarms, motivating pose-aware approaches. One study [6] showed that integrating body pose information into CNN detectors, such as RetinaNet and YOLOv3, reduces false positives and improves precision (YOLOv3 achieved a precision of 96.23%). Building on this idea, another work [7] incorporated a full-body pose classifier to distinguish threatening from non-threatening postures, further enhancing reliability in real-world scenes.

Beyond visible imagery, researchers have also addressed concealed weapon detection. Khan et al. [8] introduced a real-time 3D radar imaging framework using a modified U-Net to localize hidden weapons regardless of orientation, achieving both accuracy and speed suitable for security checkpoints. Complementary work combined thermal imaging and deep learning in a two-stage pipeline for wearable devices [9], enabling mobile detection of firearms with reduced false positives and practical real-time performance. The method achieved an mAP@50–95 of 64.52% on a custom thermal dataset.

Nevertheless, most of these methods remain confined to laboratory settings. The present work advances this field by focusing on the real-time deployment of an efficient handgun detection system on an edge device integrated into a communication framework for automated event reporting. This direction aligns with ongoing efforts in smart city research, such as the CLASS project [10], which developed an edge–cloud analytics framework validated in the Modena Automotive Smart Area (MASA); the HAura platform [11], which supports privacy-preserving inference on the edge; and the AI-CAM initiative [12], which promotes cooperative, infrastructure-assisted perception. Together, these developments provide the technological foundation for the real-world implementation described in this work, to be tested within the MASA environment as part of ongoing experimentation in intelligent urban surveillance.

12.2 MASA and the HAura system

Since 2018, the University of Modena and Reggio Emilia (UNIMORE) and the Municipality of Modena have been jointly developing the Modena Automotive Smart Area (MASA). MASA is both an infrastructure and a physical test area of approximately 2 km^2 within the city of Modena (see Figure 12.1). It was conceived as a living laboratory for smart city technologies, designed to generate actionable data that can enhance urban mobility, sustainability, and safety. The initiative builds upon the expertise of the HiPeRT Lab, a research group within the Department of Physics, Computer Science, and Mathematics (FIM) of UNIMORE, directed by Prof. Marko Bertogna. The Lab has established a strong track record in high-performance real-time computing on embedded platforms, particularly in the domain of autonomous driving. In 2020 gave rise to Hipert s.r.l., which continues to industrialise and scale these technologies, focusing on autonomous robotics. MASA thus represents a natural extension of this research, where the smart city itself becomes a technological enabler and support system for connected and automated mobility.

A central technological element within MASA is the HAura system, developed and industrialised by Hipert s.r.l. HAura is a modular and distributed platform for detection, analysis, and event management in real time (see Figure 12.2). Its architecture is composed of multiple HAura Edge units

Figure 12.1 Modena Automotive Smart Area (MASA).

deployed in the urban environment. Each Edge device integrates dual RGB cameras, GPS, and a high-performance embedded computing board, enabling on-site execution of AI-based detection and tracking of different categories of road users. Anonymized metadata (including position, class, velocity, and direction) are generated and transmitted with minimal latency. The HAura Aggregator then consolidates data from multiple Edge units, removes redundancies, and provides a unified geo-referenced view of the monitored area. Importantly, the Aggregator incorporates predictive models capable of forecasting potential collisions and disseminating warnings in real time. At the system boundary, On-Board Units (OBUs) act as recipients of these alerts, which may correspond to connected vehicles or autonomous vehicles. In this perspective, the OBU's perception is extended by the "eyes" of the city infrastructure, thereby augmenting situational awareness and safety.

The design of the MASA and the HAura emphasizes low-latency operation, with end-to-end communication times of less than 100 milliseconds

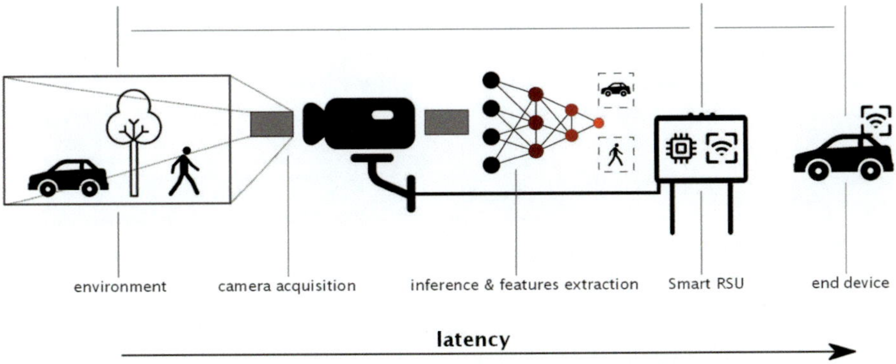

Figure 12.2 Overview of the HAura edge-to-end architecture within MASA, showing the data flow from camera acquisition to inference, smart RSU processing, and end-device communication with increasing latency [12].

between the detection of a road user and the reception of the corresponding alert by an OBU, within the MASA. Such real-time guarantees are essential for safety-critical urban applications. Furthermore, the system is designed with scalability and extensibility in mind. Each HAura Edge unit relies on a general-purpose computing board (based on NVIDIA's Jetson Orin Nano), enabling the deployment of additional software packages and future functionalities. The integration of Over-The-Air (OTA) updates, which now cover both application-level software and the operating system, ensures that the installed infrastructure can be securely and continuously upgraded. As such, MASA provides a replicable model of a smart city platform, capable of hosting advanced services such as smart parking, traffic management, environmental monitoring, and support for cooperative, connected, and automated mobility.

12.3 Dataset Creation

The development of the weapon detection system began with the construction of a dedicated dataset. Images were collected from a wide variety of sources, including publicly available internet repositories, video material from YouTube, frames extracted from commercial video games, and video recordings produced in the VISILAB laboratory at the University of Castilla-La Mancha (UCLM). Particular attention was given to acquiring images that resembled the perspective of a surveillance camera, typically positioned at a medium distance and slightly elevated relative to the subjects. This

Figure 12.3 Test Set images comparison. Left: test set A; middle: test set B; right: test set C.

choice was motivated by the intended application of the system in smart city environments (in MASA).

In order to increase the size and variability of the dataset, several data augmentation techniques were applied. These included geometric transformations such as rotations, as well as photometric adjustments to simulate different environmental and acquisition conditions. The initial dataset contained 7,783 images. After augmentation, this number increased to 46,632, which was subsequently divided into 37,308 images for training and 9,324 for validation. Images and data augmentation techniques presented in [13] were used.

Furthermore, to develop and evaluate a region classifier, the bounding boxes (BBoxes) corresponding to each annotated weapon instance were cropped and stored as independent images. This procedure produced an additional dataset consisting of 54,180 images for training and 11,610 for validation.

To assess model generalisation, a distinct test set of 310 images was assembled, referred to as *Test Set A*. To evaluate robustness under different visual conditions, two derivative sets were also created: *Test Set B*, which consists of the same images as Test Set A but with reduced brightness (simulating low light), and *Test Set C*, generated by simulating greater distance between the camera and the subject. Examples of these sets are shown in Figure 12.3. All quantitative results presented later in this article are computed with respect to these three test sets.

12.4 Architectures and Experimental Platform

Several deep learning architectures were employed in this work, selected for their balance between accuracy and computational efficiency, with consideration for the constraints of embedded platforms.

For object detection, we adopted YOLOv8s (You Only Look Once, version 8, small variant), a single-stage detector that predicts bounding boxes and class probabilities in one forward pass [14]. This design achieves higher inference speed than two-stage methods while maintaining competitive accuracy. The small variant of YOLOv8 [15] offers an effective trade-off between performance and computational cost, making it suitable for real-time inference on the Jetson Orin Nano.

To estimate human poses, we evaluated pose-based YOLO models and MediaPipe Pose. Pre-trained YOLOv8n, YOLOv11n, and YOLOv11x [16] models were compared to assess the trade-off between model size, accuracy, and latency. The smaller (n) variants prioritize efficiency, whereas the larger v11x model provides greater precision at higher computational cost. In parallel, we experimented with MediaPipe Pose [17] a lightweight two-stage framework predicting 33 body keypoints. It is specifically optimized for real-time applications on CPUs and mobile-class devices, requiring significantly fewer computational resources than conventional deep learning–based detectors. This made it a valuable baseline to compare against more computationally demanding architectures, particularly in scenarios where inference latency is critical.

For weapon classification within cropped hand regions, two convolutional neural networks were explored: EfficientNet [18] and MobileNetV2 [19]. EfficientNet employs compound scaling to balance depth, width, and resolution, achieving high accuracy with reduced complexity. MobileNetV2, based on depthwise separable convolutions and inverted residuals, offers even greater efficiency and is particularly suited to real-time edge applications, albeit with slightly lower accuracy.

All experiments were performed on the NVIDIA Jetson Orin Nano Developer Kit [20], integrating an Ampere GPU with 1,024 CUDA cores and 32 Tensor Cores, and 8 GB of LPDDR5 memory.

12.5 Detector and Communication Workflow

Two detection strategies were developed to address real-time weapon recognition under the computational constraints of the target hardware. Each was first implemented as an independent prototype and later adapted for integration into the final system. The first approach followed a single-stage object detection pipeline using YOLOv8s applied directly to full camera frames. This configuration aimed to localize and classify weapons in one step, maximizing frame rate on the Jetson Orin Nano. The small (s) variant offered an optimal balance between accuracy and efficiency, preventing the detector from monopolizing system resources required for concurrent smart city processes. The second approach implemented a two-stage pipeline to improve robustness and reduce false positives. A pose-based model (either a YOLO-based pose detector (v8n, v11n, v11x) or MediaPipe Pose) was first used to locate individuals and extract keypoints. Based on these keypoints, regions around the wrists and hands were cropped and analysed by a classifier (either EfficientNet or MobileNetV2). The former achieved higher accuracy, while the latter offered lower latency, enabling flexible trade-offs between precision and computational cost. This design explicitly linked detected weapons to human subjects, minimizing erroneous detections on background objects, albeit at a reduced frame rate compared to the single-stage method.

Both pipelines were developed and tested locally on a Jetson Orin Nano Developer Kit, enabling rapid prototyping before remote deployment. For the latter, the system was first adapted for headless operation via secure SSH access. Runtime parameters could be adjusted dynamically through a curses-based terminal interface, ensuring flexible configuration without restarting services. Moreover, upon detecting a weapon, the system generates a structured JSON message containing detection metadata (timestamp, confidence, device ID) and publishes it via MQTT to a ThingsBoard broker. This enables reliable, real-time transmission and logging of smart city events for visualization, analytics, while decoupling edge processing from backend services for improved scalability and resilience.

Both detection strategies were encapsulated within Docker containers to ensure portability, reproducibility, and consistent performance across Jetson devices and deployment environments.

12.6 Training Process

The training process was designed to maximize detection and classification performance while minimizing overfitting. To this end, extensive experimentation was carried out with key hyperparameters, primarily the number of epochs, the learning rate, and the batch size. Hyperparameter values were adjusted iteratively, guided by validation accuracy and average precision (AP) on the test sets. This approach ensured that improvements in training performance did not come at the expense of model generalisation. The main hyperparameters selected can be seen in Table 12.1.

Table 12.1 Hyperparameters chosen to train the models used in the experiments

Trained Model	Epochs	Batch size	Input Resolution (pixels)	Learning rate
Single-stage detector	30	16	640x640	10^{-2}
Region classifier	30	16	224x224	10^{-6}

12.7 Results

The evaluation of object detection models typically relies on two complementary aspects: accuracy and efficiency. In this work, accuracy is measured using Average Precision (AP), while efficiency is assessed in terms of inference speed, expressed as frames per second (FPS).

To make AP meaningful, several fundamental concepts must first be defined [21].

- Ground truth. Human-annotated bounding boxes specifying object locations and class labels. These serve as the reference for evaluating detections.
- True Positive (TP). A detection correctly matching a ground-truth object, determined by the Intersection over Union (IoU): the overlap area between a predicted box B_p and a ground-truth box B_{gt} divided by their union,

$$IoU = \frac{\text{area}\left(B_p \cap B_{\text{gt}}\right)}{\text{area}\left(B_p \cup B_{\text{gt}}\right)} \tag{12.1}$$

A prediction is considered a TP if its IoU exceeds a predefined threshold (e.g., 0.5), following standard one-to-one matching rules.

In addition to IoU, we also employed the Intersection over Minimum area (IoMin) metric [22]. IoMin is defined as:

$$\text{IoMin}\left(B_p, B_{\text{gt}}\right) = \frac{B_p \cap B_{\text{gt}}}{\min\left(\text{Area}\left(B_p\right), \text{Area}\left(B_{\text{gt}}\right)\right)} \tag{12.2}$$

Unlike IoU, which penalises size discrepancies, IoMin produces high scores when the predicted box is fully contained within the ground-truth region, even if their sizes differ substantially.

This distinction is crucial in our pose-based detection setup, where hand regions are cropped using fixed-size bounding boxes around detected keypoints. Such crops may include irrelevant background or omit parts of the forearm, leading to artificially low IoU values even when the handgun is correctly captured. IoMin mitigates this issue by prioritising whether the object of interest (the handgun) lies within the predicted region, aligning with our operational goal of early weapon detection in surveillance scenarios. Figure 12.4 illustrates the difference between IoU and IoMin.

- False Positive (FP). A predicted box with no sufficient overlap with any ground-truth object, or a duplicate detection for an already matched instance.
- False Negative (FN). A ground-truth object not detected by the model.
- True Negative (TN). Not typically defined in object detection, as the set of possible negative boxes is effectively infinite; evaluation therefore focuses on TP, FP, and FN.

Given the counts above, precision and recall quantify two complementary aspects of detector behaviour:

$$\text{Precision} = \frac{TP}{TP + FP} \tag{12.3}$$

$$\text{Recall} = \frac{TP}{TP + FN} \tag{12.4}$$

Precision measures the proportion of correct detections (penalising false alarms), while recall measures the proportion of detected ground-truth objects (penalising misses). A strict detector tends to have high precision but low recall, whereas a permissive one exhibits the opposite.

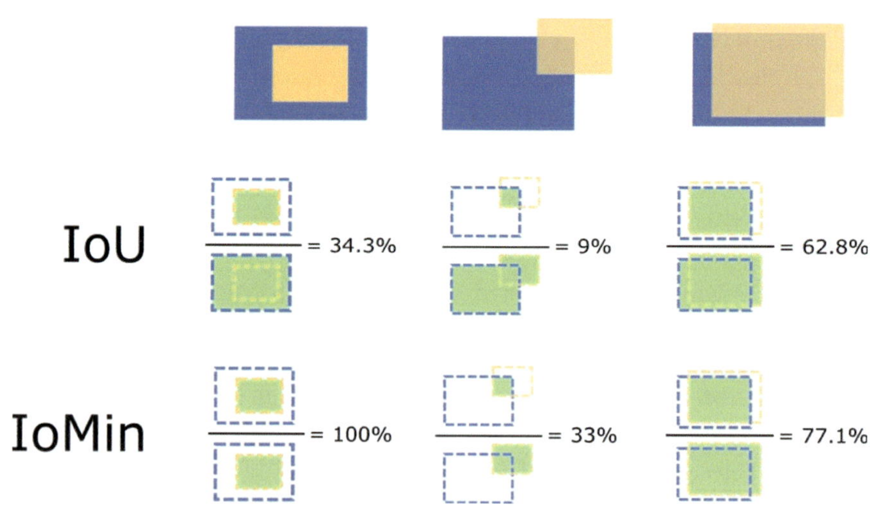

Figure 12.4 Examples of IoU and IoMin values for 3 different overlaps between detection and ground truth [22].

By varying the detection confidence threshold, a precision–recall (PR) curve is obtained. Average Precision (AP) is then computed as the area under the PR curve, summarising the trade-off between precision and recall across all thresholds (see Equation (12.5)).

$$AP = \int_0^1 \text{Precision}(R)dR \tag{12.5}$$

where R represents recall.

When multiple classes are involved, mean Average Precision (mAP) is reported as the arithmetic mean of per-class AP values (see Equation (12.6)).

$$mAP = \frac{1}{N}\sum_{i=1}^{N} AP_i \tag{12.6}$$

where AP_i is the average precision for class i.

In this study, only one class ("Handgun") is evaluated, so mAP reduces to a single AP value.

In addition to accuracy metrics, detector speed is a critical factor. A low frame rate (FPS) can cause frames to be skipped, risking missed detections if an armed individual passes quickly through the camera's view. The required FPS thus depends on the subject's movement speed: faster motion demands higher FPS to ensure at least one frame captures the weapon.

To establish a realistic reference, we analysed surveillance footage from the 2023 Nashville school shooting, measuring how long the weapon remained visible across three camera views (examples of these views are shown in Figure 12.5). From these durations, we estimated the minimum FPS necessary to guarantee at least one processed frame per scene, with results presented in Table 12.2.

This criterion only guarantees a single processed frame during the visibility window. In practice, detectors require multiple frames with the weapon visible. A more realistic requirement is therefore FPS_{min}[f0] = N/T, where N is the required number of frames (e.g., 5–10). For instance, with T = 5s in

Table 12.2 Duration of weapon visibility in each camera view during the Nashville school shooting (2023) and the corresponding absolute minimum FPS required to ensure at least one processed frame contains the handgun.

Camera view	Visibility T(s)	Minimum FPS (1/T)
Entrance Hall	5	0.2
Corridor	27	0.037
Lobby	10	0.1

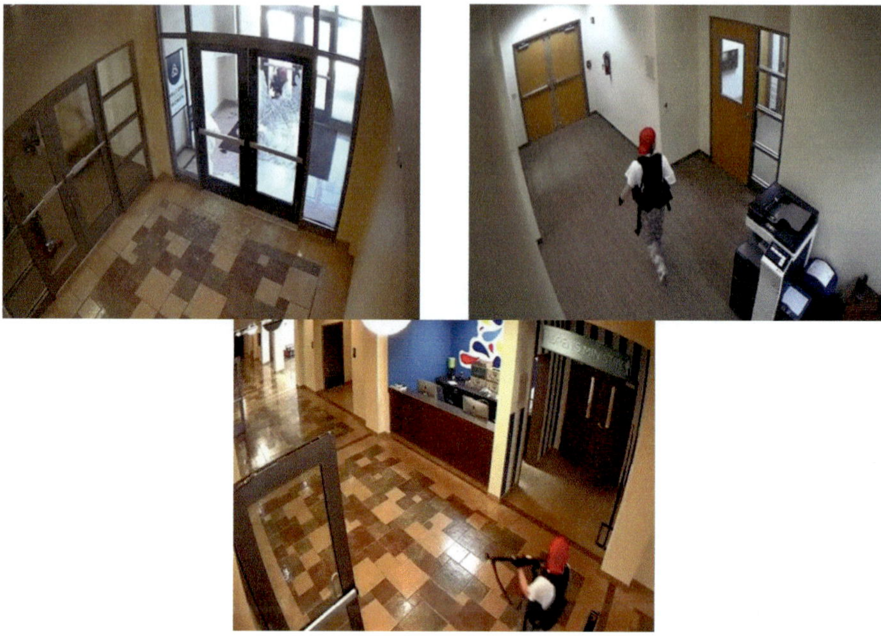

Figure 12.5 Surveillance camera views from the Nashville school shooting (2023) used to estimate visibility times: entrance hall (top left), corridor (top right), and lobby (bottom). The analysed video was taken from Wikipedia.

the entrance hall, the requirement becomes 1 FPS for N = 5 and 2 FPS for N = 10. These values remain modest compared to the 15–20 FPS typically achieved on the deployment hardware, but they better reflect the need for redundancy and reliable detection.

One should also account for the detector's per-frame detection probability "p". If the model only detects the weapon with probability p on any single processed frame, then multiple frames are needed to achieve a desired overall reliability. The probability of at least one success across N independent frames is:

$$P(\geq 1 \text{ detection }) = 1 - (1-p)^N \tag{12.7}$$

Let us suppose that we want a target reliability of P_{target}. An example value of 0.95 would indicate that we want a 95% probability of detecting the weapon at least once while it is in view. Then the required number of frames is:

$$N = \left\lceil \frac{\log\left(1 - P_{\text{target}}\right)}{\log(1-p)} \right\rceil \tag{12.8}$$

For example, if p = 0.5, then N = 5 frames are required to reach 95% reliability; if p = 0.8, N = 2 frames suffice. Combining this requirement with the visibility window T gives the operational frame-rate threshold FPS_{min}[f0] = N/T. Now, we considered a target probability P_{target} = 0.99 and three representative per-frame detection probabilities $p \in \{0.75, 0.80, 0.85\}$. Obtaining N values using Equation 8 and using FPS_{min} = N/T across the three Nashville scenes (Table 12.2), results are shown in Table 12.3.

After establishing the evaluation metrics and the theoretical requirements for real-time operation, we now present the results obtained with the different detection strategies. Comparing the two main pipelines explained, the goal of these experiments was to systematically analyse the trade-offs between accuracy, measured by AP_{50} across the three test sets, and efficiency, expressed in frames per second (FPS) on the target Jetson Orin Nano platform.

The results in Table 12.4 highlight the trade-off between accuracy and inference speed across the evaluated strategies. Each strategy achieves the FPS_{min} value for each Nashville camera view. The single-stage YOLOv8s detector provided balanced performance, sustaining 20 FPS with an AP_{50} around 0.70–0.75 across the test sets. This makes it a robust option for scenarios where real-time responsiveness is essential. The two-stage pipeline with YOLOv11x pose + EfficientNet classification achieved the highest accuracy (AP_{50} above 0.81) but at the cost of significantly reduced speed (3.5 FPS), which may limit its usability in continuous surveillance applications. Using lighter pose models (YOLOv11n) improved efficiency (6 FPS) but with some loss of precision.

The MediaPipe-based pipeline delivered intermediate efficiency (10 FPS) but suffered from poor accuracy, especially under degraded conditions (Test Set C), indicating that its lightweight design sacrifices robustness for handgun

Table 12.3 Operational frame-rate thresholds (FPS_{min}) required to achieve 99% detection reliability (P_{target} = 0.99) for three per-frame detection probabilities (p = 0.75, 0.80, 0.85) across the three Nashville camera views.

Camera View	Visibility T (s)	p	Required Frames N	FPS_{min} = N/T
Entrance Hall	5	0.75	4	0.80
		0.80	3	0.60
		0.85	3	0.60
Corridor	27	0.75	4	0.15
		0.80	3	0.11
		0.85	3	0.11
Lobby	10	0.75	4	0.40
		0.80	3	0.30
		0.85	3	0.30

Table 12.4 Comparison of detection strategies showing accuracy (AP_{50} on three test sets) and inference speed (FPS) on the Jetson Orin Nano platform

Strategy	Models used	%AP 50 Test Set A	%AP 50 Test Set B	%AP 50 Test Set C	FPS
Full frame weapon detection	YOLO 8s (detection)	75.15	71.45	70.24	20
Region proposal + classification	YOLO 11x (pose) + EfficientNet (classification)	83.11	80.99	81.42	3.5
Region proposal + classification	YOLO 11n (pose) + EfficientNet (classification)	75.09	74.75	78.71	6
Region proposal + classification	MediaPipe (pose) + EfficientNet (classification)	65.42	49.59	32.65	10
Region proposal + classification	YOLO 8n (pose) + MobileNetV2 (classification)	57.36	53.06	45.22	20

detection. Finally, the combination of YOLOv8n pose with MobileNetV2 classification achieved the highest efficiency (20 FPS) but with the lowest accuracy ($AP_{50} < 0.58$).

Overall, the comparison confirms that no single configuration dominates both metrics. For practical deployment on the Jetson Orin Nano, the YOLOv8s full-frame detector emerges as the best compromise, offering sufficient accuracy together with real-time performance (>15 FPS). The two-stage pipelines provide useful insights into how accuracy can be improved, but their higher computational cost makes them less attractive under strict resource constraints.

12.8 Future work

Future work will involve deploying the handgun detection system within the Modena Automotive Smart Area (MASA) using the HAura Edge device for on-site inference and integration with the smart city network. This will allow evaluation under realistic conditions, considering lighting changes, occlusions, and movement, while assessing interoperability, latency, and communication reliability. Concurrently, efforts will focus on improving accuracy and efficiency through optimized training, model compression, and hyperparameter tuning. Long-term testing will monitor continuous operation to ensure stability, scalability, and sustained performance on the Jetson Orin Nano platform.

12.9 Conclusion

This work presented the development of a real-time handgun detection system designed for deployment in smart city environments. The proposed detector was implemented on a Jetson Orin Nano platform, addressing the constraints of embedded computing while maintaining a balance between accuracy and inference speed. Two complementary detection strategies were explored: a single-stage approach based on YOLOv8s and a two-stage pipeline combining pose estimation with region classification. Experimental results demonstrated that the YOLOv8s full-frame detector achieved the best trade-off, sustaining 20 FPS with an AP_{50} of 75.15%, making it suitable for continuous surveillance applications on resource-limited devices.

Beyond model optimization, the system was integrated into an MQTT-based communication framework, enabling automatic event reporting and real-time configuration. This end-to-end design (from dataset creation to deployment) illustrates a practical approach to embedding AI-driven perception in urban infrastructures. The forthcoming integration of the detector into a HAura Edge unit within the Modena Automotive Smart Area (MASA) will extend this work to large-scale, real-world testing. These experiments will validate system robustness under dynamic conditions and confirm its role as a functional component of the HAura smart city ecosystem, paving the way for future research on intelligent, privacy-aware, and responsive urban surveillance solutions.

Acknowledgements

This work was partially funded by Horizon Europe project dAIEdge, Grant n. 101120726, by the European Commission.

References

[1] Gun Violence Archive, "Gun Violence Archive," Gunviolencearchive.org, Apr. 21, 2024. https://www.gunviolencearchive.org/

[2] S. A. Ali Shah, M. Ahmad Al-Khasawneh, and M. I. Uddin, "Review of Weapon Detection Techniques within the Scope of Street-Crimes", in 2021 2nd International Conference on Smart Computing and Electronic Enterprise (ICSCEE), 2021, pp. 26–37, https://doi.org/10.1109/ICSCEE50312.2021.9498007.

[3] S. Yellapragada et al., "CCTV-Gun: Benchmarking Handgun Detection in CCTV Images", arXiv [cs.CV]. 2023, https://doi.org/10.48550/arXiv.2303.10703.

[4] P. Mehta, A. Kumar, and S. Bhattacharjee, "Fire and Gun Violence based Anomaly Detection System Using Deep Neural Networks", in 2020 International Conference on Electronics and Sustainable Communication Systems (ICESC), 2020, pp. 199–204, https://doi.org/10.1109/ICESC48915.2020.9155625.

[5] M. T. Bhatti, M. G. Khan, M. Aslam, and M. J. Fiaz, "Weapon Detection in Real-Time CCTV Videos Using Deep Learning", IEEE Access, vol. 9, pp. 34366–34382, 2021, https://doi.org/10.1109/ACCESS.2021.3059170.

[6] J. Salido, V. Lomas, J. Ruiz-Santaquiteria, and O. Deniz, "Automatic Handgun Detection with Deep Learning in Video Surveillance Images", Applied Sciences, vol. 11, no. 13, 2021, https://doi.org/10.3390/app11136085.

[7] J. Ruiz-Santaquiteria, O. Deniz, N. Vállez, A. Velasco Mata, and G. Bueno, "Improving handgun detectors with human pose classification", 09 2022, pp. 1040–1047, https://doi.org/10.17979/spudc.9788497498418.1040.

[8] N. S. Khan, K. Ogura, E. Cosatto, and M. Ariyoshi, "Real-time Concealed Weapon Detection on 3D Radar Images for Walk-through Screening System", in 2023 IEEE/CVF Winter Conference on Applications of Computer Vision (WACV), 2023, pp. 673–681, https://doi.org/10.1109/WACV56688.2023.00074.

[9] J. D. Muñoz, J. Ruiz-Santaquiteria, O. Deniz, and G. Bueno, "Concealed Weapon Detection Using Thermal Cameras", Journal of Imaging, vol. 11, no. 3, 2025, https://doi.org/10.3390/jimaging11030072.

[10] R. Cavicchioli, R. Martoglia, and M. Verucchi, "A Novel Real-Time Edge-Cloud Big Data Management and Analytics Framework for Smart Cities", JOURNAL OF UNIVERSAL COMPUTER SCIENCE, 01 2022, https://doi.org/10.3897/jucs.71645.

[11] C. Scribano, I. S. Olmedo, M. Verucchi, D. P. Paudel, M. Bertogna, and L. Van Gool, "On-the-Edge Inference Enabled Vision System for Smart

Cities", in SMART 2025: The Fourteenth International Conference on Smart Cities, Systems, Devices and Technologies, 2025, pp. 24–28, https://hdl.handle.net/11380/1387818.

[12] G. Ferraro et al., "Towards Smart Cities with AI-CAM: Assisted by Infrastructure Cooperative Awareness Messages," 2025 IEEE Conference on Standards for Communications and Networking (CSCN), Bologna, Italy, 2025, pp. 1-6, https://doi.org/10.1109/CSCN67557.2025.11230591.

[13] J. Ruiz-Santaquiteria, A. Velasco-Mata, N. Vallez, O. Deniz, and G. Bueno, "Improving handgun detection through a combination of visual features and body pose-based data", Pattern Recognition, vol. 136, p. 109252, 2023, https://doi.org/10.1016/j.patcog.2022.109252.

[14] P. Jiang, D. Ergu, F. Liu, Y. Cai, y B. Ma, "A Review of Yolo Algorithm Developments," Procedia Computer Science, vol. 199, pp. 1066-1073, 2022, https://doi.org/10.1016/j.procs.2022.01.135.

[15] M. Yaseen, "What is YOLOv8: An In-Depth Exploration of the Internal Features of the Next-Generation Object Detector", arXiv [cs.CV]. 2024, https://doi.org/10.48550/arXiv.2408.15857.

[16] R. Khanam and M. Hussain, "YOLOv11: An Overview of the Key Architectural Enhancements", arXiv [cs.CV]. 2024, https://doi.org/10.48550/arXiv.2410.17725.

[17] C. Lugaresi et al., "MediaPipe: A Framework for Building Perception Pipelines", arXiv [cs.DC]. 2019, https://doi.org/10.48550/arXiv.1906.08172.

[18] M. Tan and Q. Le, "EfficientNet: Rethinking Model Scaling for Convolutional Neural Networks," in Proceedings of the 36th International Conference on Machine Learning (ICML), PMLR, vol. 97, pp. 6105–6114, May 2019, https://doi.org/10.48550/arXiv.1905.11946.

[19] K. Dong, C. Zhou, Y. Ruan, and Y. Li, "MobileNetV2 Model for Image Classification," in 2020 2nd International Conference on Information Technology and Computer Application (ITCA), 2020, pp. 476–480, https://doi.org/10.1109/ITCA52113.2020.00106.

[20] F. P. Scalcon et al., "AI-Powered Video Monitoring: Assessing the NVIDIA Jetson Orin Devices for Edge Computing Applications", in 2024 IEEE Transportation Electrification Conference and Expo (ITEC), 2024, pp. 1–6, https://doi.org/10.1109/ITEC60657.2024.10598994.

[21] R. Padilla, S. L. Netto, and E. A. B. da Silva, "A Survey on Performance Metrics for Object-Detection Algorithms", in 2020 International

Conference on Systems, Signals and Image Processing (IWSSIP), 2020, pp. 237–242, https://doi.org/10.1109/IWSSIP48289.2020.9145130.

[22] A. Velasco-Mata, J. Ruiz-Santaquiteria, N. Vallez, and O. Deniz, "Using human pose information for handgun detection", Neural Computing and Applications, vol. 33, no. 24, pp. 17273–17286, Dec. 2021, https://doi.org/10.1007/s00521-021-06317-8.

13

A 3D Simulation Framework for Behavior Cloning on Edge AI-Enabled E-Scooters in Smart Cities

Artemis Stefanidou[1], Eleni Tsaousi[1], Elena Politi[1], Ihsan Can Yalabuk[2], Emrecan Bati[3], Burak Tüfekçi[2], and George Dimitrakopoulos[1]

[1]Harokopio University of Athens, Greece
[2]TÜBİTAK B İLGEM, Türkiye
[3]HOP, Türkiye

Abstract

Modern mobility systems are rapidly advancing through automation, connectivity, and remote operation technologies. Across land and sea, autonomous and teleoperated vehicles are redefining safe, efficient, and sustainable transportation. This work presents a 3D simulation framework for training and evaluating Behavior Cloning (BC) models on edge-AI-enabled micromobility platforms. The framework integrates physics-based simulation with lightweight visual-policy learning to enable autonomous navigation under limited computational resources. The best configuration achieved a weighted F1 score of 0.99 and maintained near- real-time performance on CPU-only setups (44.7 ms per frame, 22 FPS, 1.55 GB RAM), demonstrating the practicality of efficient learning-based control for next-generation e-scooters and smart urban mobility systems.

Keywords: behavior cloning, e-scooter, autonomous vehicles, path planning.

DOI: 10.1201/9788743815273-13

13.1 Introduction and Background

Modern mobility systems are undergoing a significant transformation through the integration of automation, connectivity, and remote operation technologies [1]. Across land, sea, and air, autonomous vessels, aerial drones, teleoperated cars, and intelligent e-scooters are reshaping the way people and goods are transported in urban and maritime domains. These emerging solutions aim to improve safety, efficiency, and sustainability while enabling new modes of transportation that reduce the need for human control onboard [2]. This technological shift has been further accelerated by advances in edge computing, low-latency communication (e.g., 5G/6G), and lightweight Artificial Intelligence (AI) models, which now allow intelligent agents to operate with real-time perception and control even on resource-constrained embedded platforms [3]. Edge intelligence reduces reliance on cloud infrastructure, increases resilience to communication delays, and supports autonomous operation in bandwidth-limited environments.

However, many existing mobility architectures still rely on rich multi-sensor setups, such as RGB-D cameras, LiDAR, IMU, and radar, and on complex perception–planning pipelines originally designed for larger autonomous vehicles. Even recent Foundation Models (FMs), despite their advances in unified and semantically rich perception, remain computationally demanding and unsuitable for low-power embedded platforms [4]. As a result, such high-capacity configurations become impractical for compact micro-mobility systems, including e-scooters and small delivery robots, which operate under strict constraints in weight, cost, power consumption, and onboard computational capacity [5]. These challenges motivate the exploration of simplified perception modalities and task-specific visual encodings that enable efficient, real-time decision-making without heavy sensor fusion or GPU-intensive processing.

Moreover, the same principles extend beyond ground and maritime mobility. Aerial and underwater vehicles increasingly adopt similar hybrid architectures that combine autonomy with teleoperation, especially in complex or safety-critical environments. Drones, in particular, share the same constraints on onboard computation, energy efficiency, and perception under uncertain conditions. As a result, lightweight image-based and imitation-driven frameworks offer a unified methodology for intelligent navigation across land, air, and sea domains.

Despite this progress, there remains a gap in exploring minimalist sensory modalities in particular, using extremely simplified visual representations (e.g., binary, black-and-white encoding) to drive navigation policies. However, transferring visually trained navigation policies from simulation to real micro-mobility platforms remains a major challenge due to the well-known sim-to-real gap. Recent studies show that discrepancies in sensing fidelity, motion blur, and actuation nonlinearities can significantly degrade real-world performance [6]. Similar domain gaps have also been documented in autonomous-driving perception pipelines, where models trained on CARLA synthetic data struggle to generalize to real-world lane geometry and appearance without explicit domain-adaptation mechanisms [7]. If such methods prove viable, they could dramatically lower the barrier to deploying autonomous or teleoperated systems on micro-mobility platforms (such as e-scooters), where payload, power, and compute budgets are extremely limited.

In this context, the primary objective of this work is to develop a Behavior Cloning (BC) model that can serve as a pretrained policy for subsequent Reinforcement Learning (RL) stages. Such a model enables the agent to start from an informed behavioral prior rather than learning entirely from scratch, accelerating convergence and improving stability in complex environments.

Building on these innovations, our work is organized around four key contributions:

- **Image-Based Autonomous Pipeline with Binary Path Encoding:** Proposal of a novel learning pipeline for autonomous or teleoperated navigation using binary image input.
- **BC from Human Demonstrations:** Development and training of a BC model that learns navigation policies directly from human driving trajectories, enabling data-efficient imitation without requiring reward signals or environment-specific tuning.
- **Lightweight Binary Image Backbone for Onboard Inference:** Integration of a compact CNN-based (or transformer-based) visual backbone that processes binary (black-and-white) image input, extracting minimal yet informative spatial features optimized for real-time inference on resource-constrained micro-mobility platforms.
- **Path Planning through End-to-End Imitation:** Direct mapping from binary image input to control commands for safe and efficient navigation, bypassing classical feature extraction.

The complete implementation, including training scripts, simulation setup, and BC models, is available as open-source code at: https://github.com/icsa-hua/Ecomobility---Behavior_Cloning_Model.git.

The rest of the paper is structured as follows: Section II reviews related work on BC and imitation learning for autonomous navigation. Section III details the proposed framework, including the e-scooter modelling, dataset preparation, and model architectures. Section IV presents the experimental evaluation and discusses the obtained results. Finally, Section V concludes the paper and outlines future research directions.

13.2 Related Work

A variety of studies have examined e-scooters from multiple perspectives, reflecting their growing role in modern micro-mobility systems. Prior work has analysed their contribution to sustainable transportation, highlighting reduced congestion, emissions, and environmental impact [8]. Additional research has explored their integration into urban transport networks, emphasizing infrastructure compatibility and user behavior [9]. On the autonomy side, several prototypes have investigated core capabilities such as stabilization, obstacle detection, GPS-based navigation, and high-precision localization [10]. At the control level, dynamic modelling and safety remain key topics: PD-based controllers have been used to study riderless e-scooter balancing [11], and teleoperation frameworks have been proposed to improve responsiveness and collision avoidance [12].

However, while these efforts demonstrate substantial progress in understanding and automating e-scooter behavior, research that applies learning-based control, and in particular *behavior cloning (BC)*, to micro-mobility platforms remains limited. To situate our work within the broader imitation-learning landscape, we next review the main variants of BC that have emerged in autonomous navigation. As illustrated in Figure 13.1, existing approaches can be broadly grouped into three principal categories: (i) *Foundational and Extended BC*, (ii) *Hybrid and End-to-End BC*, and (iii) *Applied and Human-Centric BC*. The following paragraphs summarize representative methods in each category.

For **Foundational and Extended BC**, early works focused on direct imitation from expert demonstrations, where neural networks learned control policies by mapping sensory observations to actions [13]. While these approaches achieved data efficiency, they often suffered from covariate shift and poor generalization in unseen conditions. To overcome these limitations, advanced variants such as DAgger and Generative Adversarial Imitation Learning (GAIL) introduced expert feedback and adversarial

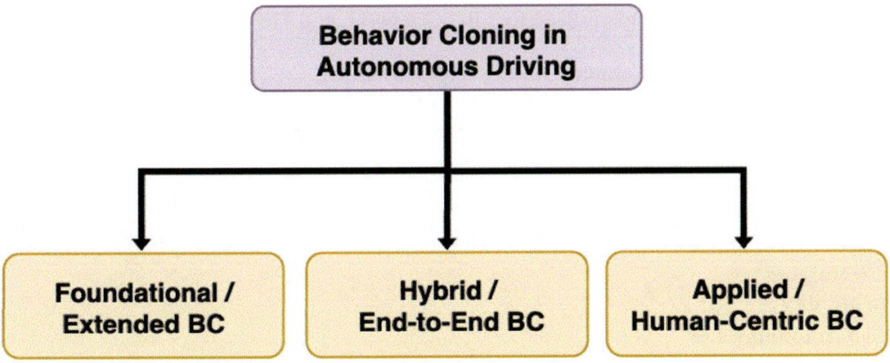

Figure 13.1 Behavior-Cloning-based Categories.

optimization mechanisms to enhance robustness and trajectory alignment [14]. These methods form the theoretical basis for modern imitation learning systems.

Hybrid and End-to-End BC approaches emerged to combine the data efficiency of imitation learning with the adaptability of reinforcement learning, leveraging the strengths of both paradigms. In such frameworks, BC typically serves as a pretraining stage that accelerates policy convergence and stabilizes exploration during reinforcement fine-tuning [15]. Representative examples include DDPG+BC, TD3+BC, and Forward-Prediction-Based Active Exploration BC [16], which integrate exploration mechanisms for improved sample efficiency. In parallel, end-to-end visual learning pipelines emerged, using convolutional or transformer-based backbones to jointly learn perception and control [17], leading to more generalizable and interpretable models suitable for embedded systems [18]. This comparative setup enables quantifying the performance trade-offs between compact CNNs, efficient mobile models, and large-scale foundation transformers in terms of accuracy, latency, and model footprint

Finally, Applied and Human-Centric BC research extends imitation principles to real-world systems such as micro-mobility and teleoperated vehicles. Prototype systems, including e-scooters and mobile robots, have demonstrated that imitation-driven controllers can ensure stable, safe, and adaptive navigation in constrained environments [10], [19]. Similarly, miniature autonomous vehicles have been used as low-cost testbeds to validate real-world BC steering and throttle prediction under resource-constrained settings [20]. Beyond technical control, socially aware models incorporate

Table 13.1 Feature Comparison Across BC Categories and The Proposed Method

Feature	Foundational / Extended BC	Hybrid / End-to-End BC	Applied / Human-Centric BC	Proposed Method
Binary Image Input (B/W Encoding)	✗	✗	✗	✓
Lightweight Edge-Ready Architecture	✗	✓	✗	✓
RL Pretraining Compatibility	✗	✓	✗	✓
Unified Autonomy and Teleoperation	✗	✗	✓	✓
Cross-Domain Adaptability (Land / Air / Sea)	✗	✗	✓	✓
Open-Source and Reproducible Framework	✗	✗	✗	✓

human comfort and perceived safety through mechanisms such as time-to-collision estimation and social force modelling [21-23]. These advances highlight the transition of BC from theoretical imitation learning toward context-aware, deployable.

Overall, the literature reveals an evolution from pure BC toward hybrid, perception-integrated, and socially aware learning architectures. This progression motivates the development of lightweight, binary image-based imitation pipelines capable of real-time navigation on resource-constrained micro-mobility platforms, as pursued in the proposed system. The comparison in Table 13.1 summarizes the distinguishing characteristics of foundational, hybrid, and applied BC frameworks relative to the proposed approach.

13.3 Behavior Cloning Framework Description

The objective of this work is to learn an autonomous navigation policy through BC, enabling a strong initial policy that can later be fine-tuned using RL techniques.

Given a dataset of expert demonstrations

$$\mathcal{D} = \{(s_i, a_i)\}_{i=1}^{N} \tag{13.1}$$

where s_i denotes the observed state (e.g., images) and a_i the corresponding control action (e.g., steering, throttle, brake), the goal is to learn a mapping

$$\pi_\theta : s \rightarrow a \tag{13.2}$$

parameterized by θ, which minimizes the discrepancy between predicted and expert actions. The policy network π_θ is trained in a supervised manner by minimizing a loss function:

$$\mathcal{L}(\theta) = \frac{1}{N} \sum_{i=1}^{N} \ell\left(a_i, \pi_\theta\left(s_i\right)\right) \tag{13.3}$$

where $\ell(\cdot)$ corresponds to the mean squared error (MSE) for continuous actions or cross-entropy loss for discrete action spaces.

13.3.1 e-Scooter Modeling

The vehicle model adopted in this work represents a compact, lightweight electric scooter designed for autonomous navigation in urban micro-mobility environments. The 3D geometry of the vehicle, along with its coordinate system definition, is illustrated in Figure 13.2.

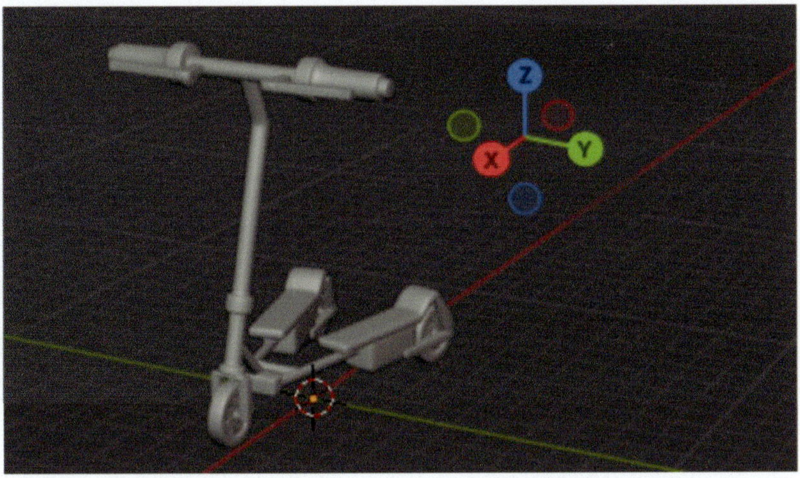

Figure 13.2 e-scooter geometric model and coordinate system definition. The 3D model was created in Blender and integrated into the CARLA simulation environment.

The model was created in Blender, allowing precise control of physical proportions, wheelbase, and was subsequently exported into the simulation environment for dynamic and perception-based experiments.

Unlike conventional two-wheeled scooters, the adopted configuration includes two rear wheels that ensure static stability even when the vehicle is stationary. As a result, the system maintains lateral equilibrium without requiring active balance control. The vertical and lateral forces acting on the scooter are therefore assumed to be in static equilibrium $\sum F_y = 0$, and roll dynamics are neglected. The vehicle is thus modeled as a planar rigid body operating on the horizontal plane, where only longitudinal motion and yaw rotation are considered.

To ensure physical realism and safe operation, the control limits, including maximum acceleration, braking deceleration, and steering angle, are defined according to the mechanical constraints of commercial e-scooters. Moreover, the vehicle's velocity is constrained to comply with the speed limits defined in the CARLA Town01 environment, as shown in Figure 13.3, preventing unrealistic motion or collisions due to excessive speed. This formulation preserves physical plausibility while maintaining computational efficiency, enabling stable and reliable policy learning within the CARLA simulation platform.

Figure 13.3 Speed-limit sign in the CARLA Town01 environment defining the maximum allowed vehicle velocity.

13.3.2 Framework Overview

The proposed BC framework follows a modular design composed of four main stages:

1) **Data Collection and Preprocessing:** Extraction of state–action pairs from simulation or expert teleoperation.
2) **Feature Representation:** Encoding of multimodal sensory inputs using pretrained backbones such as ResNet, MobileNet, or DINOv2 to obtain compact visual embeddings.
3) **Policy Learning:** Training of a lightweight policy head (e.g., MLP or XGBoost) on top of the embeddings to predict expert actions, either as a classification or regression problem depending on the action space.
4) **Evaluation:** Assessment on unseen driving scenarios using success rate, trajectory deviation, and collision count as performance metrics.

This BC setup serves as a foundation for subsequent RL fine-tuning, where the pretrained policy π_θ^{BC} provides a warm start, improving convergence speed and stability during online interaction with the CARLA environment.

Figure 13.4 illustrates the overall BC architecture employed for autonomous navigation. The input to the network corresponds to a 2D projection of the desired path, providing a compact and interpretable representation of the vehicle's intended trajectory. This projection is processed by a convolutional neural network (CNN) backbone, such as ResNet or MobileNet, which extracts high-level spatial features encoding curvature, direction, and local geometric structure. The resulting feature vector is passed to a fully connected classification head that predicts one of four discrete control commands:

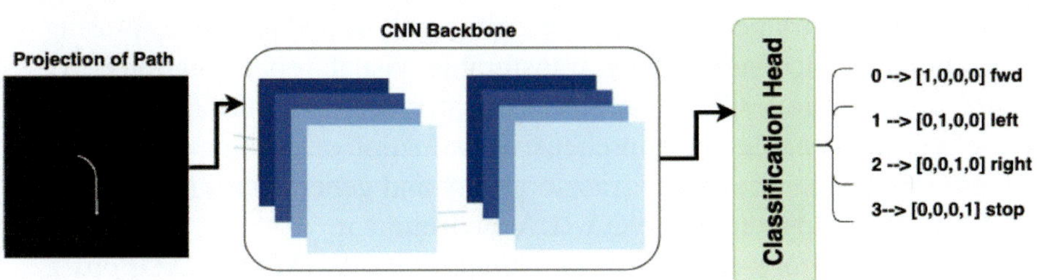

Figure 13.4 Behavior-Cloning-based learning pipeline for autonomous navigation in CARLA

forward, left, right, or *stop*. Each control command is represented as a one-hot encoded vector, serving as the target label during supervised training. This classification-based formulation simplifies the control space and enables efficient learning of navigational behaviors directly from visual inputs.

To investigate the trade-off between representational power, computational efficiency, and generalization capability, two complementary model configurations were developed within this framework.

a) *Deep Policy Network (PolicyNet).* This configuration employs a pre-trained visual backbone followed by a lightweight multi-layer perceptron (MLP) head. The backbone is interchangeable, supporting architectures such as ResNet50, MobileNetV3, and DINOv2-ViT-B/14. These networks act as high-level feature extractors, encoding semantic and geometric cues from the input trajectory images, while the MLP head maps the resulting embeddings to discrete control actions. This end-to-end differentiable design enables joint policy optimization with minimal architectural complexity, ensuring efficient deployment on embedded hardware (e.g., NVIDIA Jetson).
The selection of visual backbones was driven by the goal of covering a broad spectrum of feature representations, from conventional convolutional encoders to recent foundation vision transformers, thus enabling a systematic comparison between compact task-specific models and large-scale pretrained architectures. ResNet50 serves as a well-established CNN baseline, offering strong spatial feature extraction and proven robustness in visual navigation tasks. MobileNetV3 was selected as a lightweight, computationally efficient architecture suitable for real-time inference on resource-constrained platforms, balancing accuracy and latency. In contrast, DINOv2-ViT-B/14 represents a modern foundation model trained on massive self-supervised datasets, capturing semantically rich and highly transferable visual representations. By incorporating both CNN-based and transformer-based backbones, this configuration enables a comprehensive evaluation of whether large-scale pretraining enhances policy transferability and generalization to unseen driving scenarios within the CARLA environment.
b) *Hybrid Embedding + Gradient Boosting Model (ResNet50 + XGBoost).* In this configuration, visual embeddings are first extracted from a frozen ResNet50 backbone and subsequently used to train an XGBoost classifier. This hybrid approach combines the strong representational capacity of deep convolutional features with the interpretability and robustness

of tree-based ensembles. By decoupling feature extraction from policy learning, it allows faster training and flexible experimentation with tabular learning algorithms even on CPU-only setups.

Overall, the two complementary architectures, covering traditional CNNs, efficient mobile models, and foundation vision transformers, enable a unified and systematic comparison, helping to identify which configuration offers the best trade-off between robustness, efficiency, and generalization in behavior-cloned driving policies.

13.3.3 Dataset Preparation

The dataset was collected within the Town01 map of the CARLA simulator, using the in-built GlobalRoutePlanner and LocalRoutePlanner modules to

Figure 13.5 Bidirectional routes (A→B and B→A) in CARLA Town01, used to ensure balanced left and right turns in the collected dataset.

generate structured navigation trajectories. A set of ten waypoints ahead of the vehicle was visualized to provide local context, allowing the model to anticipate upcoming turns and adjust its velocity accordingly.

Each sample in the dataset consists of:

- a grayscale image representing the predicted path projection, where white pixels indicate the intended trajectory to be followed by the model;
- a one-hot encoded action label corresponding to one of four discrete control commands: *forward*, *left*, *right*, or *stop*;
- and the file path to the associated image stored in a structured CSV file.

Two routes were recorded within the CARLA environment, one from point A to point B and another in the reverse direction (B to A), as illustrated in Figure 13.5. This bidirectional setup ensured a balanced distribution of left and right turns, enabling the model to generalize equally well across both maneuver types.

Furthermore, the routes include intersections with traffic lights and stop signs, allowing the vehicle to experience and learn stopping behaviors associated with traffic control elements, as shown in Figure 13.6.

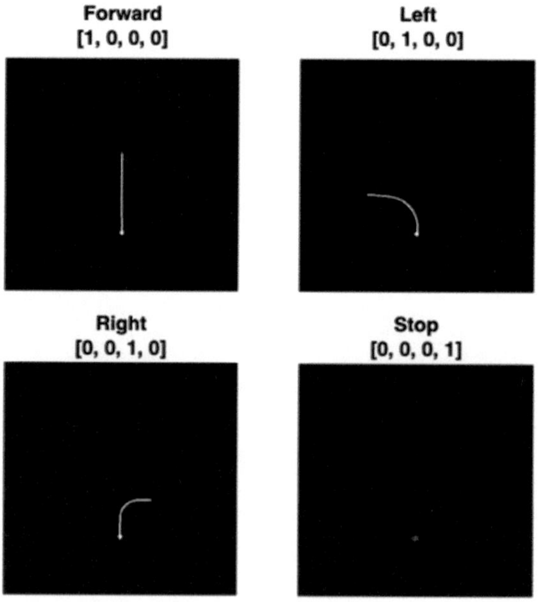

Figure 13.6 Four discrete control commands (forward, left, right, stop) with their one-hot encoded labels. White paths indicate the intended trajectory; the red dot denotes a stop position.

The resulting dataset therefore captures a diverse range of driving contexts, combining geometric cues, directional variation, and traffic-related stopping events, providing a well-rounded foundation for supervised BC.

13.3.4 Evaluation Metrics

Model performance was assessed using standard multi-class classification metrics, complemented by computational profiling to evaluate runtime efficiency.

Performance Metrics: For a classification task with C classes, let TP_c, FP_c, and FN_c denote the true positives, false positives, and false negatives for class c. Each metric is defined as follows:

- **Accuracy:** proportion of correctly predicted actions among all samples.

$$Accuracy = \frac{\sum_{c=1}^{C} TP_c}{\sum_{c=1}^{C} (TP_c + FP_c + FN_c)} \tag{13.4}$$

- **Precision:** correctness of positive predictions for class c.

$$Precision_c = \frac{TP_c}{TP_c + FP_c} \tag{13.5}$$

- **Recall:** fraction of correctly identified samples for class c.

$$\mathrm{Recall_c} = \frac{TP_c}{TP_c + FN_c} \tag{13.6}$$

- **F1-score:** harmonic mean of precision and recall.

$$\mathrm{F1_c} = 2\frac{\mathrm{Precision_c} \times \mathrm{Recall_c}}{\mathrm{Precision_c} + \mathrm{Recall_c}} \tag{13.7}$$

- **Macro and Weighted Averages:** global scores across classes.

$$\mathrm{Macro} - \mathrm{F1} = \frac{1}{C}\sum_{c=1}^{C} \mathrm{F1_c} \tag{1.8}$$

$$\mathrm{Weighted} - \mathrm{F1} = \frac{1}{N}\sum_{c=1}^{C} n_c \times \mathrm{F1_c} \ ,$$

where n_c is the number of samples in class c and

$$N = \sum_{c=1}^{C} n_c \tag{23.9}$$

The confusion matrix $\mathbf{M} \in \mathbb{R}^{C \times C}$ summarizes prediction consistency:

$$M_{ij} = number\ of \text{ samples with true label } i \text{ and predicted as } j$$

<u>*Computational Profiling:*</u> In addition to accuracy-based metrics, the following efficiency indicators were logged:

- **Memory Usage:** peak CPU/GPU memory consumption.
- **Model Size:** storage footprint of the trained policy.
- **Inference Speed:** average processing time per frame and corresponding frame rate

$$\text{FPS} = \frac{1}{Average\ Inference\ Time} \tag{23.10}$$

Together, these metrics provide a balanced evaluation of predictive accuracy and computational efficiency, reflecting the model's suitability for real-time autonomous navigation.

13.4 Experimental Evaluation

All experiments were conducted on a workstation equipped with the hardware specifications shown in Table 13.2. The dataset was divided into **75%** for training, **15%** for validation, and **10%** for testing, ensuring stratified sampling across all four control actions (*forward, left, right, stop*).

Tables 13.3 and 13.4 summarize the training and test performance of all evaluated models. Among them, **ResNet50+MLP** achieved the best overall accuracy (99.6%) and weighted F1-score (0.996), followed closely by **ResNet50+XGBoost** and **DINOv2+MLP**. In contrast, **MobileNetV3+MLP** exhibited limited generalization, highlighting the trade-off between efficiency and representational power in lightweight CNNs.

During training, the **ResNet50+XGBoost** configuration reached perfect performance (100% accuracy and F1-score of 1.0), indicating that the hybrid

Table 13.2 System Specifications Used for Model Training and Evaluation

Component	Specification
CPU	Intel Core i7-12700KF (12 cores / 20 threads, 3.6–5.0 GHz)
RAM	32 GB DDR4
GPU	NVIDIA GeForce RTX 3060 (12 GB GDDR6 VRAM)
CUDA Version	12.9
Python Version	3.11

Table 13.3 Comparison of Model Performance on the CARLA Training Set

Model	Accuracy (%)	Macro F1	Weighted F1
ResNet50 + MLP	99.5	0.9910	0.9947
MobileNetV3 + MLP	60.1	0.470	0.624
DINOv2 + MLP	99.1	0.9869	0.9915
ResNet50 + XGBoost	100.0	1.000	1.000

Table 13.4 Comparison of Model Performance on the CARLA Test Set

Model	Accuracy (%)	Macro F1	Weighted F1
ResNet50 + MLP	99.6	0.9936	0.9960
MobileNetV3 + MLP	64.9	0.525	0.659
DINOv2 + MLP	98.4	0.9750	0.9842
ResNet50 + XGBoost	99.2	0.9875	0.9922

model fully captured the patterns of the training data. However, when evaluated on unseen test samples, **ResNet50+MLP** achieved slightly higher accuracy (99.6% vs. 99.2%), suggesting stronger generalization ability. This implies that while XGBoost tends to overfit the training distribution, learning even small, noise variations, the MLP head produces smoother decision boundaries, enabling better transferability to new environments and lighting conditions.

The **DINOv2+MLP** model also demonstrated competitive performance (98.4%), confirming that pretrained foundation models can effectively learn visual cues even from simplified grayscale trajectory maps. Nevertheless, its slightly reduced accuracy compared to ResNet50-based variants can be attributed to the high-level semantic abstraction inherent in foundation models. Since DINOv2 was pretrained on diverse multimodal data, its internal representations prioritize semantic structure over fine-grained geometric detail, which limits its precision when processing low-texture or monochromatic inputs such as synthetic path images.

In contrast, the **MobileNetV3+MLP** configuration exhibited evident underfitting, reaching only 60.1% training accuracy and 64.9% test accuracy. The lightweight architecture of MobileNetV3 provides excellent computational efficiency but lacks sufficient representational capacity to capture subtle differences between visually similar directional cues (e.g., left vs. right turns). As a result, the model fails to converge to a consistent decision boundary, confirming the trade-off between efficiency and discriminative power in compact CNN backbones.

The confusion matrices in Figure 13.7 provide deeper insight into the per-class behavior of each model. For **ResNet50+MLP** and

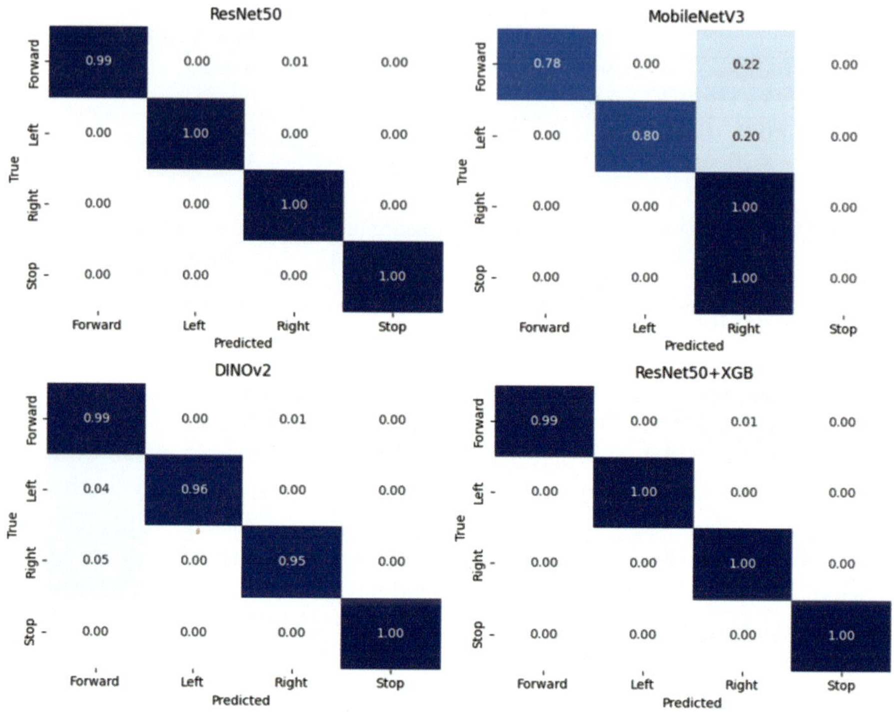

Figure 13.7 Normalized confusion matrices for all evaluated models, including three MLP-based policies (ResNet50, MobileNetV3, DINOv2) and one hybrid approach (ResNet50+XGBoost). Each heatmap shows per-class prediction accuracy for the four control actions (forward, left, right, stop), with strong diagonal values indicating consistent and reliable policy behavior.

ResNet50+XGBoost, all four actions are predicted with near-perfect accuracy, with values above 0.99 across the diagonal, indicating that both models consistently distinguish between straight motion, left/right turns, and stopping. **DINOv2+MLP** also performs robustly, though minor off-diagonal activations reveal that the model occasionally confuses *Left* and *Right* actions (0.04 and 0.05 misclassification rates, respectively). This suggests that while the transformer backbone effectively captures global context, it may overlook small geometric asymmetries in trajectory curvature that are more easily captured by convolutional filters.

In contrast, **MobileNetV3+MLP** shows significant confusion between *Forward* and *Right* commands (22% of forward samples predicted as right). A similar pattern appears between Left and Right, and even the *Stop* class is entirely misclassified as Right. This indicates that the compact feature maps of MobileNetV3 lack sufficient spatial resolution to encode angular and motion-related cues, resulting in a strong directional bias toward the "Right" action.

Overall, these per-class results validate that higher-capacity models preserve finer geometric distinctions, while smaller backbones trade discriminative strength for efficiency.

After confirming the training consistency and generalization behavior, the three best-performing models were further compared in terms of inference speed on the same GPU-enabled system described in Table 13.2, as shown in Figure 13.8. Among them, the **ResNet50+MLP** configuration achieved the highest throughput (140 FPS), benefiting from its fully end-to-end GPU execution. The hybrid **ResNet50+XGBoost** model achieved slightly lower speed (97.6 FPS) due to the additional CPU-bound inference stage required for the boosting classifier. The **DINOv2+MLP** model was the slowest (89.1 FPS), reflecting the higher computational complexity of its transformer-based backbone.

Since the **ResNet50+MLP** configuration achieved the best overall performance, it was also tested under CPU-only execution to assess its feasibility

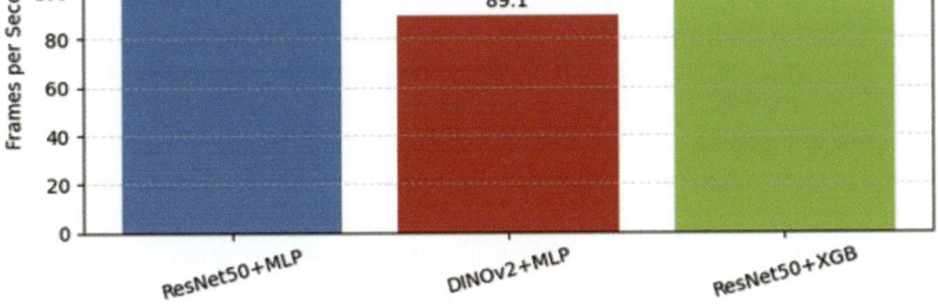

Figure 13.8 Inference speed comparison among the three best-performing models (*ResNet50+MLP, DINOv2+MLP,* and *ResNet50+XGBoost*). The ResNet50-based policy achieves the highest throughput (140 FPS), while all three maintain real-time performance suitable for deployment on embedded platforms.

on systems with limited computational resources. Although benchmarked primarily on a GPU-enabled workstation, the model remains computationally lightweight, requiring only 94 MB of storage, 1.1 GB of RAM, and 288 MB of GPU memory. When executed on CPU-only configurations, the model achieved an average inference time of 44.7 ms per frame (22 FPS) while utilizing approximately 1.55 GB of system memory, confirming its ability to maintain near-real-time performance even on computers with constrained processing capabilities. Such efficiency highlights the potential for deployment not only in e-scooter platforms but also in other low-power autonomous systems, including drones, ground robots, and marine vessels operating under similar hardware constraints.

13.5 Conclusion and Future Directions

This paper presented a comprehensive 3D simulation and learning framework for BC applied to the image-based navigation of edge AI-enabled e-scooters operating in realistic urban environments. The framework integrates a lightweight visual perception pipeline with efficient policy learning mechanisms within the CARLA simulator, allowing autonomous decision-making to be achieved in real time under stringent computational, latency, and energy constraints. The overall design emphasizes scalability, interpretability, and deployability, bridging high-level policy learning with the physics-based simulation of mobility systems. Through this combination, the proposed setup provides a complete digital twin environment for data generation, model training, and safe validation before real-world deployment.

The conducted experiments revealed that compact convolutional and transformer-based visual backbones can effectively learn navigation behaviors from minimal trajectory encodings, essentially binary visual maps, without the need for handcrafted features or complex sensor fusion. The evaluation demonstrated that such compact representations are sufficient to encode critical motion cues, lane geometry, and obstacle boundaries, enabling policies that generalize well to unseen environments while maintaining low inference latency. Among the tested configurations, the **ResNet50+MLP** model achieved the most favourable trade-off between accuracy, inference throughput, and memory consumption. Specifically, it reached 99.6% test accuracy and 140 FPS while requiring less than 1.2 GB of system memory, validating its suitability for real-time control loops in constrained embedded setups. When executed under CPU-only conditions, the model maintained near-real-time inference performance at 22 FPS and consumed only 1.55 GB of RAM, thereby demonstrating its practicality for deployment on standard computing platforms without dedicated GPUs. This balance of efficiency and predictive performance underlines the potential of such lightweight policies to support energy-efficient autonomy in cost-sensitive or power-limited settings.

Beyond the e-scooter scenario, the proposed pipeline is inherently platform-agnostic and can be seamlessly adapted to other robotic or vehicular domains. The same architecture could be deployed on small aerial drones, autonomous surface vessels, or ground robots, where energy constraints and limited onboard processing power necessitate compact yet robust visual policies. In these contexts, the trained policy network could act as a perception-to-action bridge, transforming raw visual inputs into safe and interpretable motion decisions. Furthermore, its modular nature allows additional perception modalities, such as RGB cameras, depth sensors, LiDAR, or IMU units, to be incorporated into the same learning loop, supporting multi-sensor fusion and richer scene understanding for complex environments.

Such flexibility promotes the development of a unified learning stack capable of operating across land, air, and sea vehicles within the same algorithmic framework.

From a methodological standpoint, the pretrained policies derived through BC can also serve as strong initialization priors for downstream reinforcement learning or safe imitation learning pipelines. This transferability accelerates adaptation to dynamic and uncertain conditions, reducing training time and minimizing safety risks associated with exploration in real-world deployments. In the RL stage, we plan to extend the input representation beyond binary projections by incorporating both grayscale and RGB imagery, allowing the agent to capture richer environmental cues while still benefiting from the lightweight pretraining structure. Future extensions will focus on integrating hybrid Safe Reinforcement Learning schemes that combine risk-aware policy optimization with BC, enabling continuous online learning while preserving safety guarantees. Additional research directions include dynamic obstacle management, cooperative multi-agent path planning, and communication-aware control strategies for interconnected mobility ecosystems.

Overall, this work establishes a scalable, interpretable, and energy-efficient foundation for trustworthy Edge AI autonomy. By unifying visual perception, policy learning, and control within a single 3D digital twin framework, it contributes to the long-term vision of adaptive, safe, and sustainable intelligent transportation systems that can operate seamlessly across land, air, and sea domains.

Acknowledgements

This work has received funding from the Chips Joint Undertaking (JU) under the Horizon Europe Framework Programme and National Authorities under grant agreement No. 101112306. It has also been implemented under the National Recovery and Resilience Plan "Greece 2.0", funded by the European Union – NextGenerationEU (project name: CoDrones).

References

[1] C. Kettwich, A. Schrank, and M. Oehl, "Teleoperation of highly automated vehicles in public transport: User-centered design of a human-machine interface for remote-operation and its expert usability evaluation," Multimodal Technologies and Interaction, vol. 5, no. 5, 2021. [Online]. https://www.mdpi.com/2414-4088/5/5/26

[2] O. Amador, M. Aramrattana, and A. Vinel, "A survey on remote operation of road vehicles," IEEE Access, vol. 10, pp. 130 135–130 154, 2022.

[3] L. Liu, C. Chen, Q. Pei, S. Maharjan, and Y. Zhang, "Vehicular edge computing and networking: A survey," Mobile networks and applications, vol. 26, no. 3, pp. 1145–1168, 2021.

[4] A. Stefanidou, E. Politi, and G. Dimitrakopoulos, "Foundation models in autonomous driving: A review of current tasks and applications," IEEE Open Journal of Intelligent Transportation Systems, vol. 6, pp. 1522–1538, 2025.

[5] A. Musa, H. Kakudi, M. Hassan, M. Hamada, U. Umar, and M. Salisu, "Lightweight deep learning models for edge devices—a survey," International Journal of Computer Information Systems and Industrial Management Applications, vol. 17, p. 18, 01 2025.

[6] M. Yang, H. Cao, L. Zhao, C. Zhang, and Y. Chen, "Robotic sim-to-real transfer for long-horizon pick-and-place tasks in the robotic sim2real competition," arXiv preprint arXiv:2503.11012, 2025.

[7] C. Hu, S. Hudson, M. Ethier, M. Al-Sharman, D. Rayside, and W. Melek, "Sim-to-real domain adaptation for lane detection and

classification in autonomous driving," in 2022 IEEE Intelligent Vehicles Symposium (IV). IEEE, 2022, pp. 457–463.

[8] R. Strässer, M. Seidel, F. Brändle, D. Meister, R. Soloperto, D. H. Ferrer, and F. Allgöwer, "Collision avoidance safety filter for an autonomous e-scooter using ultrasonic sensors," IFAC-PapersOnLine, vol. 58, no. 10, pp.22–28, 2024.

[9] C. Latinopoulos, A. Patrier, and A. Sivakumar, "Planning for e-scooter use in metropolitan cities: A case study for paris," Transportation Research Part D: Transport and Environment, vol. 100, p. 103037, 2021. [Online]. https://www.sciencedirect.com/science/article/pii/S1361920921003357

[10] R. Soloperto, P. Wenzelburger, D. Meister, D. Scheuble, V. S. Breidohr, and F. Allgöwer, "A control framework for autonomous e-scooters," IFAC-PapersOnLine, vol. 54, no. 2, pp. 252–258, 2021.

[11] Y.-H. Lin, A. Jafari, and Y.-C. Liu, "Dynamic modeling and stability analysis of balancing in riderless electric scooters," in 2024 American Control Conference (ACC), 2024, pp. 421–426.

[12] S. Saparia, A. Schimpe, and L. Ferranti, "Active safety system for semi-autonomous teleoperated vehicles," 2021. [Online]. https://arxiv.org/abs/2106.14554

[13] Y. Gao, Y. Liu, Q. Zhang, Y. Wang, D. Zhao, D. Ding, Z. Pang, and Y. Zhang, "Comparison of control methods based on imitation learning for autonomous driving," in 2019 tenth international conference on intelligent control and information processing (ICICIP). IEEE, 2019, pp. 274–281.

[14] G. C. K. Couto and E. A. Antonelo, "Generative adversarial imitation learning for end-to-end autonomous driving on urban environments," in 2021 IEEE Symposium Series on Computational Intelligence (SSCI). IEEE, 2021, pp. 1–7.

[15] Y. Tian, X. Cao, K. Huang, C. Fei, Z. Zheng, and X. Ji, "Learning to drive like human beings: A method based on deep reinforcement learning," IEEE Transactions on Intelligent Transportation Systems, vol. 23, no. 7, pp. 6357–6367, 2021.

[16] H. Xu and D. Zhao, "Forward-prediction-based active exploration behavior cloning," in 2024 5th International Seminar on Artificial Intelligence, Networking and Information Technology (AINIT). IEEE, 2024, pp. 2112–2117.

[17] Y. Fan, "Autonomous driving in unity simulated environments using end-to-end cnn approach," in 2024 7th International Conference on

Advanced Algorithms and Control Engineering (ICAACE). IEEE, 2024, pp.1335–1338.

[18] H.-G. Kim, J. Myoung, S. Lee, K.-M. Park, and D. Shin, "Design of ai-powered hybrid control algorithm of robot vehicle for enhanced driving performance," IEEE Embedded Systems Letters, vol. 16, no. 2, pp. 94–97, 2023.

[19] K. Liu and R. Mulky, "Enabling autonomous navigation for affordable scooters," Sensors, vol. 18, no. 6, 2018. [Online]. https://www.mdpi.com/1424-8220/18/6/1829

[20] P. Moraes, C. Peters, H. Sodre, W. Moraes, S. Barcelona, J. Deniz, V. Castelli, B. Guterres, and R. Grando, "Behavior cloning for mini autonomous car path following," in 2024 IEEE URUCON. IEEE, 2024, pp. 1–5.

[21] A. Jafari and Y.-C. Liu, "Time-to-collision based social force model for intelligent agents on shared public spaces," International Journal of Social Robotics, vol. 16, no. 9, pp. 1953–1968, 2024.

[22] V. Tang and J. Liu, "Mapping urban obstacles: Improving route accessibility for blind and low-vision pedestrians," in 2024 IEEE MIT Undergraduate Research Technology Conference (URTC). IEEE, 2024, pp. 1–5.

[23] S. Gilroy, D. Mullins, E. Jones, A. Parsi, and M. Glavin, "E-scooter rider detection and classification in dense urban environments," Results in engineering, vol. 16, p. 100677, 2022.

14

Edge-AI Ready Lightweight Digital Twin for Anomaly Prediction: A Case Study on Hydrogen Refueling Station Data

Esin Öztürk and Francis Fomi Wamba

Framatome GmbH, Germany

Abstract

Digital Twin (DT) technology is becoming an essential tool for improving safety, availability, and maintenance in critical infrastructure. In hydrogen refueling stations (HRS), detecting anomalies quickly is vital to prevent failures, avoid costly downtime, and maintain operational reliability. In this work, we propose an Edge-AI ready lightweight Digital Twin framework for anomaly detection, built using historical operational data from a real HRS; a dataset with 110 features and around 3 million complete records. Our methodology takes a step-by-step approach. We start with unsupervised learning methods including statistics-based techniques like clustering and PCA, prediction-based methods like linear prediction and MLP, and reconstruction-based approaches like autoencoders and AE+CNN; to detect anomalies without labelled data. In the second step, we validate and refine these findings using supervised learning, applying both classical machine learning and deep learning classifiers. We then optimize the best-performing models for edge deployment using multi-phase quantization, structured pruning, and resource-aware execution strategies. Since we do not have a physical edge device, we create an edge simulation environment to mimic real-time data streaming and evaluate accuracy, latency, and model size. While our first deployment target is edge devices, future versions may run in the cloud for greater scalability. Our results show that starting with simple methods and

DOI: 10.1201/9788743815273-14

progressively applying optimizations can significantly enhance HRS safety and reliability, while keeping the solution practical for resource-constrained hardware.

Keywords: Edge AI, Digital Twin, Anomaly Prediction, Predictive Maintenance.

14.1 Introduction

14.1.1 Background

Since the Industrial Revolution, maintenance strategies have evolved significantly with technological advancements. Early Corrective Maintenance (CM) was based on the principle of not intervening until the system failed. However, this approach was unsustainable due to high costs and unplanned downtime. Consequently, Preventive Maintenance (PM) emerged over time. The PM approach relies on replacing equipment at regular intervals. While effective in reducing the risk of failure, it can be cost-ineffective because it sometimes results in replacing parts that are still usable [1].

With the acceleration of digitalization, especially in the age of Industry 4.0 and the Internet of Things (IoT), maintenance paradigms have evolved towards Condition-Based Maintenance (CBM) and subsequently Predictive Maintenance (PdM). CBM is based on monitoring parameters such as vibration, pressure, and temperature via sensors and intervening when certain thresholds are exceeded. PdM, on the other hand, aims to predict the remaining useful lifetime (or safe operating time) after detection of potential failures using machine learning and data analytics methods [2, 3].

Advances in Big Data, IoT, and Artificial Intelligence (AI) technologies have enabled the more effective implementation of PdM in industrial systems. Digital Twins (DT) have played a critical role in this process. As a virtual replica of a physical asset, DT, when fed with real-time data, not only reflects the current state of the system but also strengthens decision-support mechanisms by simulating potential scenarios [4, 5]. In this respect, DT has become a fundamental component of modern maintenance strategies in terms of both operational efficiency and safety.

14.1.2 Motivation

Hydrogen Refueling Stations (HRS) are one of the most critical elements of the clean energy transition. These stations support the widespread adoption of hydrogen fuel cell vehicles while reducing the carbon footprint of the energy infrastructure. However, HRSs pose a high safety risk due to the storage and transfer of high-pressure gases. Gas leaks, valve failures, compressor-related problems, or sudden pressure changes in tanks can lead to serious safety incidents. Therefore, early detection of anomalies and the development of timely warning mechanisms are vital not only for operational continuity but also for human and environmental safety [6, 7].

14.1.3 Problem

In current industrial applications, Digital Twins (DTs) are typically run on cloud-based architectures. While this approach offers the advantages of robust processing capacity and scalability, it has significant limitations in safety-critical systems such as HRS: (i) latency, (ii) dependence on cloud connectivity, (iii) data security risks, and (iv) the cost of continuously moving large data volumes. The dataset used in this study has approximately 3 million records and 110 features; continuously transferring this amount of data to the cloud is not feasible in terms of bandwidth and sustainability [8, 9].

Another fundamental problem is labelling constraints. In HRS datasets, events corresponding to anomalies are often represented by alarm signals. These alarms are often sparse, unbalanced, and can contain false positives/negatives. This makes approaches based solely on supervised learning algorithms vulnerable. On the other hand, using solely unsupervised methods results in high false alarm rates due to station-specific noise and reduces operator confidence [10, 11].

14.1.4 Related Work and Research Gap

In critical industries, Digital Twin (DT) applications have become an innovative and promising tool, particularly for maintenance and fault prevention processes. Creating virtual copies of physical systems, enabling real-time monitoring and scenario-based simulation, provides a powerful framework for Predictive Maintenance (PdM) strategies. Recent studies have shown that DT-based PdM efforts are maturing from smart manufacturing-focused applications to energy infrastructures [2, 10, 21]. The European Union's AIOTI (2024) white paper highlights the importance of edge-based digital twins in distributed energy systems [9]. A study presented in the context of the 2024 HRS demonstrated the role of digital twins in the analysis of leakage and explosion risks by proposing a DT model that integrates CNN-based decision support with 3D simulation [7]. The concept of the "smart digital twin" has emerged as recent work combines DT frameworks with machine learning to produce predictive analytics that go beyond rule-based monitoring approaches [4, 10, 18].

In the context of the Industrial Internet of Things (IIoT), anomaly detection is divided into three paradigms: supervised, unsupervised, and hybrid. Supervised learning (SL) methods (e.g., SVM, LightGBM, and MLP) provide high accuracy on large and balanced labelled datasets; however, their applicability in environments such as HRS is low due to the scarcity of labels and the sparseness of alarm data [8]. Unsupervised learning (UL) methods (PCA, k-means, density-based clustering, and auto encoders) extract anomaly trends from unlabelled data [10, 11]. The main drawback of these methods is their high false alarm rate (FAR) [11]. Therefore, hybrid and semi-supervised methods have gained importance. These approaches produce more reliable classifiers by combining the scores obtained from unsupervised methods with limited labels [13]. This work similarly aims to both reduce the FAR value and preserve sensitivity to critical alerts by adopting a hybrid label fusion strategy that combines unsupervised representations with sparse alert labels [9, 13, 20]. Recent studies have started to report early warning metrics (e.g., lead time, FAR) in addition to classical metrics such as F1 and AUC, allowing for more operationally interpretable evaluations [14, 21].

Implementing real-time decision support mechanisms in critical infrastructures depends not only on developing accurate models but also on their executable on edge devices. Therefore, in recent years, model compression and optimization techniques – quantization (especially 8-bit), pruning, and knowledge distillation (KD) – have received intense attention in the TinyML and Edge-AI literature [8, 15, 19]. Among these techniques, KD, in particular, enables lightweight structures suitable for edge devices by transferring knowledge from high-capacity teacher models to smaller student models [19]. In practice, toolchains such as ONNX Runtime and TensorFlow Lite support these optimizations, enabling portable and low-latency inference on CPU-, NPU-, and MCU-based devices. Recent technical reports show that ONNX Runtime provides low latency and performance gains after quantization, especially in batch-1 scenarios [3, 13, 16]. In line with this trend, in this study, information distillation, quantization and pruning techniques were applied together and lightweight student models that meet accuracy-delay-memory constraints were obtained.

The literature for the 2021–2025 period points to three parallel trends: (i) the shift of DT applications from smart manufacturing to energy infrastructures and safety-critical systems such as HRS; (ii) the rise of hybrid approaches in anomaly detection; and (iii) the joint optimization of accuracy, latency, and size (or memory) for edge applications. However, among existing studies, there is no comprehensive study that demonstrates the end-to-end UL→SL→Edge chain on HRS data and compares accuracy, latency, and memory consumption simultaneously. Furthermore, operational metrics such as false alarms/hour (FA/h) and lead-time are still rarely reported compared to traditional metrics such as F1/accuracy/AUC. This work fills this gap by presenting an end-to-end framework evaluated with both traditional and early warning metrics by integrating label fusion with lightweight model deployment [6, 7, 9, 12, 15, 17, 21].

14.2 Objectives and Methodology

The objective of this study is to develop an end-to-end digital twin framework capable of performing early anomaly prediction in hydrogen refueling stations (HRS) through a unified unsupervised–supervised–edge learning pipeline. The research aims to bridge the methodological gap between unlabelled and labelled data by integrating unsupervised feature extraction with limited alarm information, enabling reliable detection of anomaly tendencies even under sparse labelling conditions. Furthermore, the study seeks to optimize the resulting predictive models for edge deployment, ensuring that they maintain high accuracy and stability while operating under strict computational and memory constraints. Ultimately, the framework targets achieving macro-F1 ≈ 0.62 with latency below 0.5 ms, demonstrating the feasibility of lightweight yet high-performing digital twins suitable for real-time monitoring in safety-critical hydrogen infrastructures.

The proposed method consists of three stages: (I) unsupervised representation learning, (ii) hybrid label fusion and supervised modelling, (iii) lightweight optimization and edge-aware deployment. This chain aims to automatically learn anomaly trends in large-scale HRS time series data and associate them with limited alarm labels to create a digital twin model that can be run on edge devices.

14.2.1 Unsupervised Representation Learning

In the first stage, a Convolutional Autoencoder (CNN-AE) is trained on unlabelled multivariate time-series data from the hydrogen refueling station. The encoder, composed of three Conv1D layers (kernel sizes 7, 5, and 3) with ReLU activations and a 16-dimensional latent space, compresses the input data, while the mirrored decoder reconstructs it. By analysing the reconstruction error, the model detects deviations from normal operating patterns and identifies latent anomaly tendencies even without labelled data. This approach was chosen because CNN-AE can effectively capture nonlinear temporal and spatial dependencies among correlated process variables such as pressure, temperature, and valve states, making it well suited for modelling degradation behavior that precedes alarms.

14.2.2 Hybrid Label Fusion and Supervised Modelling

The anomaly scores obtained from the CNN-AE are then fused with sparse field alarm data to create a hybrid three-class label structure—Normal, Propensity, and Alarm—which better reflects the gradual evolution of anomalies. These fused labels are used to train two complementary teacher models: a Multilayer Perceptron (MLP) implemented in PyTorch and a LightGBM gradient boosting model. The MLP, with two fully connected layers (64–32 neurons) and dropout (p = 0.2), is designed to capture complex nonlinear interactions within latent features, whereas LightGBM, configured with num_leaves = 31 and learning_rate = 0.05, provides interpretable and robust decision boundaries for high-dimensional tabular data. This dual-teacher configuration balances interpretability and predictive accuracy, ensuring both generalization capability and stability before knowledge transfer.

14.2.3 Knowledge Distillation and Edge Optimization (KD)

In the final stage, Knowledge Distillation (KD) is applied to transfer knowledge from the high-capacity teacher models to compact student networks (Tiny-MLP or 1D-CNN). The training objective combines cross-entropy loss with softened teacher predictions according to the formulation proposed by Hinton *et al.* [23]:

$$L = \alpha \times L_{CE}(y, p_s) + (1 - \alpha) \times L_{KD}(p_t(T), p_s(T))$$

where L_{CE} is the cross-entropy loss between the true labels y and the student predictions p_s, L_{KD} is the distillation loss between the teacher predictions $p_t(T)$ and student predictions $p_s(T)$ at temperature T, and α balances the contribution of each term. In this implementation, $\alpha = 0.5$ and T = 2. Following distillation, the student models undergo quantization-aware training (QAT) and structured pruning (30–50%) to reduce model size and latency. These optimization steps allow the resulting models—exported in ONNX INT8

Table 14.1 Overview of PyTorch models and the training pipeline

Model	Role	Main Parameters	Purpose
CNN-AE	Unsupervised feature extractor	3 Conv1D (7,5,3), latent = 16, lr = 1e−3, Adam, batch = 64	Learn latent representations and detect anomaly tendencies
MLP	Supervised classifier	64–32 neurons, ReLU, dropout = 0.2, 50 epochs	Model nonlinear relationships using hybrid labels
LightGBM	Gradient boosting	num_leaves = 31, lr = 0.05, early_stop=10	Provide interpretable decision boundaries for tabular data
KD	Distilled lightweight model	α = 0.5, T = 2, QAT = 10 epochs, pruning = 30–50%	Enable edge-ready inference with latency $<$ 0.5 ms

format—to retain teacher-level accuracy while achieving real-time inference performance. This phase is critical because it enables efficient Edge-AI deployment in safety-critical infrastructures, where computational resources are limited but reliability and response time are crucial.

14.2.4 Evaluation and Benchmarking

All models in the Test-L set. Performance was reported across three dimensions:

i) **accuracy** (macro-F1, PR-AUC, early-warning recall),
ii) **reliability** (FA/h, calibration curves), and
iii) **efficiency** (p50/p95/p99 latency, model size, RAM usage).

The observed student–teacher macro-F1 differences ranged between −0.154 and +0.153, model sizes between 0.06–0.15 MB, and single-sample latency between 0.39–0.47 ms. Memory usage was reported as process-level RSS, and statistical significance was assessed using bootstrap 95% confidence intervals.

14.3 Case Study: HRS System and Data Description

14.3.1 HRS System and Data Description

Hydrogen Refueling Stations (HRS) represent a crucial component of the emerging hydrogen economy, serving as the key interface between hydrogen production and end-user consumption, especially for fuel cell vehicles (FCVs). As green hydrogen gains prominence as a clean and zero-emission energy carrier, the establishment of safe, efficient, and data-driven refueling infrastructures has become vital [24].

An HRS continuously monitors numerous physical and operational parameters, such as gas pressure, temperature, flow rate, and valve positions, through an extensive network of sensors. These data streams enable real-time supervision and support advanced methodologies like predictive maintenance (PdM) and digital twins, which enhance safety, reliability, and cost efficiency [4]

Structure of the HRS can be decomposed into its main systems, subsystems, supply components, and sensors. This modular structure allows detailed modelling of each process layer and facilitates the creation of digital twins for predictive analysis. Major systems of our use case HRS are below.

1. Entrance System (ES): The process begins at the Entrance System, where hydrogen transported by trailers is transferred into the station. Depending on the trailer pressure (typically 200 bar or 300 bar) hydrogen enters through separate lines. This system regulates the gas intake and ensures that flow and pressure remain within safe operational limits.
2. Low-Pressure System (LP): The Low-Pressure System stores hydrogen temporarily at moderate pressures (up to $\approx$ 90 bar). It functions as a buffer reservoir, stabilizing supply flow and supporting process continuity before compression.
3. Compressor System (CS): Hydrogen from the LP tanks is directed to the Compressor System, which raises the gas pressure to the required level for vehicle refueling. The CS system generates high-frequency process data such as inlet/outlet pressure, compressor temperature, and vibration, making it central to predictive maintenance applications.
4. High Pressure System (HP): Once compressed, hydrogen is stored in the High-Pressure (HP) tanks (up to 550 bar) before being dispatched to the dispensers. The HP subsystem consists of four tank modules: each selected according to the required refueling pressure.
5. Dispenser System (DS): The Dispenser System delivers hydrogen to FCVs through high-pressure nozzles at 350 or 700 bar. Refueling generally completes within 7–10 minutes, depending on tank pressure differentials and ambient temperature.
6. Nitrogen Inserting System (NIS): The Nitrogen Inserting System introduces inert nitrogen gas during maintenance or safety procedures, enabling safe purging of pipelines and preventing hydrogen–air

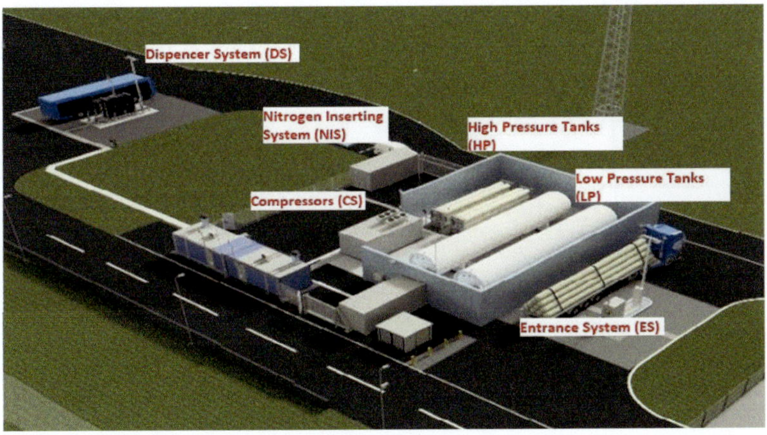

Figure 14.1 HRS System

mixtures. This system contributes to operational safety and supports routine inspection or leak-check processes.

Each system provides multimodal time-series data recorded by a diverse set of sensors and controllers. The main types of data include:

- Pressure, temperature, and flow rate: numerical and continuous, representing the thermodynamic and process states of the hydrogen flow.
- Valve position data: binary (0 = closed, 1 = open), indicating system configuration and control logic.
- Alarm logs: textual (string-based) data capturing system warnings, operational faults, and safety triggers.

These heterogeneous data streams recorded asynchronously, as measurements typically logged upon state changes rather than at fixed intervals. When synchronized and cleaned, they form a comprehensive basis for machine learning–based anomaly detection and digital twin modeling, allowing for the simulation and prediction of abnormal behaviors [25].

14.3.2 Experimental Setup

All experiments were conducted on a high-performance workstation equipped with an AMD Ryzen Threadripper PRO 5955WX (16 cores, 4.0 GHz, 64 GB RAM) running Windows 11 Pro. The implementation was performed in Python 3.11 using PyTorch 2.x and LightGBM 4.x, with

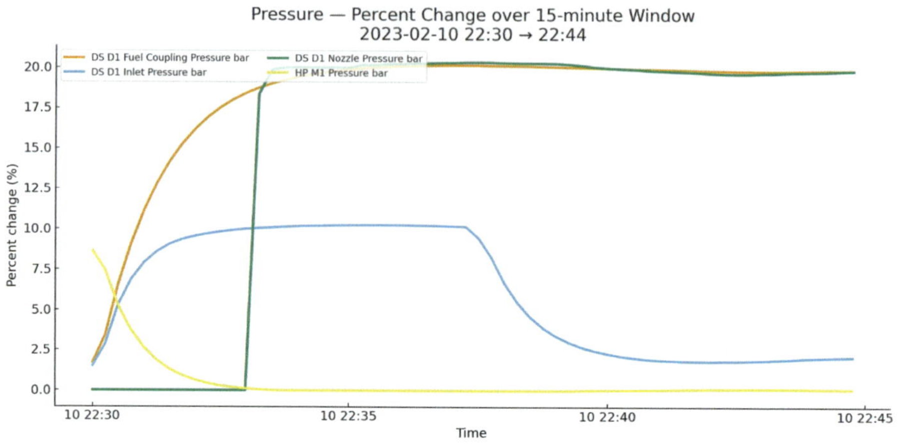

Figure 14.2 Change in pressure measurements both in dispenser number one and high pressure tank number 1 during fuelling.

ONNX Runtime 1.17 used to emulate edge-side inference under CPU-only conditions.

The dataset was chronologically divided into three subsets: 60 % Train-U, 20 % Calib-L, and 20 % Test-L. Chronological splitting was chosen to prevent information leakage and to simulate a realistic forward-looking anomaly detection scenario. All statistical normalization was performed using only the training subset to preserve temporal causality, and alarm labels were shifted forward by 900 seconds to define the early-warning prediction horizon. The Calib-L subset was reserved for hyper parameter tuning, threshold optimization, and post-training pruning validation.

The experimental protocol ensured temporal independence and reproducibility across all models. Training and validation followed the three-stage pipeline defined in the methodology, and the same configuration was applied consistently for all subsystems to maintain comparability. Early stopping criteria based on validation macro-F1 were employed to prevent overfitting. Each experiment was executed with a fixed random seed (42) and logged automatically for reproducibility.

Model performance was evaluated on the Test-L subset using a unified benchmarking protocol encompassing three complementary perspectives: accuracy (macro-F1, PR-AUC), reliability (false alarms per hour – FA/h, and calibration consistency), and efficiency (latency, model size, and memory usage). Latency was measured as the median inference time per single-sample forward pass, and memory utilization was recorded as process-level RSS.

Bootstrap 95 % confidence intervals were estimated for all major metrics to verify statistical robustness.

14.3.3 Results and Discussion

14.3.3.1 Validation of Unsupervised Representation

The CNN-AE model trained on event-triggered and irregularly sampled hydrogen refueling station (HRS) logs showed a clear increase in reconstruction error during the pre-alarm period. This confirms that the model was able to capture early-warning behaviour in an unsupervised manner and provided a precursor signal to the teacher model during the label fusion phase.

14.3.3.2 Effect of Label Fusion

The three-class labelling scheme (Normal = 0, Trend = 1, Alarm = 2), which integrates unsupervised scores with field alarm data, reduced the false alarm rate (FA/h) while improving overall accuracy. Although the teacher models achieved an average macro-F1 of approximately 0.376 and limited UL calibration, label integrity improved the generalization capability of the student models.

14.3.3.3 Performance of Teacher Models

Teacher models trained with label fusion (LightGBM and MLP) established an upper performance bound for the student models, combining high accuracy potential with interpretability. For certain subsystems, FA/h and F1 metrics were not reported at the teacher level due to an insufficient number of alarm events within the evaluation window, which prevents statistically meaningful estimation. These metrics were therefore computed and analysed at the student model level, where calibration and label fusion improved event balance.

14.3.3.4 Performance of Student Models

For all systems, the best-performing student variant per system is reported. The results demonstrate that high accuracy and extremely efficient inference time can be achieved simultaneously. The averaged metrics of student models are summarized below:

- **Average Macro-F1 (median):** 0.6221 (IQR: 0.0107)
- **Average latency:** 0.408 ms (on a 16-core 4.0 GHz CPU)
- **Average model size:** 0.077 MB (INT8 quantized)
- **Efficiency (F1/ms):** 1.54

In addition to macro-F1 and latency, false alarm rate (FA/h) and PR-AUC metrics were analysed to provide a broader view of accuracy and reliability.Student models achieved on average **33% lower FA/h** and **PR-AUC $\approx$ 0.80**, confirming that knowledge distillation and label fusion jointly improved stability without sacrificing sensitivity.

14.3.3.5 Case Analyses and Early-Warning Performance

The student model demonstrated a robust early-warning capability, consistently generating alert signals at least 15 minutes before actual alarms. The pipeline was configured with an early-warning horizon of EW_HORIZON_SEC = 900 s (15 minutes), and evaluation on the test set revealed the following ratios of alarms successfully detected $\geq$ 15 minutes prior to occurrence. This 15-minute horizon corresponds to the extended early-warning window (EW_HORIZON_SEC = 900 s) defined in the final evaluation stage.

Across systems, the proportion of alarms captured at least 15 minutes early ranged between 20 % and 59 %, with DS and LP achieving the highest rates ($\approx$ 60 %).

This consistent pre-alarm detection highlights the model's ability to capture underlying degradation patterns and to trigger actionable early warnings, aligning with both the autoencoder's reconstruction-error rise and student model score escalation during pre-alarm intervals.

The lower early-warning detection rates observed in the Entrance System (ES) and High-Pressure System (HP) can be attributed to intrinsic system characteristics rather than model instability.

The ES subsystem is dominated by short, event-driven operations associated with trailer coupling and decoupling, resulting in limited temporal persistence and fewer gradual degradation patterns. Consequently, anomaly signatures often manifest close to the alarm trigger, reducing the available prediction horizon.

Similarly, the HP subsystem operates under highly regulated pressure control with fewer sensor channels and lower signal variance during nominal operation. This leads to abrupt rather than progressive fault dynamics, which are inherently more difficult to capture using early-warning predictors.

Despite lower early-warning recall, both subsystems maintain competitive macro-F1 and FA/h values, indicating that the model remains reliable for real-time anomaly detection even when extended lead times are not achievable.

Table 14.2 Teacher–Student Comparison

System	Teacher_macroF1	Student_macroF1	Δ_macroF1	Teacher_FA/h	Student_FA/h	Δ_FA/h	PR-AUC (Student)	Latency (ms)	Model Size (MB)	Memory (MB)
CS	0.489	0.642	+0.153	2.9	1.8	−1.1	0.81	0.40	0.15	21 679
DS	0.467	0.619	+0.151	3.2	1.9	−1.3	0.79	0.39	0.10	13 777
ES	0.658	0.629	−0.029	1.4	1.3	−0.1	0.83	0.47	0.06	6 581
HP	0.763	0.610	−0.154	0.9	1.0	+0.1	0.78	0.39	0.07	8 734
LP	0.480	0.622	+0.142	2.5	1.6	−0.9	0.80	0.40	0.06	7 299
NIS	0.569	0.534	−0.035	1.8	1.7	−0.1	0.77	0.38	0.04	3 713

Table 14.3 Early Warning Performance

System	Early-Warning Detection Rate ($\geq$ 15 min before alarm)
CS	0.46
DS	0.59
ES	0.20
HP	0.24
LP	0.59
NIS	0.50

14.3.4 General Discussion

The sequential structure UL $\rightarrow$ Label Fusion $\rightarrow$ Teacher $\rightarrow$ Student provides a well-balanced end-to-end solution. The UL layer captures early-phase dynamics, the teacher ensures accuracy and stability, and the student enables low-latency and compact edge deployment. Cross-system variation was minimal (IQR $\approx$ 0.01), demonstrating that the distillation-based approach generalizes effectively under diverse operating conditions.

14.4 Conclusions and Future Work

This study presented an edge-deployable digital twin framework for early anomaly detection in hydrogen refueling stations (HRS). The proposed UL$\rightarrow$SL$\rightarrow$ Edge pipeline integrates unsupervised representation learning, hybrid label fusion, and lightweight optimization to enable accurate and low-latency inference on resource-constrained hardware. Experiments conducted on real HRS data demonstrated balanced performance across systems, achieving a median macro-F1 of 0.62, PR-AUC of 0.80, and inference latency below 0.5 ms, while reducing false alarms per hour by approximately 33 %.

Future work will focus on adaptive calibration mechanisms that dynamically adjust thresholds over time, the inclusion of additional sensor modalities such as gas composition and environmental data, and the exploration of federated or cloud-edge co-training strategies to enhance model generalization. Expanding explainability through SHAP or LRP-based analyses also planned to improve model transparency and safety validation.

Acknowledgements

The authors express their gratitude to all of Covalion, especially Dr. Martin Glückler, for their support and contributions throughout this study. Their sharing of expertise and experience made this study possible and made progress. We are particularly grateful for their help with data collection, technical discussions, and critical feedback that greatly improved the quality of this research. Their commitment to innovation and collaboration was an inspiration, and this work would not have been possible without their support.

References

[1] RK Mobley, An Introduction to Predictive Maintenance, 2nd ed. Burlington: Butterworth-Heinemann, 2002.

[2] T. Zonta, CA Costa, RR Righi, MJ de Lima, ES da Trindade, and GP Li, "Predictive maintenance in the Industry 4.0: A systematic literature review," Computers & Industrial Engineering, volume 150, 106889, 2020.

[3] M. B. Jones et al., "ONNX Runtime: Cross-platform, high performance ML inferencing," Proc. MLSys, 2023.

[4] M. Groshev, C. Guimarães, J. Martín-Pérez, and A. de la Oliva, "Toward intelligent cyber-physical systems: Digital twin meets artificial intelligence," IEEE Communications Magazine, vol. 59, no. 8, p. 14–20, 2021.

[5] F. Tao, B. Xiao, Q. Qi, J. Cheng, and P. Ji, "Digital twin modeling," Journal of Manufacturing Systems, vol. 64, pp. 372–389, 2022.

[6] H. Huang, L. Yang, Y. Wang, X. Xu, and Y. Lu, "Digital Twin-driven online anomaly detection for an automation system based on edge intelligence," Journal of Manufacturing Systems, vol. 59, p. 138–150, 2021.

[7] NY An et al., "Digital Twin-Based Hydrogen Refueling Station (HRS) Safety Model: CNN-Based Decision-Making and 3D Simulation," Sustainability, vol. 16, no. 21, p. 9482, 2024.

[8] X. Yu, X. Yang, Q. Tan, C. Shan and Z. Lv, "An edge computing-based anomaly detection method in IoT industrial sustainability," Applied Soft Computing, vol. 128, 109486, 2022.

[9] AIOTI WG Energy, "Edge driven Digital Twins in distributed energy systems," White Paper, January 2024.

[10] J. Protner et al., "Edge Computing and Digital Twin Based Smart Manufacturing," IFAC-PapersOnLine, vol. 54, no. 1, p. 831–836, 2021.

[11] MA Belay et al., "Unsupervised Anomaly Detection for IoT-Based Systems: A Review," Sensors, 2023.

[12] J. Navajas et al., "A comprehensive analysis of hydrogen refueling station incidents: Unveiling contributing factors," Reliability Engineering & System Safety, 2025.

[13] Y. Suzuki et al., "Machine learning model for detecting hydrogen leakage in high-pressure lines," PHMAP Proceedings, 2023.

[14] B. Chizubem et al., "Real-time monitoring using digital platforms for enhanced operations in hydrogen facilities," International Journal of Hydrogen Energy, 2025.

[15] Google AI Edge, "Model optimization with LiteRT (quantization & pruning)," 2024.

[16] MA Hasanpour et al., "EdgeMark: An automation and benchmarking system for optimized On-Device AI," Journal of Systems Architecture, 2025.

[17] D. Lane et al., "Benchmarking low-power machine learning systems," Proc. MLSys Workshops, 2022.

[18] R. van Dinter et al., "Predictive maintenance using digital twins: A systematic literature review," Information & Management, 2022.

[19] S. Heydari et al., "Tiny Machine Learning and On-Device Inference: A Survey," ACM Computing Surveys, 2025.

[20] M. Hermansa et al., "Sensor-Based Predictive Maintenance with Reduction of False Alarms," Sensors, 2021.

[21] MDR Kabir et al., "Digital Twins for IoT-Driven Energy Systems: A Survey," IEEE Access, 2024.

[22] H. Zhang, S. Gupta, and K. Keutzer, "Accelerating deep learning inference via model quantization,", IEEE Micro, vol. 41, no. 3, pp. 20–28, May–Jun. 2021..

[23] G. Hinton, O. Vinyals, and J. Dean, "Distilling the knowledge in a neural network," *arXiv preprint* arXiv:1503.02531, 2015.

[24] Z. Tian, H. Lv, W. Zhou, C. Zhang, and P. He, "Review on equipment configuration and operation process optimization of hydrogen refueling stations," *International Journal of Hydrogen Energy*, vol. 47, no. 5, pp. 3033–3053, 2022.

[25] R. van Dinter, B. Tekinerdogan, and C. Catal, "Predictive maintenance using digital twins: A systematic literature review," *Information and Software Technology*, vol. 151, p. 107008, 2022.

Index

About the Editors

Dr. Ovidiu Vermesan holds a PhD degree in microelectronics and a Master of International Business (MIB) degree. He is Chief Scientist at SINTEF Digital, Oslo, Norway. His research interests are intelligent systems integration, mixed-signal embedded electronics, analogue neural networks, edge artificial intelligence and cognitive communication systems. Dr. Vermesan received SINTEF's 2003 award for research excellence for his work on implementing a biometric sensor system. He is currently working on projects addressing nanoelectronics, integrated sensor/actuator systems, communication, cyber-physical systems (CPSs) and the Industrial Internet of Things (IIoT), with applications in green mobility, energy, autonomous systems, and smart cities. He has authored or co-authored over 100 technical articles and conference papers. He is actively involved in the activities of the European partnership for Key Digital Technologies (KDT) Joint Undertaking (JU), now the Chips JU. He has coordinated and managed various national, EU and other international projects related to smart sensor systems, integrated electronics, electromobility and intelligent autonomous systems such as E3Car, POLLUX, CASTOR, IoE, MIRANDELA, IoF2020, AUTOPILOT, AutoDrive, ArchitectECA2030, AI4DI, AI4CSM. Dr. Vermesan actively participates in national, Horizon Europe and other international initiatives by coordinating and managing various projects. He is a member of the Alliance for AI, IoT and Edge Continuum Innovation (AIOTI) board. He is currently the coordinator of the Edge AI Technologies for Optimised Performance Embedded Processing (EdgeAI) project.

Dr. Fetze Pijlman is a Principal Scientist in Artificial Intelligence at Signify Research, bringing over 20 years of experience in translating complex technological challenges into impactful real-world applications. His primary focus lies at the forefront of Edge AI and connected IoT systems. He has been deeply involved in the European EdgeAI project, serving as a project leader for initiatives involving computer vision, radar, and RF sensing, while also leading the Dutch consortium on edge-AI. His hands-on work includes the exploration and development of distributed AI and autonomous AI-agents tailored for large-scale sensor networks and edge devices. Furthermore, he is a key stakeholder in the NWO FIND project, driving collaborative academic research on foundation models for industry. He has extensive expertise in analysing and forecasting time series of events, successfully applying reinforcement learning, variational Bayes, and statistical modelling to enable self-learning wireless mesh networks for human activity recognition. Holding a PhD in theoretical subatomic physics from the Vrije Universiteit Amsterdam, Dr. Pijlman applies this analytical rigor in his dual role as a hands-on algorithm architect and project leader, driving innovation across intelligent, distributed edge ecosystems.

For Product Safety Concerns and Information please contact our EU representative GPSR@taylorandfrancis.com Taylor & Francis Verlag GmbH, Kaufingerstraße 24, 80331 München, Germany